The Professional Developments Series

These eight books provide you with a wealth of insight into all aspects of nursing practice. The series is essential reading for qualified, practising nurses who need to keep up-to-date with new developments, evaluate their clinical practice, and develop and extend their clinical management and teaching skills. Through reading these books, students of nursing will gain an insight into what the essence of nursing is and the wide range of skills which are daily employed in improving patient care. Up-to-date, referenced and appropriately illustrated, The Professional Developments Series brings together the work of well over two hundred nurses.

Other titles in The Professional Developments Series:

Dunne   **How Many Nurses Do I Need: A Guide**   1 870065 24 7
to Resource Management Issues
This book provides valuable advice and information for all nurses facing the challenge of taking direct responsibility for managing human resources and planning, providing quality assurance and managing financial resources.

Glasper   **Child Care: Some Nursing Perspectives**   1 870065 23 9
In three sections, this book covers many pertinent issues that are associated with caring for babies, young children and adolescents, in hospital and community settings.

Horne   **Effective Communication**   1 870065 14 X
This book examines a wide range of communication topics, including counselling, confidentiality, group and team work, compliance and communicating with children.

Horne   **Patient Education Plus**   1 870065 11 5
This book helps to develop nurses' teaching roles, and covers an extensive range of clinical topics. Each chapter contains a useful handout which can be freely photocopied or adapted for use with clients.

Horne   **Practice Check!**   1 870065 10 7
Each Practice Check presents a brief description of situations which may arise in practice together with open-ended questions and discussion to enable problems to be explored and effective solutions to be found.

Horne   **Staff Nurse's Survival Guide**   1 870065 13 1
Relevant to recently qualified and experienced nurses working in all healthcare settings, this brings together chapters on a wide range of clinical and non-clinical issues in patient care.

Horne   **Ward Sister's Survival Guide**   1 870065 12 3
This book is essential reading and a valuable reference for all nurses with direct clinical management responsibility.

Other titles of interest:

Morison   **A Colour Guide to the Assessment and**   1 870065 25 5
Management of Leg Ulcers
This book takes a practical, problem-solving approach to the most effective management, treatment and prevention of leg ulcers, and is a valuable reference for practitioners involved in the care of patients with these wounds.

Morison   **A Colour Guide to the Nursing**   1 870065 20 4
Management of Wounds
This book is a highly practical, research-based guide to wound management giving valuable advice to practitioners on the optimum nursing management of chronic, traumatic, or surgical wounds.

Taylor and Goodinson-McLaren   **Nutritional Support: A Team Approach**   1 870065 21 1
This book takes a team approach to nutritional support and offers practical information on all aspects of enteral and parenteral nutrition to enable the patient to be managed effectively at ward level and at home.

Dedication

For Rhiannon and Huw.

Contents

Preface

Dedication

Ageing and current trends
1 Ageing: a collective and an individual experience   1
   Gill Garrett
2 Current issues in the care of older people   6
   Stephen G. Wright and Lynne Swiatczak

Daily Living
3 A safe environment?   15
   Gill Garrett
4 Good food for long life: nutrition for elderly people   21
   Susan Holmes
5 The senses in old age   27
   Lynne Swiatczak
6 Relationships in later life   34
   Gill Garrett
7 Killing time   40
   Steve Goodwin
8 Family care and the elderly   46
   Gill Garrett
9 Caring in the UK today   52
   Gill Garrett
10 Care, mis-care, abuse?   55
   Gill Garrett
11 Death and bereavement in old age   62
   Gill Garrett

Health Problems in Old Age
12 Hypothermia in elderly people   71
   Gill Garrett
13 Falls in the elderly   76
   Karen A. Webb
14 Pain and its management in later life   82
   Jane Latham
15 Mobility problems of the new stroke victim: supporting the carer   89
   Elizabeth M. Horne
16 Leg ulcers: the nursing assessment   94
   Jacqueline Dale and Barbara Gibson

17 Treatment of leg ulcers   100
    Jacqueline Dale and Barbara Gibson
18 Compression bandaging for venous ulcers   106
    Jacqueline Dale and Barbara Gibson
19 Prevention of venous ulcers   113
    Jacqueline Dale and Barbara Gibson
20 Incontinence: who cares?   118
    Marian Egan, Thelma Thomas and T. W. Meade
21 Continence in later life   124
    Lesley M. Irvine
22 Care of the urinary incontinent patient   131
    Janet Gooch
23 Management of male incontinence using a sheath   137
    Virginia Playford
24 Care of the catheter at home: a patient education handout   141
    Janet Gooch
25 A new kind of loving? The effect of continence problems on
    sexuality   144
    Veronica Wheeler
26 Early assessment of pressure sore risk   150
    Moya J. Morison
27 Pressure sores: assessing the wound   156
    Moya J. Morison
28 Managing pressure sores: local treatment   161
    Moya J. Morison
29 Pressure sores: removing the causes of the wound   167
    Moya J. Morison
30 Mental health problems in old age   175
    Lesley Donovan
31 Management of mental health problems in old age   181
    Lesley Donovan
32 Tablets to take away: why some elderly people fail to
    comply with their medication   188
    Sally Quilligan
33 When should you take your tablets? Teaching elderly
    people about their medication   194
    Sally Quilligan
34 Surgery in old age   197
    Gill Garrett

Working With Older People
35 Teamwork: an equal partnership?   205
    Gill Garrett
36 The dynamics of ageing: their implications for care   210
    Brendan McMahon and Patricia Fitzgerald

37 Communicating with elderly people   215
    Kevin Teasdale
38 Coping with other people's emotions   220
    Philip Burnard
39 Helping clients to come to terms with loss   225
    Teresa Lombardi
40 Bereavement: patients with advanced cancer and their
    families   230
    Jenny Penson
41 Screening elderly people   235
    Maggie Rogers
42 The age gap: teaching students about health education for
    the elderly   241
    Beverly Holloway
43 Happy to be home? A discharge planning package for
    elderly people   246
    Jo Booth and Cath Davies
44 Encouraging compliance   252
    Ruth E. Smith and Jill Birrell
45 Patient advocacy   256
    Mary Watkins
    Index   263

Preface

This book grew out of a series of articles on the care of older people published in the *Professional Nurse* journal. The need for the discussion of such issues, not simply by specialist nurses in elderly care but by practitioners, educators and managers in all spheres, increases daily with our growing ageing population. Far more older people are found in general medical and surgical wards, orthopaedic and ophthalmic units, and accident and emergency departments than in areas specifically designated for their care; in the community the nurse's caseload has a strong bias towards this age group.

The book cannot hope to be, nor does it attempt to be, a definitive text on the nursing care of older people. References will direct the reader to other and more diverse literature for further study. It is however essential that all health professionals coming into contact with older people and their carers have a working knowledge of their situations, their needs and the current trends in the provision of care and support to meet these. It is to promote such knowledge and to open up discussion that this book is offered.

Gill Garrett,
Bristol, July 1991.

Ageing and Current Trends

1

Ageing: a collective and an individual experience

Gill Garrett, BA, RGN, RCNT, DN (London), Cert Ed (FE), RNT, FP Cert
Freelance Lecturer, Bristol

Human beings may be amongst the longest living animal species on the planet, but in common with all branches of the plant and animal kingdoms (and despite the way some behave!) they are not immortal. The biblical 'three score years and ten' has certainly been exceeded in many areas of the developed world, and many people are now living into advanced old age; existence however remains finite. This fact of life is preceded, for the majority who survive accidents or fatal illnesses in earlier years, by another – senescence, the processes of ageing which render us 'old'. These do not occur overnight but over a prolonged period of time; just as we develop to maturity through infancy, childhood and adolescence, over a number of years we 'age'.

For centuries the mysteries of ageing have fascinated many and varied cultures – some have welcomed them, some feared their onset, depending on the role and relevance of the aged in the contemporary society. But any serious scientific study of the processes has only been carried out during the past century. Gerontology could be said to be still in its academic infancy – though now progressing rapidly as population changes prompt urgent enquiry and planning.

Demographic change

Over the past hundred years developed nations have witnessed a tremendous increase in the numbers of people living out their full life-span and dying in old age; many third world countries still reflect the population profile of the now more affluent nations in the last century (see Figure 1). The 'Christmas tree' shape of the UK profile in 1891 bears little relation to the 1988 outline, the peak of which will continue to broaden in the coming decades with our ageing population. In less developed countries where infant and maternal mortality remain high and where life expectancy at all ages is much reduced, the previous pattern is likely to persist.

In the UK at the turn of the century only 4.7% of the population were past retirement age: they now comprise some 17%. By 2029 it is projected that one in four of the population (ie, 25%) will be over 60. The number of young old (ie, the 65–75 year olds) will not increase before

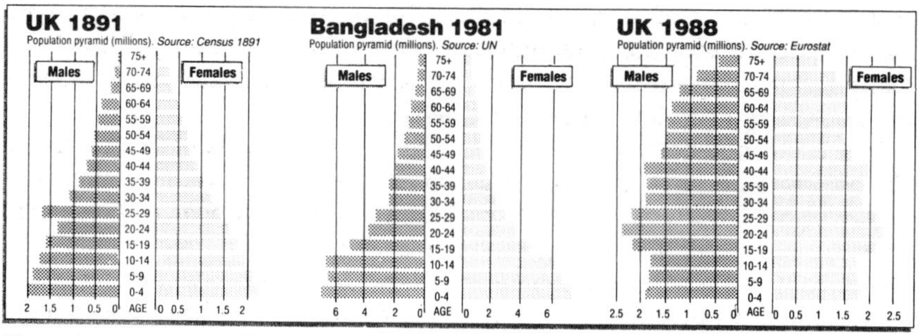

Figure 1

2010 when the post-war baby boom group begin to retire, but the numbers of the very old are increasing now and will continue to do so. In 1989 there were 2.1 million people over 80, a 50% increase on the 1961 number. As a proportion of the population they will also continue to increase. Estimates indicate that whilst the total population will increase by 9% in the next 40 years, the over 85 sector will rise by 76%. Women at present outnumber men in all the older age groups – by 4:1 in the over 85s – but this ratio may well lessen with changing behavioural and work patterns.

The alterations described result from changes in both mortality and fertility rates: the former accounts for the increased number of older people and the latter for their increased percentage within the population. Although improvements in medical care are often quoted as being instrumental in adding to the number of older people, these have been minimal in other than improving the quality of life and survival in a certain number of conditions. During this century there has been little improvement in life expectancy for people already in middle age but a vast improvement for the newborn. The dramatic fall in maternal, infant and child mortality has been consequent upon improvements in general living standards, public hygiene and nutrition as much as upon advances in medical knowledge and practice.

Some countries in the Western world are moving to the stage of zero population growth with effective fertility control meaning fewer babies born each year. This is not so in the UK, which forecasters believe will soon have the highest birth rate in Western Europe. Families of two or three children are now the norm with the Victorian and Edwardian broods of eight or more definitely a feature of the past. Yesterday's children are becoming the elderly of today with progressively fewer children and grandchildren of their own, thus reshaping the population profile.

Why do we age?

That we all grow old is undeniable and the physical manifestations are readily identifiable and described in literature as diverse as myth, historical fiction and scientific papers. But there is as yet no widespread agreement on why the phenomenon occurs. The theorists fall into two camps, some expounding random or extrinsic ideas, others pacemaker or fundamentalist views (Bennett, 1986).

The random or extrinsic theories argue that ageing is basically due to the effects of living – to wear and tear. Background radiation may be a factor, waste products may collect altering cell metabolism, or there may be increasing chemical changes affecting DNA and cell replication. The champions of the fundamentalist view however see ageing as a genetically programmed occurrence: there is an internal 'clock' governing the rate of cell activity and division and thus the timing of growth, decline and death. There may be an overall 'clock', perhaps in the hypothalamus, or each cell may have its own programmed timer. A variation on this line has been the suggestion that there is an, as yet unidentified, ageing hormone.

Normal vs pathological ageing

Logically society should celebrate the achievement of longevity for most of its members and the changes that have permitted it, eg, the great improvements in hygiene and nutrition, the conquering of most childhood killer diseases, the better provisions in sickness and in health. Conversely however it views the ageing population with alarm and labels it a 'social problem'; it sees later life as a time of social redundancy and calculates not the benefits older people could bring to their communities, but the cost the latter must bear to supposedly support them in their decline.

This would appear to follow from the 'pathological' model of ageing which has been created, largely by the professionals (medicine concentrating on the diseases of old age, social scientists dwelling on the negative impact of retirement, etc) and passed into common belief through the stereotyping of which we are all guilty at times. Such stereotypes are damaging to older people because of the expectations they promote and they contribute substantially to the problem of ageism – discrimination against people on the grounds of age. But they are more subtly damaging too, because older people themselves may come to believe the myths, which can act as 'self-fulfilling prophecies'. If an older person believes later life to be a time of illness and deprivation, she may not report health problems which could have been readily remedied but which then progress to disabling proportion.

It would be foolish to dismiss the changes of later life and the health problems which may be experienced; however many of the latter result not from ageing *per se* but from pathological processes which may be preventable (with behavioural modification such as dietary change, abstention from smoking etc) or remediable. With concentration on such aspects, it has been suggested that healthy old age may be prolonged with 'the major maladies of adulthood . . . compressed into a relatively short space of time immediately prior to death' (Johnson, 1986). Whilst this may be our overall aim for all older people in the future, it is as well to recall that it is a reality for many now. The great majority will live quite independently to the end of their lives, possibly with minor functional restrictions but much more rarely with major impairments.

Personal life histories

For those who work with older people an appreciation of the universality of ageing, the theoretical perspectives and the implications for their work are undoubtedly valuable. But those concentrating solely on these aspects or on the pathological model do so at their, and certainly their client's or patient's, peril. Malcolm Johnson of the Open University speaks of such professionals as spectators in an arena at the end of a marathon, seeing the runners enter for the last lap, tired and bruised; they are more concerned with relieving the pain and weariness than asking how the race was run or what plans the runners have for future racing. For what is important in ensuring individual care is looking at how older people themselves see and value their lives in the context of their personal life histories.

Old age has been called the 'zenith of individuality' (Brown, 1978); when, like illness, it is referred to as a great 'leveller' this is quite erroneous. For just as different people react differently to the onset of ill health, in ageing the social and class background, educational level, financial status, gender and family roles played, religious or philosophical orientation, indeed the total life experience of the ageing person will be completely individual and their response thus quite unique. To understand the meaning of ageing and old age for them it is necessary to look at the paths which brought them to their present standpoint and their personal perceptions of them.

In any society life experiences will have overall common patterns (growth and development, education, work experience, the making, sustaining and terminating of relationships – close and distant) but no two individual patterns will have the same timings, meanings or significance, no one stands on someone else's ground. The many 'strands' of life's tapestry, work, relationships, interests, run simultaneously; sometimes they interact minimally, at other times they may be closely intertwined. The picture the older person has to look back on may bear little relation to that put together by a dispassionate observer, for what emerges for the older person is not a clinical photographic record of life events but a distillation of them, some poorly recalled, some partially interpreted, some completely 'rewoven' in the light of further living.

Perhaps the tapestry analogy has a drawback, however, in that it implies that at the end there is a finished product. In reality the picture is never 'completed' as it is open to change and reinterpretation right to the moment of death. A slight turn of events can rearrange the view perhaps more kaleidoscopically. And although much of an older person's life review may be handed on to younger generations, which is immensely valuable if they choose or are encouraged to do so, the 'original' is lost with that person's life. For what remains then is incorporated into another's framework and understanding, interpreted in the light of their own experience and living.

To look at older people from such a perspective and to utilise this 'biographical' approach in care is of course not objective or scientific and as such may be quite foreign to conventionally trained nursing, medical and paramedical staff. But through it, a far more dynamic, authentic picture of the older person emerges and the carers, armed with an understanding of the very basis of that person's self-esteem and self-image, are then far better placed to assist in the planning and execution of appropriate care.

Effective survival demands constant adaptation to changing circumstances and by their very achievement of old age those in later life have demonstrated this capacity. Indeed the current generation of older old people have witnessed during their lives a rate of social and technological change unparalleled in history. The manner in which individuals cope with such changes, and perhaps more pertinently with the changes on a personal level, bears witness to the personality and coping mechanisms developed over a lifetime. If we as professionals are to augment that coping, in relation to the achievement of healthy ageing, it must be on a personal level and this can only become a reality if an individual is known, recognised and respected as such. For this, a prerequisite is a professional not simply versed in objective, scientific methodologies, but also knowledgeable and practiced in more intuitive, 'human' skills. In the past much effort has been put into training for the former; it is time the balance was redressed with equal weight now given to the latter.

References
Bennett, G. C. J. (1986) The physiology of ageing. In Redfern, S. (Ed) *Nursing Elderly People*. Churchill Livingstone, London.
Brown, M. (1978) *Readings in Gerontology*. Mosby, St Louis.
Johnson, M. L. (1986) The meaning of old age. p4. In Redfern, S. *Nursing Elderly People*. Churchill Livingstone, London.

2

Current issues in the care of older people

Stephen G. Wright, RGN, DipN, RCNT, DANS, RNT, MSc (Nursing)
Consultant Nurse, Nursing Development Unit, Tameside General Hospital

Lynne Swiatczak, RGN, RNMH
Clinical Nurse Specialist, Nursing Development Unit, Tameside General Hospital

Toffler (1973) writes of the 'roaring current of change' which is accelerating and affects all our lives. This is no more true than of the changes on the horizon for the care of older people.

Even the concept of 'old age' seems less certain than ever before. It has traditionally been very difficult to achieve a consensus on when old age begins, except that there is general agreement that arbitrary numbers of years attained (eg, 65 years) is an inadequate reference point. There is also debate about whether there is indeed such an identifiable group as 'elderly people', with special needs. This has led, in some areas, towards a trend to integrate services for the elderly person into mainstream health care specialties, a move which is accelerated by a general aversion to the label 'geriatric' with all its negative connotations.

Care provision for older people

Whoever or wherever elderly people are, there is no doubt that this is a time of significant change in relation to the services available to them. Growing consumer demand for better quality services, longer life expectancy and resource restrictions have served to concentrate the minds of politicians and health care personnel on what kind of service is desirable and achievable in the future. For some, the 'rising tide' is seen as a problem of society, for others it is an opportunity to re-evaluate the service that is offered, an opportunity to provide the kind of quality service to which all citizens are entitled and from which so many older people have been excluded for so long.

The perceived problem of rising numbers of older people is bringing new life to the debate over euthanasia, while resource restrictions reinforce the need for value judgements to be made about who shall or shall not receive care. Thus, older people may have less opportunity for certain forms of surgery, transplants, intensive care, cancer care and so on. In part this is driven by limitations to resources, but also subjective views by those with control over resources about the 'more deserving' young, or misconceptions about the older person's potential response to treatments. It is falsely assumed, for instance, that recovery after surgery for example is poorer, despite the evidence that with proper preparation and after care that this is not the case. This had led some to espouse the value of 'QALYS' (Quality added life years) where health intervention is based on someone else's judgement of how much quality will be added to the person's life by health intervention.

A positive shift in approach
There is no doubt that older people themselves are contributing to a more positive shift in approach, pensioners' action groups and similar organisations are forming a powerful lobby for political and social change. 'Ageism' is being defined and challenged, and more and more professionals in health care, not least nurses, are defining themselves, not in terms of the traditional patrician model, but, on the basis of partnership to empower the older person to get involved in and take more control over their health and the proposed changes (Wright, 1988).

This is not to say that everything in the garden is rosy, it is not. Many older people still suffer from enormous political, social and economic disadvantages. At the same time they, and the social and health care workers involved with them, are facing monumental changes in approach in the coming years.

Private sector care
There is an increased emphasis on the private sector, not only in the area of residential care but also in private health insurance. Recent Government incentives are intended to encourage people to look towards insuring themselves privately rather than relying on the NHS. It has been argued that this could lead to a two tier system, those without insurance using the NHS (RCN, 1989), many of whom would be people with chronic health problems who either were refused private insurance or could not afford the additional premiums.

It may also be argued that older people have already contributed to their health care by paying National Insurance contributions. Nevertheless, a philosophical shift in Government which places greater emphasis on personal accountability for health, has considerable implications for the older person.

Nursing and residential home care
Private and local authority nursing and residential accommodation is now increasingly used, as hospital provision of continuing care beds diminishes. In one example, which is probably typical of the average NHS district general hospital, the number of private sector beds has increased from nil in 1981 to over 600 in 1990 (Tameside Social Services, 1990). There is, as yet, no national body to monitor standards or to inspect nursing and residential homes. The legislation is complex and local monitoring very variable. This leads to problems of abuse and ill

treatment and to a great disparity in the standards of care which are given.

Abuse of older people within residential care settings is by no means uncommon and there is a lack of awareness of the problem of abuse amongst health care workers and the general public (Wagner, 1991).

There is also a problem of accommodation for the mentally ill and handicapped as few homes accept older people who exhibit any behaviour problems. As a proportion of elderly people suffer from dementia and Alzheimer's disease, this severely limits their choice of accommodation and care. In addition, clients with problems such as incontinence or reduced mobility are not always accepted by all homes. The health care system generally is accused of lack of awareness of the needs of ethnic minority groups and others such as elderly mentally handicapped or AIDS sufferers. The closure of large institutions for the mentally ill and handicapped, and the likelihood that many HIV positive patients may not develop AIDS until their late 60's, indicates that the client needs are not exclusive to younger age groups. Nurses in the care of the elderly sector also need to be aware of the skills and knowledge needed to help patients with such problems.

The future of National Health Service nursing homes is uncertain. Three were pioneered in the mid 1980s, already one of these has been put up for sale to the independent sector. This, combined with the closure of many long stay beds, and the expansion of the private sector in this field raises questions over the likelihood of much continuing care for elderly people remaining within the NHS.

Informal carers

Many elderly people are cared for at home by relatives, neighbours and friends, but receive little support from health and social services in doing so. The burden on such informal carers is very great (Mace and Rabins, 1985). Social, financial and psychological pressures can produce great strains upon the carers themselves. Health Visitor provision is changing and many elderly people no longer receive regular visits, while there are limited resources for the provision of home helps, relief care and so on. Informal carers are coping with difficulties which could be relieved by education and assistance from professional health care workers. Respite care provision varies and is not available in many health authorities. Carers need to rely on Local Authority provision or on the help of other relatives and friends in order to take time out.

There is also the problem of the 'young elderly' taking care of the 'old elderly'. Many informal carers are elderly themselves and are coping with the responsibility of older relatives. This limits their own opportunities for taking care of themselves and often exacerbates other social, economic and health problems.

Health screening

The recent initiative for health screening of the elderly by their General Practitioners appears to be a positive move towards better care. This initiative does not state that the screening must be carried out by doctors, however. Many of these assessments are carried out by Practice Nurses who have varying degrees of knowledge, skill and experience in this area. Recent guidance has been published to help address this issue (RCN, 1991). Some GP practices support development of their Practice Nurses in order to update their knowledge and to provide better standards; other practices do not do this and their screening may not be effective.

Specific health needs

The funding of the NHS remains problematic and it is questionable how far the recent purchaser and provider developments will solve the problems of longstanding underfunding. The care of elderly people, many of whom may have chronic conditions, has never been inexpensive. It is more costly to provide care for these patients and it is also difficult to improve the service without more funds. It is difficult to generate income in a Care of the Elderly setting, and Authorities with a large elderly population may have to subsidise elderly care by generating income in other areas such as day case surgery. The NHS has always had a cure rather than care approach, and as health care needs are infinite more emphasis needs to be placed on health promotion, particularly targeted at groups who are at risk.

Recent changes in nurse education have done little to improve the status of caring for the elderly. Negative attitudes to this client group appear to be still transferred and enhanced by students' learning experience (Fielding, 1988). In the Project 2000 initiatives no place was given to Care of the Elderly as a specialty. It was assumed that older people do not need specialist nursing in the same way that children or mentally ill people do, and that it could be subsumed within the branch of nursing the adult. There has long been a debate about whether care of the elderly should be a specialty or not, yet the reality is that most older patients are not nursed in specialist units. Older patients can form a large part of the caseload in most nursing settings. There is some strength in the argument, however, that the needs of older people are specific and identifiable as the territory of a specialist body of knowledge and function. The 'Cinderella' image of nursing the elderly remains and might be enhanced by the inability of some nurse leaders to recognise it as a specialty.

The recent PREPP proposals (UKCC, 1990) raise questions as to how they may affect the care of older people. Each nurse is expected, according to the initial proposals, to keep up-to-date with five days study leave to be provided by employers in every three years. Many nurses in care of the elderly settings already have difficulty in obtaining study leave. If employers have only to adhere to these guidelines then it may remain a major problem for many nurses.

Quality of care

The development of the role of the Health Care Assistant is a cause for concern in many settings. Most elderly care wards ten to fifteen years ago were staffed by a majority of unqualified staff. In many areas the ratio was as high as 80% unqualified: 20% qualified.

The care given was not of the standards which might be expected today, and an institutional approach tended to dominate (Martin, 1984). In recent years there have been improvements made in order to address this problem. Initiatives such as Primary Nursing have placed the emphasis on the qualified nurse giving care to the patient. These aim to ensure that the care planned and given is comprehensive, consistent and of a high standard.

The advent of the Health Care Assistant causes much concern in areas where the skill mix on wards has been improved, as there are fears of a threat to the employment of qualified nurses. The care assistant training and role is different and their function varies according to employers' requirements. There are concerns about the level of activities undertaken – seemingly very similar to nurses in some circumstances. However, without the full knowledge base of nurses, and unless support and supervision is adequate, the effects upon the quality of care delivered leave many questions to be answered. The role of the qualified nurse could quite easily become one of supervisor and the ratio of staff could quickly revert to a majority of unqualified staff. Some managers appear to see this as a cheaper way of giving care, but it also solves recruitment problems which some areas have in attracting qualified staff. Historically these areas have been Care of the Elderly, Mental Illness and Mental Handicap, the so-called 'Cinderella' services.

Current initiatives

There are, however, some initiatives which have improved the care of older people. Nursing Development Units have been set up throughout the country in many different areas of care. There are quite a number in Care of the Elderly settings where nurses have examined their practices and have improved the standards of care. These Units aim to develop more creative, thinking approaches to nursing and actively promote the image of elderly people as valued members of society. There is a greater emphasis placed upon the rights of the individual and patients are encouraged to actively participate in their care (Salvage, 1989).

The Voluntary sector is also responsive to the needs of older people and organisations such as Age Concern are more involved in the planning of projects which will affect the care of older people.

Nurses in the care of the elderly sector have been at the forefront of changes in practice in recent years, for example in adopting the use of complementary therapies, giving access to nursing records, the creation of nursing beds, pet therapy, reminiscence therapy and so on. Thus, despite many difficulties, there is evidence of great progress being made in the care of older people. How far the changes ahead will reinforce or restrict these improvements remains to be seen.

References
Fielding, P. (1988) *Attitudes Revisited*. RCN, London.
Mace, N. and Rabins, M. D. (1985) *The 36 Hour Day*. Age Concern, London.
Martin, J. P. (1984) *Hospitals in Trouble*. Blackwell Scientific, Oxford.
RCN (1989) *Response to the proposed changes in the 'White Papers'*. RCN, London.
RCN (1991) *Guidelines For The Assessment of Elderly People*. RCN, London.
Salvage, J. (1989) Nursing, developments. *Nursing Standard* **22**(3), 25–6.
Tameside Social Services (1990) Northern Western Regional Health Authority.
Toffler, A. (1973) *Future Shock*. Pan, London.
Wright, S. G. (1988) *Nursing The Older Patient*. Harper & Row, London.

Daily Living

In recent years much emphasis in working with older people has been placed on the 'activities of daily living' as defined by theorists such as Roper. Whilst such an approach provides a perfectly legitimate framework within which to assess needs and to plan care, it is not the perspective with which this section deals. For older people daily living is a total experience, much greater than the sum of its individual parts; it is the day by day experience of relating to others, structuring activity in a personally meaningful manner, continuing, developing, adapting the patterns of a lifetime in changing circumstances.

These changing circumstances reflect the physical, psychological and sociological effects of ageing – some biologically determined, others imposed by society, and by no means all of a negative nature. By choice or chance, old age may be lived out independently, with family or community support or in 'caring' institutions, large or small. The following chapters consider some of the aspects and adaptations which make for a 'good life' in old age in these very varied settings.

3

A safe environment?

Gill Garrett, BA, RGN, RCNT, DN (London), Cert Ed (FE), RNT, FP Cert
Freelance Lecturer, Bristol

Violet and Ted Taylor had lived for 53 years in a Victorian end-of-terrace, three bedroomed house in a large North Eastern city. In it they had reared their family of three children and numerous stray cats, photographs of which adorned the shelves in their small living room. Ted had worked at the bakery two streets away, they shopped at the local shop three doors down, and they had had the same next door neighbours for forty years.

At 82 Violet had been in poor health for a couple of months; she was on the waiting list for cataract surgery, and was very hard of hearing. One winter's evening Ted collapsed with a myocardial infarction and died shortly after admission to hospital. For the first time in her life Violet was alone. After the funeral however she refused to stay with any of her daughters, and returned home determined to manage unaided.

Her children were desperately anxious because of their mother's general condition, the steep stairs in the house, the outside toilet, and the fact that she lived an hour's drive from any of them; her hearing impairment made telephone contact virtually impossible. The health visitor who called shortly after Ted's death was very concerned about her open fire and her ability to manage safely in the kitchen, where she cooked by gas in a literally hit or miss manner. She felt the four current cats presented definite hazards, as Violet tripped over them with monotonous regularity.

But, despite all their misgivings, Violet managed quite successfully in the house for a further eleven months, refusing any outside assistance other than occasional shopping from her neighbour and a fortnightly visit from her youngest daughter to clean the house. One November evening however she slipped on the back door step whilst getting in some coal, hitting her head as she fell and fracturing her right wrist. It was some time before she could attract her neighbour's attention and she was then admitted to hospital.

Much to Violet's surprise her family appeared relieved to have her in there. There was a great deal of discussion as to the wisdom of her returning home and eventually, much against her better judgement, she was persuaded to apply for a sheltered flatlet on the other side of the city, a few minute's walk from her eldest daughter's home. She was discharged home for a month until a flatlet became available and then whisked off across the city with a few token items of furniture and belongings, but minus the cats, to the purpose-built unit on the edge of a new housing estate.

It was with a great sense of relief that Violet's daughters installed her in the centrally heated, ground floor flatlet with its intercom and alarm system . . . .

The reader may well have imagined by now the outcome of this real life situation. For Violet her new, modern, 'safe' environment proved far more restrictive than the old in which she was supposedly 'at risk'. The electric cooker confused her, the limited space depressed her, she desperately missed her cats and, with her hearing impairment, she found great difficulty in relating to the other residents. Only once did she venture out alone to do some shopping; that necessitated using a subway under a dual carriageway which she found intimidating in the extreme. She became increasingly dependent upon her daughters and isolated within her flatlet. A few months after her move she suffered a stroke early one morning; she was found by the warden but died in the ambulance on the way to hospital.

What is a home?
When discussing Maslow's hierarchy of needs, two American nurses write that "safety and security are in one sense co-existent with biologic integrity. At another level however (they) are a matter of feeling and perception of surroundings" (Ebersole and Hess, 1990). Nurses would do well to ponder this statement when considering the environment of older clients and its supposed 'suitability' to meet their needs. The homes which professionals scrutinize for hazards to life and limb and about which relatives worry endlessly are the ones in which older people seek secure personal space and freedom of expression. Thus respective expectations may bear little relation to each other, and may be the cause of some difficulty, when illness or infirmity raise questions about where the older person should 'appropriately' reside.

Where the home environment is the one of an elderly person's choosing – and thus it could be a room in residential care, or a flat in a sheltered housing scheme as well as independent living accommodation, providing it is home *by choice* – it fulfils many needs.

It is a place of shelter and security, in which there is a sense of belonging and mastery, which allows the person to be herself, which reinforces (by the presence of significant personal items) her life experience and identity. The extended environment – the proximity of conducive social support and facilities which meet individual needs – is of equal importance.

Choice and change
What factors then affect choice of one's living environment? Personality, family needs and one's stage in the life-cycle all have major bearings on

the demands a person makes upon her surroundings, and financial considerations obviously operate in relation to the ability to achieve the desired accommodation. Whilst personality remains a constant feature however, these other generally alter with ageing, and an ideal choice in earlier years may have decided drawbacks at a later stage, for example, room for a family to grow up in may mean too big a house to heat and care for once the children are gone (although familiarity and valued associations may compensate). A home whose features well suited younger, fitter inhabitants may, in itself, handicap them considerably should age related physical changes, or disability consequent upon illness ensue, limited mobility or sensory difficulties perhaps.

For owner-occupiers particularly, reduced retirement income especially in later old age when savings are substantially used up may lead to major problems with upkeep. The suitability of the extended environment may be similarly lessened: the twenty minute walk to park, pub or post office may render them out of reach in later life, and the house and garden on the hill, chosen for the lovely views, may be less attractive when a car is no longer available to reach it.

As with all aspects of later life however, generalisations can be dangerous, and environmental needs have to be looked at on a personal basis. As at other stages in the life-cycle, an older person's needs and their resources (both physical and social) to meet these will be highly individual. It is *their* perception of their situation which is the vital consideration. But, as Pre-Retirement Courses advocate, forward planning is a wise move. Thought given to projected future needs, with adaptations made to the home in later middle and early old age (such as ensuring a good state of repair, adequate personal safety, and an efficient and affordable heating system) may make later old age less stressful and   a lot more comfortable.

Making a move

At any age a change of home is a major life event, and the impact of a move, the preparation for it, the practicalities of dealing with it, the readjustment following it, should not be underestimated. When such a move follows hard on the heels of other significant changes, such as retirement, or the death of a spouse, the cumulative stress effect may be great and detrimental to both physical and mental health. It is not only families and friends who are guilty of pressing for a move to 'something smaller' or nearer to children, however; some health professionals, albeit well-meaningly, try to encourage such moves too. Unless the older person actively wishes to move and has made an informed decision, considering all the ramifications, a far more appropriate first course of action is to investigate ways of improving the existing environment to meet changed or changing needs.

Staying put

Home improvements on a limited income and with dwindling savings may not be easy, but with imaginative help they are certainly possible. Potential sources of help and advice include officers in local authority housing departments, local building society managers, occupational therapists in social services departments and in some areas agencies working specifically with older owner-occupiers such as Staying Put (run by the Anchor Housing Trust in conjunction with the Abbey National Building Society) and Care and Repair. The local Citizen's Advice Bureau will be able to advise on what is available in individual areas. Through such services significant improvements are achieved, making a marked difference to the older person concerned. A combination of a local authority grant for loft insulation and its installation by Age Concern or other volunteers, for example, will make the home more comfortable, cut fuel bills, and lessen the risk of accidental hypothermia.

In addition to structural improvements, domiciliary services available to older people (such as home care assistance) may make for a more satisfactory environment, providing practical support and a channel for social communications. There are also schemes intended for disabled clients who require help with personal care in additional to domestic help (such as Crossroads and local authority home aide services). Such schemes do not provide twenty-four hour cover of course, but there has been a significant increase in the numbers of frail older people using personal alarms which they can activate in the event of sudden illness or accident. Systems such as Lifeline use a telephone link to a trained operator who can summon help to the home; some of the systems can be activated by a cord worn around the neck or wrist so that the person using them does not have to get to a telephone.

In the financial climate at the time of writing however the supply of formal, statutory services may be limited in some areas, even where clients bear part of the cost themselves. Furthermore such services all too often only become involved in an older person's support after a crisis has arisen: had they been brought in sooner the crisis may have been averted. Thus older people increasingly need information on what services are available to them by right and how to get them provided at the appropriate time. In the absence of sufficient local authority provision, other types of support may need to be investigated, and charitable and private concerns are now making inroads in this area, some quite imaginatively.

Sheltered housing

Sheltered housing can be defined as "housing which has been purpose built or converted exclusively for the elderly and which consists of grouped independent accommodation linked to a resident warden by an alarm system". It is not a new concept, witness the almshouses of the

Middle Ages, the cottage homes referred to in the 1909 Royal Commission on the Poor Law and Rowntree's suggestion in 1947 that 5%of housing stock in the country should be specifically designated for the elderly.

The number of people living in such accommodation however has grown considerably since the 1960s. Local authorities, aware of changing demographic trends, are now building more small units rather than 3-bedroomed houses intended for family occupation (although not all of these of course will go to older people); Housing Associations are continuing to increase the amount of accommodation they provide.

As Alan Butler points out (Butler, 1983), some rather extravagant claims have been made on behalf of sheltered housing: that active life is extended for older people, loneliness reduced, medical emergencies averted, and the need for institutionalisation reduced. He indicates that some studies have not borne out these claims; whilst many older people have expressed satisfaction with moves to such accommodation and many have benefited in terms of improved structural surroundings (eg, leaving behind outside sanitation), a significant percentage speak of 'dislocation' problems, missing friends, neighbours and localities to which they were attached and in which they felt supported. Additionally many older people in such schemes speak of having wanted smaller, more easily managed accommodation, but not the additional facilities that go with it in sheltered housing. Instead of being *a* choice however it was the *only* choice in their area.

Quality of life

Although it is possible to speculate on other possible outcomes in the story of Violet Taylor had her placement been different, it cannot be known with certainty how she would have fared in any other situation. It is a reasonable assumption however that her remaining quality of life was markedly reduced by her change in circumstance further to her accident.

It has been said that "Apart from his spouse, housing is probably the single most important element in the life of an older person" (DHSS, 1978); thus it merits very serious consideration by those working with clients in later life. These clients often have to make very difficult decisions, and both community and hospital nurses may be involved in discussions concerning the suitability of current accommodation, projected needs and possible courses of action. Some of the points have been outlined here which they might keep in mind. But it is not only good background and specific knowledge, and the ability to refer appropriately, that are required of the nurse in this situation. Equally important is an understanding, non-judgmental approach and the ability to be non-directive in putting forward and discussing possibilities. Suitability and acceptability remain ultimately the decision of the individual.

References

Butler, A. (1983) Housing and the Elderly: A Sheltered Response. In *Housing Alternatives for the Elderly*, Alan Butler and Anthea Tinker. Centre for Applied Social Studies, University of Leeds, Occasional Paper no. 10.

DHSS (1978) *A Happier Old Age: A Discussion Document on Elderly People in our Society.* HMSO, London.

Ebersole, P. and Hess, P. (1990) *Toward Healthy Ageing: Human Needs and Nursing Response.* C V Mosby, St. Louis.

4

Good food for long life: nutrition for elderly people

Susan Holmes, PhD, BSc, SRN, FRSH
Lecturer in Cancer Nursing, University of Surrey, Guildford

Growth, development, maturity and ageing are all phases in the continuum between birth and death. From conception to maturity, the main characteristics are an increase in mass and a development of function until peak performance is reached; there then follows a continuing but subtle decline in many body functions.

All body cells and tissues are affected by age. There is, however, a wide variation in their ability to resist deterioration, and the lifespan of some cells and tissues is unrelated to that of the body as a whole. Erythrocytes, for example, survive just 120 days between formation and destruction, and it has been estimated that 2.3×10^{11} erythrocytes die and are replaced daily (Lamb, 1977); the epithelial cells lining the intestine are being replaced approximately every two days. Ageing is, therefore, a natural, intrinsic characteristic, representing a progression of changes throughout life. It involves all aspects of the body and proceeds at different rates among body cells and tissues. It also varies between individuals, and age is a poor indicator of general condition.

The process of ageing involves a gradual decline in body function, vitality and resistance to stress, making elderly people more susceptible to disease (pathological change). It is important to distinguish between the intrinsic effects of ageing, which may not be subject to modification, and the consequences of disease, which may respond to treatment or be exacerbated by nutritional deficiency.

Frank malnutrition is rare in the UK, although it is occasionally found in elderly people (Exton-Smith, 1988) when the physical, psychological and social effects of ageing affect the ability to obtain or prepare food or to ingest, digest or absorb nutrients. Alternatively, the processes of metabolism, utilisation or excretion of nutrients may be impaired.

Physiological effects

Ageing is associated with physiological changes; for example, between 30 and 80 years, resting cardiac output is reduced by 30 per cent, renal blood flow by 50 per cent, and maximum breathing capacity and oxygen uptake by 60-70 per cent (Shock *et al*, 1963; Shock, 1972). Furthermore, when additional demands are imposed on elderly people, they recover physiological function more slowly than younger individuals.

A variety of physiological effects may directly affect nutritional status. Studies have shown a reduction in the number of taste and olfactory nerve endings (Bowman and Rosenberg, 1983), and an age-associated decrease in the number of taste buds (Arey *et al*, 1935). A decrease in taste and smell acuity may, therefore, markedly reduce the pleasure of eating, and an inability to smell food odours increases the risk of food-borne illness (eg, food poisoning). Visual impairment may increase the difficulties associated with shopping and food preparation, as well as posing problems while eating.

Gastrointestinal (GI) changes may reduce salivary flow, gastric secretion and GI motility, thus disrupting ingestion, digestion or absorption. As many of today's elderly are edentulous, suffer severe periodontal disease or dental caries (Bellfield, 1987), eating can become more difficult or painful. Inadequate dentition may distort the appetite, while wearing dentures can disrupt normal chewing mechanisms, and this may lead to dietary change, with soft and bland foods being preferred. Although easy to eat and often high in calories, these can be relatively nutrient dilute and low in dietary fibre, and can lead to constipation - particularly when combined with a decline in GI motility.

Digestion is often impaired by reduced gastric secretion; decreased bile and digestive enzyme secretion may disrupt absorption, increasing the volume of the intestinal residue; bacterial fermentation of the residue may cause flatulence thus enhancing GI discomfort.

Metabolic changes

Basal metabolic rate (BMR) falls an average of 20 per cent between the ages of 30 and 90 years (Shock, 1970), due to a loss of actively metabolising tissue (lean body mass - LBM) and a relative increase in adipose tissue. Since adipose tissue is relatively insulin resistant, a loss of LBM also contributes to a decline in glucose tolerance, manifested by a reduced tissue response to insulin and a decreased insulin response to a glucose load (Horowitz, 1982). These effects may reflect ageing *per se*, rather than pathological changes, and diabetic therapy may not be required (Horowitz, 1982). However, the decline in BMR is associated with a fall in body temperature which, when energy (calorie) intake is inadequate, may fall even lower, resulting in hypothermia.

The level of physical activity often declines with age and, when combined with reduced BMR, the demand for energy is reduced. Since many dietary changes associated with age result in increased energy intake, obesity is not uncommon (Bellfield, 1987; Raab and Raab, 1985), and may cause other problems such as hypertension or osteoarthritis and consequent immobility. Obesity may also, however, be accompanied by deficiency of a range of micronutrients such as vitamins and minerals.

Psychosocial and environmental factors

Both psychological and environmental factors may influence food consumption: anxiety, depression, dependence on others, loss of a loved one and reduced income can all affect eating patterns (Holmes, 1987). Depression and social isolation may reduce the appetite - living and eating alone can reduce the pleasure of cooking and eating so that they become chores, especially if the taste of even familiar foods is altered, or dentures or other oral problems make eating difficult.

People on low incomes have a limited amount of money to spend on food, and selection can be dictated not by personal choice but by economic factors. The cheapest foods, however, do not always have the highest nutritional value or contain the most appropriate balance of nutrients, so they can adversely affect overall nutrient consumption. Similarly, economic constraints may cause a lack of dietary variety and increase disinterest in food/eating. Combined with inadequate housing, poor cooking facilities and reduced mobility, such factors can significantly affect food intake.

Physical and mental disability often cause considerable difficulty in obtaining and preparing foods, and this may be exacerbated by the increasing trend of replacing local shops with large supermarkets in shopping centres or on the outskirts of town. These centres can be difficult to get to without a car, and even more difficult to get back from with heavy shopping.

Although, as we have seen, many elderly people are at significant nutritional risk, this must be set in context. While it is predicted that the numbers of elderly people will increase, this does not mean they are all at risk, nor will they all suffer from degenerative diseases and poor health. On the contrary, most people over 65 years (75 per cent) remain physically fit and alert (Fallowfield, 1990), living either independently or with family or friends with little or no limitations on their activity.

Health problems in elderly people, however, present different characteristics to those of younger individuals. Lower body reserves, reduced resistance and the tendency to have more than one debilitating condition at a time make them less able to cope with infections and diseases, and these may exert synergistic effects. Illness may, therefore, impose significant stress, and the reduced rate of recovery means it tends to be chronic rather than temporary, while therapy is often palliative rather than curative, and aggressive nutritional support may be necessary.

Nutrient requirements

The increasing prevalence of degenerative change in elderly people combined with alterations in nutritional requirements due to physiological and metabolic changes and the possibility of chronic use of medications, will all influence the need for nutrients (Table 1).

Primary
- Ignorance of basic facts of nutrition
- Social isolation, particularly in older people
- Physical/mental disability
- Iatrogenic factors eg, due to inappropriate dietary advice
- Chronic use of medications
- Poverty

Secondary
- Impaired appetite - transitory/long-term
- Chewing/swallowing difficulties
- Malabsorption
- Alcohol abuse
- Chronic drug use
- Increased nutrient needs

Table 1. Causes of nutritional deficiency in elderly people. (Based on Exton-Smith, 1988).

Due to the fall in BMR and the likely decrease in physical activity, the need for energy decreases but with little or no change in the need for protein and other nutrients. However, the less efficient digestion and absorption resulting from reduced production of digestive enzymes, bile and other compounds essential for the utilisation of nutrients may mean that the volume of food required changes little. It is, therefore, appropriate for energy to be derived from a variety of nutrient-dense foods, such as lean meat, wholegrain breads and cereals, fruit and vegetables. Starchy foods, which are oxidised more slowly than sugary foods and supply other dietary essentials (such as vitamins, minerals and dietary fibre) should be included. The slow release of glucose from these foods will also help to minimise glucose intolerance.

Although the precise protein requirements for elderly people have not yet been determined, it is suggested that for most 0.6g/kg body weight is appropriate (Young *et al*, 1976). High protein foods are significant sources of vitamins and minerals, and assume greater importance when energy intake is restricted. Since dietary studies often suggest elderly people consume only small amounts of high quality proteins (those supplying all the essential amino acids), these should be actively recommended.

Meat and meat products are both expensive and difficult to chew, whereas mixtures of grains, legumes and pulses are cheaper and may be easier to eat, although they may require considerable effort to prepare and cook; eggs may also be a suitable substitute. Fat is an important source of energy, particularly when glucose tolerance is impaired; it is also the only source of both fat-soluble vitamins (A, D, E, and K) and essential fatty acids (linoleic and linolenic acid), and at least some fat is an essential dietary component. In general, fat should comprise 30-35 per cent of the total calorie intake (National Advisory Committee on Nutrition Education, 1983; DHSS, 1984). However, due to the reduced production of bile, large amounts of fat may cause indigestion and abdominal discomfort which may cause some individuals to reduce their fat consumption below the necessary level. Distributing the fat intake across all meals will aid digestion and absorption, and help to maintain the palatability of the diet.

Protein derived from meat, fish, eggs and poultry, or a mixture of vegetable proteins combined with the vitamins and minerals it contains, is essential. As in childhood, milk and dairy products remain important foods, being the major source of calcium and an important source of vitamin B_2. Fruits and vegetables are also important, providing not only vitamins and minerals but also dietary fibre which will help to stimulate GI function and prevent constipation. Energy-dense foods which provide few nutrients, such as sweets, cakes and biscuits, should not be totally restricted from the diet but reserved as 'special treats' when a 'boost' is needed.

A varied diet

As with all other age groups, elderly people require a well-balanced diet drawn from a wide variety of foods. In general, nutritional deficiency is not an inevitable consequence of ageing if such a diet is consumed in adequate amounts and, as previously stated, frank malnutrition is rare. In 1979, only 7 per cent of elderly people were found to be malnourished (DHSS, 1979) although, when translated into real terms, this represents a significant number of people (Holmes, 1987).

• Living alone
• No regular cooked meals
• Receipt of income support
• Social class IV or V
• Reduced mental test score
• Depression
• Chronic bronchitis/emphysema
• Poor dentition
• Difficulty in swallowing
• Housebound

Table 2. Risk factors predisposing to malnutrition in elderly people (based on DHSS, 1979).

Malnutrition rarely occurs in isolation and the factors responsible for its development can usually be readily identified (Tables 1 and 2). Since it is usually associated with a variety of medical and social needs (Exton-Smith, 1988), it is here that nurses can play a major role in identifying vulnerable patients, and advising them on how to maintain a well-balanced diet.

References
Arey, L.B. *et al* (1935) The numerical and topographical relations of taste buds to human circumvallate papillae throughout the lifespan. *Anat Rec*, **64**, 9–13.

Bellfield, P. (1987) Nutrition and ageing. Lecture delivered at course in clinical nutrition. Leeds, September, 1987.

Bowman, B. and Roseberg, I.H. (1983) Digestive function and ageing. *Human Nutrition: Clinical Nutrition*, **37C**, 75–89.

Department of Health and Social Security (1979) Nutrition and health in old age. Report on Health and Social Subjects, No. 16. HMSO, London.

Department of Health and Social Security (1984) Diet and cardiovascular disease. Report on Health and Social Subjects No. 28. HMSO, London.

Exton-Smith, A.N. (1988) Nutrition in the elderly. In: Dickerson, J.W.T. and Lee, H.A. (Eds) Nutrition in the Clinical Management of Disease. Edward Arnold, London.

Fallowfield, L. (1990) The quality of life, Souvenir Press (E & A) Ltd., London.

Holmes, S. (1987) An acquired taste. *Nursing Times*, Community Outlook, **83**, 16–19.

Horowitz, D.L. (1982) Diabetes and ageing. *Am. Journal Clinical Nutrition*, **36**, 803–08.

Lamb, M.J. (1987) Biology of Ageing. John Wiley and Sons, New York.

National Advisory Committee on Nutritional Education (1963) A discussion paper on guidelines for nutrition education in Britain. Health Education Council, London.

Raab, D. and Raab, N. (1985) Nutrition and ageing: an overview. *The Canadian Nurse*, **79**, 24–28.

Shock, N.W. (1972) Energy metabolism, caloric intake and physical activity of the ageing. In: Carlson L.A. . . . Almquist and Wiksell, Uppsala.

Shock, N.W. *et al* (1983) Age differences in the water content of the body as related to basal oxygen consumption in males. *J. Geront*, **18**, 1–8.

Young, V.R. *et al* (1976) Protein and amino acid requirements of the elderly. In: Winick, M. (Ed) Nutrition and Ageing, John Wiley and Sons, New York.

5

The senses in old age

Lynne Swiatczak, RGN, RNMH
Clinical Nurse Specialist, Nursing Development Unit, Tameside General Hospital

The senses: sight, hearing, touch, taste and smell, are all affected by the ageing processes. The usual changes tend to be associated with some degree of deterioration. This degeneration usually occurs as a result of wear and tear, biological factors and occurs at different rates. The various theories of ageing are documented in many texts (Garrett, 1987; Wright, 1988) as are the physiological characteristics of ageing and it is not intended to discuss either of these subjects here. The focus will be on the effects of the ageing processes and how these may be overcome.

Each of us will experience the changes associated with ageing; these may range from minor problems such as needing reading glasses to severe problems such as total hearing loss. These changes will affect the way in which we carry out our usual daily activities and we may need to make adaptations to our environment. The senses also help us to participate in the world around us, there may be social consequences such as withdrawal if there are sensory deficits.

These adaptations aim to minimise the detrimental effects of the ageing processes and will maximise our individual potential.

Hearing
Wright (1984) suggests that some deafness is inevitable as we grow older and that in some cases complete hearing loss may result from degenerative changes within the ear. Presbycusis is a progressive hearing loss which affects the inner ear and occurs as a result of ageing. Hearing loss affects a number of the daily activities of an older person.

Communication   Satir (1967) states "We cannot not communicate". All the time from our appearance, our gestures etc we are giving out signals about ourselves and taking in messages from the environment. Communication may be impaired by hearing loss. Non-verbal communication has been well documented and it has been argued that it is more effective than verbal communication alone (Argyle, 1978). Most individuals use a mixture of verbal and non-verbal communication in their daily activities. Verbal communication becomes impaired through hearing loss and non-verbal techniques, ie, gestures, facial expression and touch take on a more important role.

Hearing often deteriorates slowly, giving time to adapt new ways of coping with hearing loss. Initially people may compensate without realising it, turning up the volume on the television set, turning their head slightly in order to hear a conversation or facing the person who is speaking to them. Hearing aids may be supplied which will enhance the remaining hearing, these may however also add problems. Some hearing aids are unsightly causing embarrassment for the wearer. They may also cause discomfort and need to be adjusted. There may also be operational difficulties. Hearing aids give many people with hearing loss the opportunity to carry out their usual daily activities with a minimum of problems.

Hearing loss may be due to other problems which can be dealt with simply such as the removal of ear wax, or more serious problems which may require surgical intervention.

Total hearing loss presents more severe difficulties and often sign language and lip reading are the only options available. These techniques whilst invaluable are not without problems, they often take years to learn well and need visual acuity which may not be present in an elderly person.

The role of relatives and other carers is important, they may help to identify the problems, recommend help and give support. Nurses and other health care professionals should be assessing patients' hearing and should not treat all older people as if they were deaf.

Safety Hearing loss can cause several problems associated with safety. A gradual deterioration of hearing may go unnoticed for some time and problems may not arise until the loss is severe. A deaf person may not hear approaching traffic on a busy road or an intruder entering their house. They may be unable to respond to shouts of warning or alarms and sirens, therefore increasing the dangers from accidents.

Elderly people with hearing loss need to be taught to use their other senses more fully. Crossing a road may need to be re-learned using vision and vibration rather than hearing. Home security is also important, windows and doors should be easily secured and entrances should be well lit. Visual alarms for fire and intruders can be placed at strategic points. Voluntary and social services can often assist with the cost and fitting of these alarms.

A telephone can be adapted for use for hearing impaired people with amplifiers and lights. Doorbells can also be adapted by the use of flashing lights instead of ringing to alert the occupant to their visitor.

Work and leisure Many older people may still be in employment when they lose their hearing, this will have varying effects dependent upon the type of employment. It may be that the person will have to change their work or leave if the hearing loss is severe. Leisure activity is also affected by hearing loss, the theatre and cinema become less enjoyable if the dialogue cannot be heard. Listening to music or watching television may also be difficult. The volume may need to be increased to compensate for the hearing loss, this may distort the sound and disturb the neighbours! Some hearing aids need to be turned down in order for the user to listen to conversation when there is background noise such as a television. This creates problems if, for example at a party, there is background music.

It is important to encourage people to try alternatives to their usual pastimes if these can no longer be pursued. Individual likes and dislikes need to be considered when looking for appropriate leisure activities. Isolation can be a major problem caused by hearing loss and this should be avoided. There are social clubs for the hard of hearing and self-help groups which provide useful advice and hopefully new friends.

Learning A person with hearing loss needs to learn about his or her condition. It may be difficult to do this due to a number of factors. Initially the hearing loss itself provides a barrier to effective communication. There may be a reluctance on the part of the individual to accept the loss and there may also be a lack of understanding about the techniques available to help.

Each person is an individual and should be treated as such, it is important to tailor any education programme to meet the individual's need.

Sight

Degenerative visual changes can have an adverse affect on many of our daily activities. Presbyopia begins in middle age and is compensated for by wearing glasses, which may need to be changed regularly in order to meet the changing needs of the wearer. There are more serious conditions, which affect the eye, such as cataract and glaucoma both of which require treatment and which may otherwise lead to severe loss of vision.

Communication Visual deterioration affects the ability to communicate. In order to communicate effectively we use a number of skills including eye contact, this can be seriously impaired in an older person. Many elderly people also have hearing loss and cannot rely on their hearing to compensate for loss of visual acuity. Each person will need different aids to help with communication, glasses often help as does adequate lighting. It is important to assess each person to find the correct techniques for their needs.

Safety and mobility The safety aspects of daily living are severely impaired by visual loss. It becomes more difficult to move about and to feel safe. Elderly people often become anxious and depressed due to loss of vision as they are unable to orientate themselves in new situations as quickly as they once could. Going out becomes a problem particularly if alone. Reading a bus timetable or finding a street sign are extremely difficult if sight is poor. There are many measures that can be taken to help overcome difficulties including the use of magnifying aids. However for many elderly people the fear of falling because of visual difficulty keeps them a prisoner in their own home. Brocklehurst *et al* (1976) suggests that visual deterioration is closely linked with the incidence of fractured femur in the elderly.

Within the home it is relatively easy to prevent accidents, keeping furniture in the same places in order for elderly people to become familiar with its position, removing or securing mats and rugs which could contribute to falls, and improving lighting in places such as staircases and halls can all help. In the community it is more difficult although much could be done to help visually impaired people, pavement edges could be painted in a contrasting colour in order to make them seen more easily, signs in libraries, banks and surgeries could also be in contrasting colours. These are small changes which could make a large difference to the lives of elderly visually impaired people. Local councils and pressure groups could perhaps help.

Work and leisure   Many leisure pursuits are affected by loss of vision. Knitting, sewing, tapestry, carpentry, electrical work etc are all more difficult and in some cases impossible. Aids are available such as magnifying glasses which can be worn around the neck which enlarge any needlework, also there are page magnifiers to help read a pattern, instruction leaflet or book. Many books are available in large print and there are also 'talking books'. These are books which are read and recorded onto cassette. Going to the theatre or cinema is one area which is difficult to enhance for visually impaired people and many find they have to give up this pursuit or attend only to listen.

It is important to encourage elderly people to find new leisure pursuits or to adapt old ones in order to maintain their sense of self and to prevent isolation.

Personal cleansing and dressing   This area of daily activity may also be affected, it may become difficult to dress when buttons and zips cannot be seen. There is also the problem of choosing clothes if distinguishing between colours or being seen clearly in a mirror are restricted. If possible a friend can be taken on a shopping trip in order to assist when choosing clothes and there are now many suppliers who manufacture clothes for disabled people which have easier openings and less difficult fastenings.

Eating and drinking   This area is affected as there may be difficulties preparing food and also eating it. A visually impaired person may have difficulty in the kitchen with the risk of accidents whilst preparing food. Good lighting is essential as are aids and appliances which minimise safety risks such as guard rails on the cooker. Buying food which takes a minimum of preparation may be one option although these foods tend to be expensive for people on a small budget, as many older people are.

One of the factors considered when serving food is its presentation and it is suggested that well presented food can encourage people to eat. If one cannot see the food then it is unlikely to be tempting. It is important to encourage the other senses such as smell and taste in order to prevent a poor appetite developing. It may also be necessary to use aids such as plate guards in order to make it easier to eat the food.

Touch

Touch may become less sensitive with ageing. The receptors within the skin deteriorate and the skin becomes less elastic. These receptors are sensitive to pressure, pain and temperature as well as providing tactile sensations which allow discrimination between rough and smooth, and sharp and blunt. They provide a measure of safety enabling a rapid response to avoid things which are too hot or cold.

If these receptors are not as effective, this can affect both the safety and communication of an older person.

Safety   An elderly lady may sit next to the fire and burn her legs quite badly as she does not feel the heat. A man may take a hot water bottle to bed to warm his feet and in doing so cause burns which require frequent dressings. These problems are obviously very serious but may not be the only safety problems associated with diminished sensations. Pressure sores may develop as a result of lack of feeling in the person's skin. These problems do not take long to occur but can take months to resolve. Elderly people need to understand the nature of these problems, and need help with developing methods of coping. Simple measures such as using a bath thermometer or regularly relieving pressure are easily taught.

Communication   Touch can be very important in communication. Many people touch when speaking, a hand on someone's arm may hold his or her attention or may convey a message. Not everyone likes to be touched and it is important to remember this when communicating, it is an individual preference and should be assessed as such. Problems with diminished sensation may lead people to touch less which may inhibit their communication. There may be social problems as a result of touch deprivation in older people, there is often a loss of family friends and it is assumed that older people require less contact. Touch may be related to a sense of psychological well-being.

Taste and smell

Taste and smell can be discussed together in that they both affect the same daily activities and are in some ways linked. Goldman (1971) suggests that there is an 80% reduction in the number of functioning taste buds in the elderly. There are only four taste sensations which the taste buds identify, these are sour, salt, bitter and sweet. All other tastes are as a result of these four being modified by the accompanying olfactory sensations (Tortora, 1987). The sense of smell is also believed to diminish with age but is, as yet, poorly researched and documented. However, changes in the ability to detect different odours also has implications for the sensation of taste.

Eating and drinking   For many elderly people the pleasure of food may decrease with the loss of taste sensation. This may lead to malnutrition as eating is no longer enjoyable. It may also lead to an increased use of salt and sugar to heighten the taste, with resulting weight gain or heart problems. An alternative would be to modify the diet to include more spices and stronger tasting foods. These would also have to be suitable for the person as many elderly people are more likely to have digestive problems such as hiatus hernia or peptic ulceration. Food needs to be well presented and look attractive in order to tempt the person to eat.

Eating is also a social activity, people living alone may have little incentive for preparing food for themselves and need to be encouraged to eat well. At the same time there is an economic factor as the cost of feeding one person is proportionately greater than feeding two.

Safety   A diminished sense of taste and smell may have an effect on the safety of the individual. Serious problems may be the inability to smell a gas leak, minor problems may be eating or drinking something which has decayed and is contaminated leading to further health problems.

Minimising the difficulties

Thus to some degree, all older people experience a decline in the response of the special senses. The effects are profound as the loss touches on almost every other aspect of the older person's life. However, much can be done by older people themselves and those who help them, to minimise the difficulties, provide practical help and social contacts and compensate for the loss of senses. The older person can still, with help, keep in touch with the world.

References

Argyle, M. (1978) *The Psychology of Interpersonal Behaviour*. Penguin, Harmondsworth.
Brocklehurst, J.C. *et al* (1976) *Fracture of the femur in old age: A two centre study of associated clinical factors and the cause of the fall. Age Ageing*. **7,** 7–15.
Garrett, G. (1987) *Health Needs of the Elderly, 2nd edn*. Macmillan, London.
Goldman, R. (1971) *Decline in organ function with ageing. In Rossman, I. Clinical Geriatrics*. 19–21. Lippincott, Philadelphia.
Satir, V. (1967) *Conjoint Family Therapy*. Science and behaviour books, California.

Tortora, G.J. and Anagnostakos, N.P. (1987) *Anatomy and Physiology, 5th edn.* Harper and Row, New York.

Wright, S.G. (1988) *Nursing the Older Patient.* Harper and Row, London.

Wright, W.B. (1984) *Common physical conditions of old age. In Young P., Nursing The Aged. 11–28.* Woodhead-Faulkner, Cambridge.

6

Relationships in later life

Gill Garrett, BA, RGN, RCNT, DN (London), Cert Ed (FE), RNT, FP Cert
Freelance Lecturer, Bristol

The nature of sexuality: its implications

Sexuality has been defined as "those aspects of the human being that relate to being boy or girl, man or woman . . . an entity subject to lifelong dynamic change. (It) reflects our human character, not solely our genital nature" (Lion, 1982). As such an integral feature of the human condition it is one which merits serious consideration by nurses. Its inclusion in the curriculum, however, has only been a very recent occurrence, and even now it is often defined and taught in far narrower terms, with many vital areas overlooked.

The comprehensive Lion definition stresses the ongoing development of sexuality throughout the life-cycle, and this chapter seeks to look at this in later life. Webb has described how human sexuality is intimately tied up with the self-concept, self-esteem, body image and social roles (Webb, 1985). All of these are affected by the ageing processes, and nurses working with older people consequently need to give some thought to the implications for the everyday living, and caring situations, in which their clients find themselves.

Many nurses, however, do not feel entirely comfortable in considering, let alone dealing with, older people's sexuality. Perhaps this reflects the general societal belief that older people are, or should be, asexual. Whilst changing social moves over the last two or three decades have permitted the liberation of the young, this does not hold true for those in later life. Some older people, having inherited the Victorian legacy of beliefs and attitudes of their parents during their formative years, may themselves feel confused or unsure as to the 'appropriateness' of their needs and feelings. As today's young and middle aged people age they may well be far more assertive about their continuing needs, but the asexual image that the current generation of older people bears is a clear example of the present ageist stance of our society.

A further reason why some nurses may find the area difficult is because, as young people, they may still be developing and coming to terms with their own sexual identity and its expression. It has been said that "There is no one way to love or be loved; there is no one liaison which is superior to another. No one lifestyle in singlehood or marriage, heterosexual or homosexual, will suit all persons" (Weg, 1983). However, dealing with people whose feelings, beliefs and behaviour may be very different from one's own can be very threatening, and to accept other's lifestyles, as equally valid as one's own, demands a maturity of outlook perhaps beyond the years of some. From more experienced staff, it is often expected that there will be a more confident approach but for many older nurses, too, sexuality remains "one of the most difficult areas . . . to explore honestly with patients" (Nursing Times, 1991).

Approaching later life

People approaching later life may be in a whole variety of relationship situations. Some may be in close continuing relationships; with a sibling, a long term friend, a marriage partner; some of these relationships may be of an overtly sexual nature (hetero- or homosexual), others may be platonic. Some older people continue to enter into a series of relationships as they did in earlier life. Others may be alone: some by choice, others by circumstance such as separation, divorce or early widowhood.

It is all too easy to define other people's relationships in the light of one's own experiences, perhaps of singlehood or marriage. Recognition and acknowledgement of the absolute individuality of older people's relationships is essential. Whatever their situations, all older people will have arrived at them by pathways unique to themselves. Decades of experiences – some happy, some sad, some public, others intensely private – will have shaped their feelings and expectations, their responses and their chosen or imposed ways of living.

In an interesting chapter in her book on ageing Margaret Hellie Huyck asks whether we age or *grow* older (Huyck, 1974). In later life there may be involvement in fewer relationships but those that remain become increasingly precious and meaningful. The opportunities for extending, for deepening relationships which a greater life experience, more unmortgaged time and a less cluttered existence afford are very real for many older people. But ageing is so commonly thought of as a time of loss, which it undoubtedly is on the one hand, that these opportunities for personal growth, which occur on the other hand, are often overlooked. Youth is portrayed as the time for relationships, their formation and cementing; age is seen as simply a continuation stage, or as a time of discontinuity with a partner's death. Yet so unhelpful a depiction is challenged daily by the thousands of older people living and loving to capacity around us.

Features of later life which affect relationships

In ageing there are many challenges to be met as the individual faces physical, psychological and social change. But people age in different ways, at different times and at different rates; they approach ageing with different attitudes. Generalisations are thus always questionable when discussing the subject. However, there are common features in most older people's later existence from which useful points can be made, and the observations which follow are offered from this standpoint.

Physical change

Western society still clings to youthfulness and vitality as the embodiment of physical beauty. Although the concept is now beginning to be challenged (even in the continuing onslaught of advertisements and portrayals on film and television) today's elderly grew up with the idea. Women especially were brought up to conform to the pattern of attracting and pleasing men by 'taking care of' their appearance. In later life the hair and skin changes, the postural and other physical attractions may signal to some the loss of attractiveness and may be difficult to accept. Some of the physical changes in men may conversely be seen as rendering them more attractive and this has led to the description of a 'double standard' in attitudes to ageing. However, the decline in physical strength and capacity may be equally problematic and frustrating for some older men, who grew up with the idea of male dominance and images of powerfulness, sometimes difficult to maintain in the circumstances.

Sensory changes in later life, such as failing eyesight or hearing impairment, can, in addition to presenting barriers to ordinary social interaction, adversely affect closer relationships. Between established couples, other channels of communication may have built up over the years, but developing new relationships may be more difficult if the deficits are not satisfactorily corrected. Some changes in touch perception may also be experienced, some older women for example find their lips less sensitive, but these are not always of a negative nature and some bodily areas may become more sensitive, enhancing intimacy.

The menopause, marking the end of female reproductive life, may effect an older woman's relationships positively or negatively. If sexuality and procreation are intimately connected for her she may view 'the change' as drawing a curtain across any future activity. If she views relationships in a more recreational light (in the true meaning of the word) however, the new freedom from the fear of unwanted pregnancy and from the need for contraception may be very welcome indeed. Some of the physiological changes consequent upon hormonal alterations (such as vaginal dryness) may occasionally be bothersome but respond readily to treatment (for example with the use of a lubricant or the prescription of oestrogen cream or pessaries).

Although reproductive capacity is not lost by the older man, there are changes in sexual performance, such as lower arousal and a decrease in the number and force of ejaculations. But, as with women, the physiological changes in no way preclude the continuation of physical intimacy in all its manifestations (masturbation, fondling, penetrative intercourse, oral sex) into extreme old age; of far more import are social changes and personal attitudes. To quote one elderly gentleman – 'Sex has far more to do with what's between your ears than between your legs!'

Social change

Later life almost inevitably heralds social changes of some magnitude: retirement from paid employment, family changes (such as adult children becoming independent, the onset of grandparenthood, perhaps the taking on of responsibility for dependent elderly parents), and, in partnerships, the often devastating blow of bereavement. All these changes demand adaptation, but the outcomes are not all negative and the potential for growth, mentioned above, is an ever present reality.

Most of the discussion on retirement has until recently concentrated on the male viewpoint; women were seen as either not working outside the home or only doing so as a 'second' occupation, with homemaking their prime interest and responsibility. For a variety of reasons this is often no longer the case, and it is becoming obvious that women too may miss the companionship and paid income work afforded, the status of a 'working' (ie, contributing) person and a structured and meaningful employed lifestyle.

Because of the changed workforce profile over the past couple of decades, couples are now more likely to be retiring together or within a short space of time of each other. In the generation currently retiring, however, male and female roles in relation to home care are still likely to be clearly defined, with the woman taking by far the larger share. 'Twice as much husband on half as much income' is a true aphorism for many women; when retiring husbands naively imagine that they can help out around the house, disrupting the routine of decades, the disagreements are likely to reverberate in other areas of relationships as well as in the kitchen. Some partners have only got on well because they have seen comparatively little of each other during their working lives, and retirement, which throws them together, can precipitate crises undreamed of beforehand.

Alternatively, time to talk, walk, garden, visit friends and family, read, watch films together after years of concern with childrearing or employment can be truly liberating and can witness the deepening of relationships on both emotional and physical levels. Couples may still wish to pursue individual interests rather than 'living in each other's pockets', but with the pressure of other commitments relieved they may discover new energy and resources to do both.

Bereavement after a long partnership (of whatever nature) can be shattering. It has been termed 'the cost of commitment'. The loss of the person who provided companionship, friendship, practical help and support and emotional and physical closeness shakes the very foundations of the survivor's world. Whilst society acknowledges the practical and social implications, the intimacy needs of the bereaved, especially in later life, tend to be disregarded. For younger bereaved people there are opportunities through normal social channels for the eventual formation of new relationships: this tends not to be the case with older people. Similarly, little thought tends to be given to the additional burden borne by the older bereaved gay or lesbian whose relationship may have been the source of some stigma to begin with (Courtney, 1985). In some areas these difficulties are beginning to be acknowledged and addressed, through the work of organisations such as CRUSE and the Gay Bereavement Project, but a widespread understanding has yet to be engendered.

Disability

Whilst physical and social changes are inevitable in ageing, the onset of illness or disability in later life is not, and many older people remain healthy and capable of independent living virtually to the end. For others minor or major problems may dog their later years with consequences for all aspects of their lives, including their relationships.

In recent years there has been a growing realisation of the sexual implications of surgical procedures affecting body image, eg mastectomy, stoma creation, amputation (all of which are frequently carried out on older patients), but less thought appears to have been given to the effects on sexuality of chronic medical conditions, such as arthritis, stroke, diabetes, Parkinson's disease, urinary incontinence. Whilst, properly controlled, these may not be life threatening, they are certainly life altering and may have decided effects upon an older person's relationships.

Physical difficulties may well be experienced with such chronic conditions, perhaps the inability to position oneself comfortably for lovemaking, but of equal importance are the perhaps less obvious implications. An older man hemiplegic following a stroke may be demoralised, frustrated by his dependence for personal care, unable to relate to his partner in their established manner. Where intimate functioning can be encouraged and restored, however, it is truly part of the rehabilitation process: "the intimacy and warmth often associated with sexual expression have a significance beyond the pleasurable release of sexual tension – an important assertion and commitment of self and a reaffirmation of the connection with life itself" (Weg, 1983). To make such restoration a reality, nursing and medical staff must familiarise themselves with the agencies offering the necessary help and advice, such as SPOD and the Disabled Living Foundation, and refer appropriately.

Many older people regularly take a variety of drugs, both prescribed and bought over the counter. Some drugs are known to have frequent effects upon sexual functioning, eg narcotics, tranquillisers, antidepressants, hypotensive agents; others, such as cimetidine and propanolol, may occasionally give rise to problems. Older people need to be made aware of possible side-effects of their therapy and it often falls to the nurse to do this. One drug used by many older people can have very marked effects. Whilst alcohol in moderation may be acceptably enjoyed, the associated socialising often increasing interaction outside the home, sexual functioning can be impaired by over indulgence and close relationships generally may be wrecked by problem drinking as in any other age group.

The onset of disability or frailty in later life may mark the advent of the need for care either in a family home or in a more institutional setting. Such relocation often assigns the older person a 'sick role', removes from them the opportunities for independent social interaction and denies them the privacy necessary to conduct intimate relationships. Dependence upon others for help in the activities of daily living lowers self-esteem and in turn changes the self-concept. Unless carers consistently make the effort to respect privacy and to react sensitively and appropriately to expressed or apparent need, they may, albeit unwittingly, effectively neuter the older person and in so doing destroy part of his or her essential humanity.

Quality of being human

It has been said that "For a growing person, time passing is parallel with the growth of self – you become ever more who you really are" (Huyck, 1974). In the absence of any gross pathological change further to accident or illness, there are no great alterations in personality or character in ageing: there is a continuation of the traits, the idiosyncrasies, the endearing ways, the annoying habits developed in earlier years. Circumstances change and the expression of different aspects of our nature may thus alter with time, but the essential personal remains the same; an integral feature of this is our sexuality.

This chapter can serve only as a brief introduction to a broad and enormously important area. It is one which nurses must pursue and integrate into their professional perspective, as it is impossible to speak of 'whole person care' without due regard for that "quality of being human, all that we are as men and women" (Hogan, 1980) which our sexuality comprises.

References
Courtney, M. (1985) The sexual needs of widowed people. *Bereavement Care,* **4,** (1).
Editorial Comment (1991) *Nursing Times.* **87** (18).
Hogan, R. (1980) *Human sexuality. A Nursing Perspective.* Appleton-Century-Crofts, New York.
Huyck, M.H. (1974) *Growing Older: What You Need to Know About Ageing.* Prentice Hall, New York.
Lion, E.M. (Ed) (1982) *Human Sexuality in Nursing Process.* John Wiley, New York.
Webb, C. (1985) *Sexuality, Nursing and Health.* John Wiley, Chichester.
Weg, R.B. (1983) *Sexuality in Later Years. Roles and Behaviour.* Academic Press, New York.

Bibliography
Greengross, W. and Greengross, S. (1989) *Living, Loving and Ageing.* Age Concern, England.

Useful Addresses
Association to Aid the Sexual and Personal Relationships of People with a Disability (SPOD), 286 Camden Rd., London N7 0BJ.
Cruse – Bereavement Care, Cruse House, 126 Sheen Rd., Richmond, Surrey TW9 1UR.
Relate, Herbert Gray College, Little Church St., Rugby CV21 3AP.
Gay Bereavement Project, Unitarian Rooms, Hoop Lane, London NW11 8BS.

7

Killing time

Steve Goodwin
Cosmic Nursing Projects, Lancashire

Imagine the stir that would be caused if on the death certificate of some elderly deceased person cause of death was recorded as 'bored to death'.

Though this may seem fairly outrageous we should not underestimate the problems that boredom and the lack of mental and social stimulation can have on the health and wellbeing of any person young or old.

The nurse's role in recreation

Nurses throughout the years have often found it difficult to relate social and recreational activities to their roles, more likely seeing it solely as the responsibility of the Occupational Therapist or voluntary agencies. Particularly in the more acute setting of health care provision for older people, nurses might consider lending precious time to such activities as unproductive, surely not a matter of life or death, yet quality of life may certainly be at risk.

Having the clinical expertise to help an elderly person to recover after surgery, a stroke or heart attack may not be enough to guarantee their full rehabilitation or return to their maximum potential. Without the will, motivation and purpose to get better, many elderly people will be left along life's hard shoulder rather than returning to the slow or fast lane of their previous lifestyle.

For many elderly people who do not enjoy good health, days can seem very long and years short. With time on their hands, whether in a hospital ward or in their own front lounge, there is usually more opportunity to reflect on the pains, aches and sorrows of life. Preoccupations with minor ailments and petty concerns often grow out of elderly people losing a purpose in their lives and a lack of expectation that pleasures will come. The focus of their own and their carer's attention, even trained professional staff, rests on what is wrong with them, and the important area of what is right with them loses its relevance. Nurses too sadly, over the years have been more interested in elderly people's disabilities and handicaps rather than building on their strengths and experiences that have often been well tested and tried over the passing decades.

Contact with the real world

Many nurses may feel that most elderly people are generally boring full stop. It might be that they are just young bores grown old or it is more likely that in their old age, and because of restricted opportunity to continue with life long interests, hobbies and leisure activities, they have little new or of interest to talk about. This may be worsened by a lack of contact with others around them, or through sensory deprivation, particularly the hard of hearing. In these different ways they may have been cut-off or protected from the real world. Once elderly individuals lose contact with the real world they are in danger of no longer being seen as real people with real values, beliefs and expectations.

Once value, worth and status of an elderly person is lost, particularly those who are confused, frail or handicapped, then they become open to all forms of infringements of their civil and legal rights even to the extent of abuse. Can it really be that helping old people to maintain and develop interests, hobbies and recreational activities will also ensure they are not maltreated or undervalued? Would you mix words with an elderly person who you know can complete The Times crossword daily? Will we, as nurses, stand by and let medics try to convince an elderly lady that her hip replacement operation is not essential, recognising her love of ballroom dancing? Could we glibly ask an elderly gent with a heart condition to give up his allotment, when his dying wish is to be buried beneath his artichokes?

Of course not all interests and activities that elderly people are involved in are particularly good for them. The same again, however, could be said about ourselves. There may be some elderly people who smoke too much or consume too much alcohol. They may spend a large percentage of their income on these and neglect their nutritional needs. This could be as a result of spending a lot of time in the pub or alone with a bottle because they are lonely, or socially isolated. By helping them rediscover or develop interests, make social contacts, and by making a healthy lifestyle option more interesting, we may not just save quality of life but quantity of life as well.

Activities in care planning

When nurses are first introduced to an elderly patient or client, it is usually when they are ill or in need of treatment or assessment. Not only will they perhaps be feeling unwell but they will very likely be looking and perhaps behaving unwell. This can influence the nurse's opinion and expectations about them. The nurse can easily form early impressions underestimating elderly people's potential and circumstances. As the Care Plan is drawn up little attention may be paid to the person's social and recreational interests, yet these could be used as part of treatment processes to help some elderly people recover. If patients need to partake in physiotherapy sessions, they can be linked to activities they already enjoy and are practiced in. The more relevant and interesting a treatment is the more successful it is likely to be for the patient. Elderly people do not have to recognise it as 'treatment' for it to be doing them good, this is a form of 'invisible mending'.

Many older people may be reluctant to join in a 'keep fit' or movement to music session in groups but enjoy a game of carpet bowls with another patient. Mysteriously an elderly gent with arthritic shoulders may fail miserably his dressing assessment in a morning because he cannot get his arms high enough, yet in a pub that same lunchtime with a member of staff he can get a pint glass well up to his chin. Even walking practice may be more beneficial if done in a garden area, out with the dog or even the grandchildren. Finger dexterity can be much improved by games of dominoes, cards or even a keyboard, all of which may also exercise mental agility.

Important role that pets can play

The simple activity of stroking a cat or dog can be much underestimated as well, not only encouraging essential limb and joint movement, but perhaps relieving stress and exercising the old facial muscles when a smile breaks out. With patients who are less popular or who just find other human contact difficult, very often a pet is less discriminitive. Many elderly people refuse operations, or day and respite care because they do not want to leave their pet who can very often be also a best friend, lending a concerned look when everyone else has had enough of their grumblings and complaints.

The use of visiting PRO and PAT Dogs in hospital and nursing home settings have proved a great help where such animals cannot be permanently kept. These charities use volunteer handlers to bring specially selected dogs into tangible contact with old people which stimulate a great deal of fuss, stroking, petting and conversation.

Enjoying time spent with patients

Whilst people are enjoying themselves they often forget about their current aches, pains and symptoms. This is particularly so off the ward away from their own home or normal environment. From time to time we all enjoy a trip out, a change of scene, a purpose to put on best clothes and a splash of make-up or to shave. For elderly patients who have been unwell for some time but now much on the mend, or who are about to be discharged after a period of rehabilitation, or who just need to regain confidence and practice conversation and social interaction again, a trip out in a small group or individually can be a great tonic. There is no need for them or the nurses involved to feel guilty about enjoying these few hours, after all it's not against the code of conduct to enjoy yourself with patients. Perhaps only one nurse may be available to be escort on such an excursion, relatives, friends and volunteers can be used to assist and make such outings possible.

Once nurses cease to consider recreational and social activities as a 'luxury' and realise it is an important and essential ingredient to good health, then it will no longer be seen as 'optional extra' but as an integral part of care planning. Not only this but also it should be recognised as a basic human right, even criminals in prison have daily access to recreation. Of course elderly people have equal right to disengage from any leisure activity or pastime. Some may genuinely not have the physical strength or mental capacity to do anything but sit and watch others enjoy themselves or watch the world go by. Good assessment may, however, be able to differentiate between those who are depressed and unmotivated, and those who are just lazy, or who quite simply do not want to know thankyou.

The more we know about their previous habits, lifestyles and histories the better our understanding of what interests or motivates them. Coupled with this desire for more useful information is the elderly person's right to remain anonymous or give limited details about themselves or their past. They may even be involved in pastimes, clubs and societies that they would rather not have made known.

Reminiscence and life history review

In the last few years an ever increasing interest has been shown in the use of reminiscence therapy. Some nurses see it as a useful tool in the process of helping some elderly people take a retrospective view of their past lived experiences, and build on these to put a perspective and purposeful view on their present state and future wellbeing. Others quite simply see it as a pleasant and valuable pastime that is perhaps of more benefit to staff than the elderly people participating. Certainly it can help nurses and other carers have a more positive and factual view of certain elderly individuals, particularly those who are at risk of being undervalued such as the mentally frail or stroke victims.

Reminiscence is something we all naturally do whether young or old therefore there is nothing to discourage nurses from contributing to individual or group sessions. Reminiscence work often incorporates the use of props to stimulate conversation and interaction. These may include old photographs and newspapers, memorabilia, tapes of songs and tunes from past eras, quizzes, bottled aromas or selecting special occasions or aspects of our daily living to discuss. These may be as simple as wash day, the Sunday School Outing or as momentous as the outbreak of war.

A whole industry around the use of reminiscence has developed with many useful packs and publications available. A great deal of careful consideration also needs to be used with reminiscence work as many elderly people have very private and sad memories amongst the fascinating and pleasurable ones.

Looking back at elderly people's pastimes does reveal key indicators as to the type of activity and interest most suitable to them now. Some leisure pursuits have changed little, others have changed dramatically. Napoleon described Britain as a nation of shopkeepers, certainly the corner shops that elderly people were once heavily dependent on are increasingly becoming video and take-away establishments.

The older generations of today were brought up on live entertainment, queueing to get in the theatre, cinema or football match. Dancing was popular as was a family get together either down in the pub or at home for a sing along around a piano. Here also a whole industry has been created around videos and records and tapes that capture the artists and milestones from those eras, including Pathe News reels and great sporting achievements of the past.

Using modern technology

Individual patients in hospital can listen to music of their own selection without disturbing others if they have a personal stereo and they can have it as loud as they like without annoying others around them. The television is often abused in hospitals but here again a video recorder could be used to show relevant programmes or appropriate video films at times when children's programmes are on. Many elderly people in hospital miss out on favourite programmes because of treatments or when visitors interrupt. Video recordings could be made to ensure their interest in a series or television in general is maintained.

Patients with special difficulties

Patients with sensory problems often miss out on activities or give up interests as their sight or hearing fails. Proper spectacles and a good hearing aid are major factors in maintaining a good quality of life for many elderly people. Large print books and news or novels on tapes are widely available and the variety is improving all the time. Magazines in hospital tend to be female orientated and the print size rather small. Elderly people who have moved away from their own home town to be nearer family can be kept in touch by newspapers being sent from their old locality. Many people are only too willing to get rid of the free press that come through their doors. Ethnic elders may also appreciate papers from their own country of origin or books, films and foodstuffs peculiar to their own culture and taste.

Matching activities to the individual

Many elderly women and even some men enjoy the occasional cooking session, knitting, sewing or embroidery while some truly detest it. It is very often more the social contact and chit chat around these sessions that proves most beneficial and enjoyable. Some elderly patients, perhaps chair or bed-fast, can still partake in quizzes, competitions and even games such as table top skittles. Nurses must be careful not to insult elderly people's integrity or competiveness. Many very old people are highly skilled bridge or whist players. There is perhaps nothing worse than asking them to play 'snap' because that's all the nurse knows.

The nurse may have few opportunities to spend long periods with patients before being called away to other duties so they need to act as a catalyst. They can assess and choose patients who will get on well together, are matched in interests and skills or who can help each other along whether consciously or not. All recreational equipment needs to be well kept, accessible to patients and encouragement given to their use. If a garden facility is available then patients may be encouraged to lend advice or take an active interest. Raised flower beds for less agile patients can be developed or simple pots and planters. Competitions for individual participants may be interesting for the more keen or experienced.

Broadening interests

Some interests that can be maintained or developed may not just be for leisure, they may be professional or business interests or even an active involvement in a church or society. Most churches, clubs and societies are only too willing to send out newsletters, publications and even visitors.

There are a number of holiday companies who specialise in breaks for retired and older people including holidays in nursing homes or hotels which have facilities for incontinence and mobility problems. Many societies have special interest holidays or week-end breaks. Many elderly focus much of their time and interest on their families, sometimes nurses can overlook this, and so involving them and their wider carers in all these issues is very important.

The confusion about boredom

For elderly people with dementia or confusion the problem of boredom is also a major challenge. How much of their confused behaviour is really just sheer boredom? Any person left without mental or social stimulation will act strangely or behave disruptively even after a relatively short period of time. Over a long period, mental and physical health can decline, depression and despondency set in and for those who have much time to kill we may find surprisingly it ends up slowly killing them instead.

8

Family care and the elderly

Gill Garrett, BA, RGN, RCNT, DN (London), Cert Ed (FE), RNT, FP Cert
Freelance Lecturer, Bristol

Just as marriage and the strength of the family unit in earlier times are often lauded, a popular belief holds that in the 'good old days' the elderly were clasped to the bosom of the extended family. On becoming infirm or simply too old to work, they were supposedly taken in to the hearth and home of kith and kin and cherished by their offspring and the offspring of their offspring. The available evidence simply does not support such a belief, however, and Peter Laslett considering the present management of the elderly, writes "(it) remains irreducibly novel; it calls for invention rather than imitation" (Laslett, 1978).

This chapter sets out to examine what may be meant by the word 'family' in relation to the elderly, to discuss factors affecting past and present living and caring situations, to describe the supportive role the elderly themselves play in 'family' life and to consider different situations in which 'family'-type care may be offered to them when required.

What is a family?
The term family is often used very loosely and may mean various things to various people. In most definitions however, in addition to blood or marriage ties, certain other features are generally considered characteristic of 'family' relationships. Leonard and Speakman (1983) have listed them as follows:
- they are not monetary based; services within them are done for love.
- there are strong feelings of obligation to give and receive help.
- there is a sharing of income, goods and property.
- there is continuing social contact and often cohabitation.
- there is often more physical contact than in other settings.

The implication is that 'the family' is a unit of economic, social and emotional support. When relatives are seldom seen, socially distant or financially calculating, they may be said to form little more than a 'legal' family; equally, biologically or maritally unrelated individuals who maintain close, affectionate and supportive relationships could be seen to demonstrate many of the positive aspects of 'family' involvement. At a time when much is said and written about young people seeking alternative life-styles, it should be remembered that some of the elderly are already involved in them, and more will become so – perhaps living in long-term friendships, or with family groups other than those which are, strictly speaking, their own.

Why is it so vital for nurses to consider the broader social perspective when studying age and ageing individuals? In his classic publication *The family life of old people* Peter Townsend writes in his conclusion: "If many of the processes and problems of ageing are to be understood, old people must be studied as members of families . . . and (treated) as an inseparable part of a family group, which is more than just a residential unit . . . whether or not they are treated as such largely determines their security, their health and their happiness" (Townsend, 1963). His study had concentrated on the elderly in the east end of London, mainly in conventional family relationships. A broader view will be taken here which encompasses other living and caring situations which may demonstrate features of a 'family' (ie where two or more people share a relationship which is economically, socially and emotionally mutually supportive).

Moving on from all our yesterdays

It has been only in the last 70 years that a sizeable proportion of the population has survived into old age. For those who did survive in the pre-industrial era, though they may well have lived in closer proximity to their immediate relatives, care and support depended far more on mutual affection than on external social pressures. Indeed, some early records indicate that it was so unusual for elderly parents to be housed with married children that those who were, might have been described as 'lodgers, receiving parish relief' (Laslett and Wall, 1972).

Social and demographic changes during the twentieth century have accounted for the very different caring situations and attitudes experienced by present-day families as opposed to those experienced by their grandparents. One feature however remains constant; the majority of carers are still women. The Government has decreed that for the elderly: "Care in the community must increasingly mean care by the community" (DHSS, 1981); with financial restraints and cuts in the provision of many welfare services, community care can only be seen to equal 'family' care, which in turn equals care by women (spouses, daughters, nieces and neighbours). Thus to understand past and present situations, it is necessary to look primarily at the women in them.

The age group most likely to be caring for the elderly are the 45–59 year olds. In 1901 for every one hundred elderly people in the general population, there were 83 women in this age group. The increasing number of people who survived into old age and the falling birth rate (exacerbated by the tremendous loss of life in the First World War, which left many women unmarried and childless) reduced this ratio to 100:49 by 1971. This is the age group which has also experienced the biggest change in employment status; five times as many women of this age are now in paid employment than in 1921. A delay in the age of parenthood, an increasing divorce rate and a rise in the number of single parents has meant that women are often heavily committed to child care. Women are often spoken of as undertaking a dual role; in reality, it is a treble role, often encompassing paid work, caring for the nuclear family and caring for the extended family.

Another change in living situations is the nature of employment. Earlier generations sought employment in local trades and industries and people sometimes remained at their original jobs for the whole of their working lives. Mobility is often now vital to ensure continuing employment and may require the offspring of elderly parents to live many miles from their parental home in another city or even in another country.

It has been suggested, however, that many people prefer not to be involved in sometimes claustrophobic family situations, that they prefer 'intimacy at a distance' (ie living separately from families, but close enough for visiting and mutual assistance). Such situations may be considered to demonstrate 'the modified extended family'. If the attitudes of society are changing, it must not be forgotten that the elderly are an integral part of that society; 'older adults often enjoy the independence and freedom from responsibility that nuclear family life offers' (Eliopoulos, 1979).

The elderly as carers

All too often, stress is placed on inter-generation conflict and problem family situations. It is wise to remember that 'the world is full of families in which there is a minimum amount of discord and a maximum amount of respect and love between the generations' (Millroy, 1964). Family relationships seldom change dramatically in later years; if individuals have got on well beforehand and have been sensitive and adaptable to each other's needs and life-styles, the pattern is generally maintained. This does not mean that difficulties are not experienced (sometimes they are insuperable ones), but makes the point that situations are often far more positive than they are negative.

It is equally vital to remember the active caring role that elderly people may play in family situations. In a study in Cumbria in 1978, almost 60% of the elderly people who had children were found to be actively engaged in babysitting, shopping, lending money or caring for and cooking for school-age grandchildren, often freeing mothers to undertake paid work (Butcher and Crosbie, 1978). In the wider 'family' sense, elderly people are often the source of help for other elderly people to whom they are close; one study found that 30% of the disabled elderly were receiving help from such a source (Green, Creese and Kaufert, 1979).

The old maxim states that 'it is more blessed to give than to receive'; for the elderly there is often a stigma attached to simply receiving and being cast in a state of dependency (ie of being in a subordinate relationship). For them an 'exchange relationship' in which both giving and receiving take place in family situations is vital; the inability to reciprocate may lead to an unwillingness to accept help (Townsend, 1963). Even when advancing age, limited income and restricted mobility may preclude practical assistance, the elderly have less tangible gifts to give, the value of which should not be underestimated.

Their value is acknowledged by nuclear families who have no elderly relatives of their own who have joined 'Adopt a Granny' schemes in this country, and when the elderly offer their services to organisations such as 'Foster Grandparents' in the USA.

Many nurses have personal experience of the closeness that often exists between elderly people and their grandchildren; to them the elderly offer an historical perspective, a sense of their roots and of continuity; they may give advice and affirmation in young adulthood and support in trying situations (often involving their parents!); they help in the achievement of an understanding of ageing and of mortality.

When the time comes: caring for the elderly

Conventional family care It must be remembered that most of the frail elderly are cared for at home; there are three times as many bedbound and severely disabled at home than in all institutions put together (Townsend, 1981), and more women are now caring for elderly and handicapped dependents than for 'normal' under 16-year-olds (this includes elderly women caring for their spouses).The reality of that caring experience must be appreciated; one small but very detailed study of families caring for severely disabled elderly relatives found that the average time spent on weekdays simply on personal care activities was 3 hours 24 minutes – 3 hours 11 minutes by wives, 13 minutes by their husbands (Nissel and Bonnerjea, 1982). The effect upon family and social life in addition to the physical strain and inevitable tiredness experienced may readily be imagined; for most of the carers, outside paid work is an impossibility but the financial costs of caring are high.

Health and social care professionals must adopt a dual approach in such situations which focuses both on the needs of the elderly person and on those of the carers. It may be difficult to meet both requirements simultaneously (for example where the carer is in urgent need of respite care to which the elderly person is opposed). Professionals must try to understand the internal dynamics of the family and, if there are inherent difficulties, to accept that long-standing rivalries, anxieties or ambivalences are unlikely to change and must be worked within. The point has been made that family, friends and neighbours are 'informal' carers simply because they do not originate from any formal organisations but, in truth, "The family and their allies are the primary care team" (Bayley, 1978). It is salutary to reflect on how often their perception of their needs is determined let alone acted upon.

There is also a need to look critically at personal attitudes and prejudices when involving supportive services for an elderly person cared for perhaps by a husband, a son or a brother which would have been withheld had there been a female carer available. Services are scarce and their cost effective use is mandatory; but the hidden costs of long-term caring take their toll on women and their families. Additional expenditure on health and social services may be necessitated later and most of this expense could have been pre-empted by judicious intervention at an earlier stage. Referral to voluntary support groups (such as the Association of Carers) will for some clients be invaluable, but attendance at meetings may be difficult when alternative care for the elderly person has to be arranged.

Other continuing care settings

In some areas, when physical or mental frailty or social isolation means that an elderly person can no longer live in his own home or 'family' situation, imaginative schemes arranged by the social services departments may provide substitute families to ensure continuing community care. These are still mainly in the experimental stages, however, and many elderly people enter residential or hospital care.

Great efforts have been made in recent years to create a more home-like environment in continuing care situations, but home means more than attractive crockery and matching duvet covers and curtains. For the elderly it is the setting in which relationships are forged and maintained, or intimately recalled when lost to death or time; where living and loving have taken and still take place. For children in care, units are designated Family Group Homes; staff attempt to create stable, warm and supportive relationships within them. Do the elderly not merit the same in continuing care at the end of their lives?

As horizons narrow with the concomitants of advanced age, it is within their 'family' (whatever its nature) that the elderly must meet their basic human needs. Nurses may be familiar with Maslow's hierarchy of human needs (Figure 2). Despite its limitations and the simplistic representation, it demonstrates the different levels of need experienced. Its hierarchial framework indicates how the satisfaction of needs at one level is a prerequisite for the attainment of those at the next.

It seems that professional staff involved in continuing care often concentrate their energies on assisting the elderly to meet their needs at the two lower levels; they are fed and watered and their physical safety is ensured. It is time to think about meeting higher level needs, maintaining existing relationships, encouraging social integration and permitting the development of affectionate interaction with staff. For the staff to allow themselves to be used as substitute daughters or grand-daughters, however, demands the ability to constantly give of themselves and reciprocally to take from the elderly in relationships which, by their very nature, are transient. Perhaps, in nursing, such possibilities have not yet even begun to be truly explored.

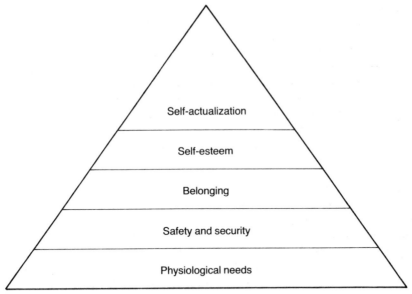

2 Maslow's hierarchy of needs. (From Maslow A. *Towards a Psychology of Being.*
New York: D. Van Nostrand, 1962.)

This article was first published in *Nursing*, 1161–3, and reproduced with permission from Baillière
Tindall.

Further reading

Bayley, M. (1978) Someone to fall back on. *Community Care.*

Butcher, H. Crosbie, D. (1978) *Pensioned Off.* Cumbria Development Project, University of
York.

Department of Health and Social Security. (1981) *Growing Older.* London, HMSO.

Eliopoulos, C. (1979) *Geriatric Nursing.* Harper & Row. London.

Green S, Creese, X, Kaufert, J. (1979) Social support and government policy on services for
the elderly. *Social Policy and Administration* **13**: 210–18.

Laslett P. (1978) The history of ageing and the aged. In: Carver V, Liddiard P., eds. *An
ageing population.* Open University Press. Milton Keynes.

Laslett, P., Wall R. (1972) *Household and Family in Past Times.* Cambridge University Press,
Cambridge.

Leonard, D., Speakman, M.A. (1983) *The family: daughters, wives and mothers.* (Open
University Course u221 Unit 9). Open University Press, Milton Keynes.

Millroy M. (1964) Casework with the older person and his family. *Social Casework* **45**: 406.

Nissel M., Bonnerjea, L. (1982) *Family care of the elderly – Who pays?* Policy Studies Institute,
Np. London 602.

Townsend, P. (1963) *The Family Life of Old People.* Penguin Harmondsworth.

Townsend, P. (1981) Elderly people with disabilities. In: Walker, A., Townsend, P., eds.
Disability in Britain. Martin Robertson, Oxford.

9

Caring in the UK today

Gill Garrett, BA, RGN, RCNT, DN (London), Cert Ed(FE), RNT, FPCert
Freelance Lecturer, Bristol

Over the last few years, healthcare professionals have become increasingly aware of the vital nature of 'informal' caring networks supporting frail, disabled and elderly people in the community. The considerable burden which many of the carers shoulder has at last been acknowledged, but hard facts about the numbers of people involved, their circumstances, and other detailed information have been difficult to obtain. What was known of the national picture came largely from surveys carried out almost a decade ago.

New information has recently been made available based on the 1985 General Household Survey (Green, 1988). Based on that document, this chapter gives a profile of the caring situation to stimulate thought as to how we can more effectively 'care for the carers'.

The carers

There are now six million carers in Great Britain (four times the number previously estimated), and 1.7 million of these care for a person (or persons) in their own household. The rest support a dependant (or dependants) in a separate home, possibly some distance from their own.

The 'classic' carer (a single woman) now only makes up 11 per cent of the female caring population. As was commonly believed, women generally have a bigger caring commitment than men, but the difference is less marked than was thought – 15 per cent of women and 12 per cent of men are carers. Caution needs to be exercised in interpreting these percentages, however, as the adult female population is greater than the male; the six million figure actually breaks down to 3.5 million women and 2.5 million men. Of those in employment, the majority of women work part time, but a significant number work full time.

The majority of carers (44 per cent) live in a family comprising a couple with children, while 34 per cent have no children but live with a partner, and 33 per cent have responsibility for dependent children as well as the person cared for. Twenty per cent of carers look after more than one person (eg, both parents).

Carers come from all social groups and educational backgrounds. All age groups from youth to old age are also represented, but the peak age for caring lies between 45 and 64 years. In this age range, almost 50 per cent of carers report personal poor health, and among the caring population generally almost 33 per cent have a longstanding illness themselves.

The cared for
Of those cared for, 80 per cent are related to their carers – about 50 per cent are their parents or parents-in-law. The majority are elderly and have physical disabilities (73 per cent); those with mental and physical disabilities account for another 16 per cent, with only 5 per cent having mental disabilities alone.

A significant proportion of carers, many of them elderly, are looking after a grown up child at home; these cared for are more likely to have mental handicap or multiple disabilities (72 per cent). Where the person cared for does not live in the carer's household, they are most likely to be living alone elsewhere, although some may cohabit with elderly spouses or other family members.

What does caring mean?
Caring is a time consuming business – 20 per cent of carers devote at least 20 hours a week to the care of their dependant. When the person cared for lives in the same household, their dependency is usually greater, and a commitment of at least 50 hours a week is common – with 59 per cent of carers over 65 giving this amount of time.

The type of care given tends to vary with the location of the person cared for. If the dependant lives with the carer it more frequently involves personal assistance (such as dressing, help with walking) and nursing care (such as giving medication), whereas if the dependant lives elsewhere, the caring role tends to be more supervisory and supportive (such as shopping, taking the person out).

While most carers can manage a couple of hours break, a two day absence from the dependant is impossible for the vast majority. Many have not had a break since they began caring, some more than 10 years ago (18 per cent of carers have been committed to care for more than 10 years, and a further 25 per cent have been involved for between five and nine years). Where the dependant lives in the same household as the carer, only 2 per cent are away for any period of time (eg, in respite residential care).

Who supports the carers?
Only 50 per cent of carers have any contact with health or social service personnel; 24 per cent have no help whatsoever; 30 per cent have some help but remain the sole main carers, and 11 per cent share their caring with someone else. Where the dependant lives with the carer, 42 per cent cope singlehandedly. For those who get 'regular support' (ie, at least one visit a month from health or social service personnel), the GP and the community nurse are most frequently involved; other statutory and voluntary helpers account for less than 10 per cent of support.

A clearer picture

The survey provides a clearer picture of the caring situation and experience in Britain today than was previously available. It must be pointed out, however, that certain areas still remain uninvestigated, such as the number of young people under the age of 16 who are caring (often for disabled parents), and the vitally important area of black and other ethnic minority carers. Before appropriate support can be offered, specific needs have to be identified and so thorough assessment of the carers' situations is a prerequisite.

The report points out that "the role of statutory services is now seen as being to support the informal carers so that they can continue to look after their dependants in the community". With this in mind, all healthcare staff need to identify carers in their own working areas, and consider how they can best assess and then plan to meet their needs, tempering idealism with realism in the current economic climate.

When studying local situations, the outline of the national study may prove a useful basis from which to work. If this precis of the study results seems somewhat esoteric, however, the practical reality of caring situations is graphically described in three new books, details of which are given in the bibliography. All three make salutory reading for healthcare professionals. An excellent source of information is the King's Fund Carelink Informal Caring Programme, which supplies free newsheets quarterly – recent issues covered such topics as black carers in focus, and counselling carers. The Carers' National Association also has a fund of further information.

Bibliography
Hicks, C. (1988) Who Cares – Looking After People at Home. Virago, London.
  Looks at caring in many different situations, including handicap, old age, married life, men as carers.
Lewis, J. and Meredith, B. (1988) Daughters Who Care. Routledge, London.
  A study of daughters caring for elderly mothers at home.
Pitkethley, J. (1989) It's my Duty, Isn't It? Souvenir Press, London.
  Looks critically at the reality of the current caring situation and professionals' attitudes.

Reference
Green, H. (1988) Informal Carers. General Household Survey 1985, Supplement A. HMSO, London.

Useful addresses
Carelink, Informal Caring Support Unit, King's Fund Centre, 126 Albert Street, London NW1 7NF. Publish free news-sheets for carers.
Carers' National Association, 29 Chilworth Mews, London W2 3RG. Acts as a voice for people whose lives are restricted by the need to care for someone else.

10

Care, mis-care, abuse?

Gill Garrett, BA, RGN, RCNT, DN (London), Cert Ed(FE), RNT, FP Cert
Freelance Lecturer, Bristol

Sometimes violence seems almost commonplace in today's world. The media is full of child abuse, sexual abuse, lately ritual abuse, violence against women. Perhaps rather less frequently we hear of criminal violence towards the elderly, such as mugging or rape – 'granny bashing' in the tabloid expression. Even some so-called 'caring' institutions, hospitals and nursing homes, have been exposed as places of ill treatment and neglect. In common with the rest of society, health professionals have had to wake up to the reality of such problems, and to focus on their professional responsibilities in relation to them. Multidisciplinary teams have met to draw up guidelines for the recognition of non-accidental injury and its management, and to formalise overall strategies. Legislation has been passed, and professional literature and conference programmes reflect the weight of current concern.

But until recently there has been almost a conspiracy of silence concerning perhaps the saddest abuse of all – that of the vulnerable elderly by those caring for them in their own homes. Even now there are remarkably few references to it in the UK literature, and some experienced workers with older people and their families remain totally unaware of the problem. Yet this could be the fate of 500,000 elderly people a year in this country. There is now an urgent need for us to come to terms with, and to grips with, the situation.

The subject is wide and emotive, however, and this chapter can serve only as a brief introduction. It seeks to do so by looking at four main areas:
- what old age abuse is and who it affects.
- why it happens.
- its recognition.
- its management.

Old age, abuse – what it is

Perhaps it is as well to start with what, in the context of this paper, it is *not*. It is not the criminal attack to which an older person may be subjected inside or outside their home; nor is it part of the ongoing cycle of violence seen in some families – readers may be aware of the old Glaswegian rhyme:

"When I was a lad I lived with my granny
And many a hiding my granny gi'ed me;
Now I am a man and I live with my granny
And do to my granny what she did to me".

Nor does it cover the woman who has been abused by her partner throughout their relationship, and who then turns 65. She may well be ageing, but that is not old age abuse.

A wide variety of definitions of what *is* meant by the term can be found. Each of the following four give very different implications to consider. "Deprivation of the quality of life" (Peter Horrocks) which is an enormously broad definition. "Any act or behaviour by a family member or carer which results in physical or mental harm or neglect to an elderly person" (E. Podneiks) with one off incidents thus included. "The systematic and continuous abuse of an elderly person by the carer, often thought not always a family member, on whom the elderly person is dependant for care" (Christopher Cloke) which stresses the ongoing nature of the problem. And "Miscare" (Dr Elizabeth Hocking). This last definition is most interesting. Dr Hocking feels that families begin their caring commitment with genuine concern and sympathy; but that they are frequently overwhelmed by the weight of the task, and the relationship then becomes soured, with resultant harm to the elderly person.

The abusive behaviours subsumed within these definitions are wide-ranging. They include:
- physical assault (eg, force-feeding, hitting, pushing).
- threats of physical assault.
- neglect (withholding food, warmth).
- mis-medication (over-medication, withholding drugs).
- exploitation (often financial).
- abandonment.
- sexual abuse.
- psychological abuse (ridicule, humiliation).

Who it affects
Under this heading we need to look at four categories:
- the victims.
- the perpetrators.
- the professionals.
- society as a whole.

Case history: a victim   Mary X at 79 had been a widow for five years. She and her husband had taken in their daughter Pat with her two young sons when her own marriage broke up. After his death the family continued to live together in Mary's three-bedroomed semi-detached house on the outskirts of a small town. Over a period of three years Mary had become increasingly confused. She then became incontinent and began wandering at night. Pat at 46 worked part-time as a waitress. She had no support from her brother or sister and no contact with her former husband. She visited her GP frequently with anxiety and depression: he told her "You're doing a wonderful job with your Mum", and prescribed some mild sedatives.

The extent of the family's problems only came to light when a Health Visitor undertaking a research project on menopausal women visited Pat. She found Mary with a black eye and broken dentures; she seemed drowsy and unsteady. She was said to have fallen in the bathroom, but Pat eventually admitted giving her mother her sedatives, then having hit her when she soiled the bed.

Mary in facts fits what had been described as the typical victim profile. This sees the victim as classically:

- over 75.
- female.
- roleless within the family.
- functionally impaired.
- dependent for at least some basic survival needs.
- lonely.
- fearful.
- living at home with or near adult children.

It is all too easy however to be 'blinkered' by profiles such as this, accepting them as definitive. It is vital to remember that not all victims will fit this picture, and we must be alert to possible problems of clients with other backgrounds.

The perpetrators   There is an army of carers without whom the health and social services in this country would be effectively paralysed: the relatives, neighbours and friends of the elderly and the disabled. A survey of these six million people a few years ago (a precis of which can be found in *Caring in the UK Today* in this book) demonstrated that they come from all classes and backgrounds, and are of all ages. A third care for dependent children as well as elderly relatives; a fifth look after more than one elderly or disabled person. Many work full time, many more have part-time work commitments. Their burdens are indeed tremendous.

The professionals   Who are the professionals to whom the topic of old age abuse is particularly relevant? Basically any in the health and social services who work with older people and their families. Certainly nursing, medical and social work staff in the community, and members of the multidisciplinary team within the hospital; also support staff such as home care assistants, home aides.

Society   It is sobering to realise however that 50% of carers have no regular contact whatsoever with health or social service personnel. It has long been realised by organisations, such as the NSPCC, that child abuse is a collective and moral responsibility, with the whole community having a role to play in its prevention, its detection, and the support of those families affected by it.

This should be no less the case with old age abuse. Not only must we educate the professionals, we must ensure that the public at large is aware of the process of ageing, the needs of older people, and, without sensationalising the situation, about the realities of caring and the problems that may be experienced. An American writer on the subject has stated that "the number of frail elderly increases daily. We can expect the problem of elder abuse to become epidemic without societal intervention". Before society can intervene, a prerequisite is the knowledge and understanding of the problem.

Why it happens

Why should a normally sensible, sensitive and sociable adult turn on an older person for whom they care (both practically and emotionally), with resultant harm to all concerned? For let us remember that not only are the victims damaged: many perpetrators speak of being brutalised by the experience, of hating themselves for what they have done and do. For most the stress of caring, unimaginable at the beginning of the commitment, has brought them to breaking point, and they have indeed broken the family and social taboos; they have broken the faith put in them.

Three precursors to old age abuse have been described (Steinmetz, 1988). These are:
- caregiver overload and confusion.
- variable motivation.
- deficiencies in the necessary caring skills.

Deficiencies in the necessary caring skills   Many carers are undertaking skilled nursing tasks on a 24-hour basis with no professional support nor teaching in management whatsoever. They have learned their caring skills through trial and error. Additionally they may lack knowledge concerning the processes of ageing, age-related disorders, and the needs of older people: for all it is said that families in the past knew about and looked after their elderly, this is simply not true. Demographic and social change have ensured that we lack historical precedents or role models for dealing with dependent family members over prolonged periods of time.

Variable motivation   Studies have shown that when relatives take on a caring role, their major motivator is a feeling of family obligation. Some relationships have not been particularly positive before hand, but it has been pointed out that "the provision of help rests on a delicate balance of sentiments such as affection, gratitude, guilt, a desire for parental approval as well as love and compassion" (Treas, 1977). Especially when the taking on of caring results from a family crisis (such as death of an older person's partner), the decision may well be based on haste, guilt, and a sense of responsibility, rather than on a careful evaluation of the possible options.

Researchers have found that, where affection is absent in a caring situation, there is an increased level of perceived stress, and the potential for abusive responses.

Caregiver overload and confusion   The chapter is this book on *Caring in the UK Today* outlines the situation in which six million people currently find themselves. But we need to look behind the figures, to go beyond the statistics to put life into these situations, to understand the lack of freedom and privacy experienced by the 35-year-old single woman caring in a two-bedroom flat for her demented, incontinent father; the never-ending work cycle of the woman with three small children, an alcoholic husband, and an immobile mother. We need to look and listen to what families tell us both in tears and in silence.

It is also important to remember that abuse is not of necessity inflicted on the cared for by the carer: the elderly person may be the perpetrator, abusing the carer verbally, physically or psychologically. This may result from illness-related difficulties (eg post-stroke) or may be the continuation of the relationship in earlier life. To remain caring and supportive when continually abused in this way may be more than flesh and blood can cope with.

Also important to note is that the carer's sense of burden may not correspond with the actual weight of care given. Some with heavily dependent relatives may be less stressed than some with far less outwardly demanding charges. It is essential therefore for professionals to look at the carer's perception of the stress they experience, rather than at more objective criteria.

Recognising abuse

Rarely does a diagnosis of abuse follow an unsolicited complaint by an elderly patient: all too often there is extensive mental impairment and frequently communication problems to begin with. The alert elderly person may feel desperately ashamed of their situation, or may fear reprisals so will not complain. Nonetheless when complaints are made against carers, it is as well to remember, as we try to investigate the situation, that paranoia may be a feature to reckon with.

Observation of over-zealous diagnosis of abuse in other age groups should lead us to a cautious approach with the elderly. Age-related physical, mental and functional frailties do predispose to accidental injury, and subjectively our own personal values can influence judgements on abuse. Mercifully not every old lady with a fractured femur will have been pushed downstairs, not all bruising results from a shaking or a slapping. But suspicious indicators must be watched for, especially when they occur in clusters.

Hospital staff should be alert for:

- a history of falls, frequent minor injuries.
- evidence of delay in seeking help following injury.
- person other than the carer seeking help for the elderly person.
- injuries inconsistent with the history given.
- relatives who are absent on admission or during stay, or defensive or aggressive towards staff, or unwilling for patient to be interviewed alone, or unwilling to participate in discharge planning.

Community staff are often better placed to:

- understand family dynamics.
- observe subtle changes in elderly person/carers' attitude/condition.
- note disparities in hygiene between elderly person/carer.
- note evidence of poor nutrition or dehydration or absence of glasses/hearing or stability aids etc. (Garrett, 1986).

Management

As in all health issues, prevention is better than cure. The point has already been made about the need to increase professional and public awareness of the ageing process, the needs of older people, and potential problems in caring situations. Other countries such as the USA have now passed legislation on the issue of elder abuse, and consideration needs to be given to similar measures here.

In a much broader perspective, we need to be working towards ensuring that all older people have a choice in their care arrangements, and that families who choose to care are supported appropriately.

As professionals we must begin to regard the *family* as the focus of care, rather than simply the older person within it. When a caring commitment is made it may be appropriate to offer help and advice at the initial family conference. Supportive measures need to be instituted from the start, respite care, social security benefits, sitters etc, rather than when crisis points are reached. The necessary nursing skills, lifting, turning, bowel and bladder care, must be taught and reinforced.

When caring is established the situation should be monitored for changing needs, and care plans adapted accordingly. Awareness of danger signs is vital, remembering that it is the carer's perception of the situation which is a better predictor of behaviour than objective criteria. Above all it is necessary to establish an open, supportive relationship with the carer, only then can they be honest concerning their feelings, shortcomings, anxieties.

When evidence of abuse has been found, however, both the acute and the ongoing situations must be provided for. The immediate needs are to ensure the safety of the victim, and the relief and support of the perpetrator (who is in as much need of help as the victim). Occasionally to ensure the victim's safety it may be necessary to change their environment: to move them to hospital or residential care on a temporary or permanent basis. More commonly more local measures are appropriate, instituting a supportive regime to relieve the domestic and caring pressures and resulting stresses. Practical assistance from statutory and voluntary sources may need to be mobilised; also local support groups, where others in similar situations can sympathise, can be enormously beneficial.

The value of such lay support and befriending should never be underestimated, but sometimes professional assistance is essential. Where the emotional wounds in the elderly person or the carer run deep the skilled input of a social worker or counsellor are needed. In such situations anger, frustration and hostility can be dealt with in a controlled, safe manner, to the benefit of all concerned.

Raising awareness

In some ways, this chapter has portrayed the issue in very black and white terms. Under neat section headings the 'what', 'why', 'how', 'to whom' components have been separately considered; but in reality the whole area of old age abuse is far from a neat, tidy subject, readily open to study and discussion. For too many families it remains a shameful, sad secret; by too many professionals it remains unrecognised or unacknowledged.

To open up the subject for wider discussion, however, demands courage and honesty, and a high degree of compassionate sensitivity to the needs of fellow human beings under tremendous stress. But can we, as nurses, afford the Marys and the Pats of this world anything less?

References
Garrett, G. (1986) Old age abuse by carers. *Professional Nurse* **1** (11), 304–6.
Steinmetz, S. (1988) *Duty Bound: Elder Abuse and Family Care.* Sage Publications, Newbury Park.
Treas, J. (1977) Family support systems for the aged. *Gerontologist* **17**, 486–91.

11

Death and bereavement in old age

Gill Garrett, BA, RGN, RCNT, DN (London), Cert Ed (Fe), RNT, FP Cert
Freelance Lecturer, Bristol

Whilst reading through a volume of women's poetry from the First World War, I came across a poem by Margaret Postgate Cole entitled 'Praematuri'. In it she laments the loss of so many young lives and expresses the profound grief of those who loved them. She contrasts the situation with death in old age, writing:

"When men are old and their friends die,

They are not so sad

Because their love is running slow

And cannot spring from the wound with so sharp a pain;

And they are happy with many memories

And only a little time to be alone".

Whilst I could not presume to know the depth of bereavement women of that generation experienced, I could not help feeling sadness at the poet's evident dismissal of old-age emotions and their expression. To me her words epitomise the feelings of society generally, now as then that death in old age is 'natural' and the bereavement is just one of the many losses encountered at that stage of the life-cycle. Therefore little thought needs to be given to the specific needs of older people in these circumstances.

In this chapter I would like to challenge these assumptions (the 'good innings' theory), identifying the unique features of death and bereavement in later life, and suggesting areas which we must look at carefully if we are to meet individual needs. The space available allows only a brief consideration of this vast area, however, and so I would like to concentrate on two aspects with particular relevance to the nurse: the maintenance of self-esteem in the dying patient; and the recognition and acknowledgement of grief, not in the family setting but in the older person's peer group.

But firstly let us identify how death and bereavement in old age differ from similar situations in earlier life. Sudden death can obviously occur in any age group, but often for older people dying can be a protracted experience with increasing frailty, loss of mobility and perhaps continence and sometimes the onset of mental changes. Consequently their care often takes place not in acute hospital wards but in continuing care units, residential or nursing homes, or still for many, in the family home. In this latter case the main career is often an equally elderly partner: a spouse, sibling or friend; or a member of a younger generation, perhaps with many other responsibilities (paid work, childcare). In the case of very elderly dying people, their caring offspring may be well past retirement themselves.

Bereavement too has some special features in later life. The death of an elderly spouse often means the loss of one half of a previously coping partnership, the two having compensated for each other's difficulties and disabilities. Death leaves the survivor very vulnerable, both functionally and emotionally. Because of the nature of an older person's dying, there may be progressive losses to cope with. A wife may feel she has 'lost' the husband she loved for fifty years with the onset of personality changes in dementia; his admission to hospital or residential care, perhaps months later, means she then loses his care and support to others; his eventual death marks the loss of her married status with its social, emotional and financial implications. A partner's death frequently heralds other losses too – the social and caring roles just referred to, very often the family home, frequently income. Whilst roles are inevitably lost with bereavement at any age, in later life they may be extremely difficult to compensate for, and this may complicate and prolong the grieving process.

The grieving process itself may differ in older people, though few studies have concentrated on this specific age group. Extreme outbursts of overt despair are less common, but denial is often a prominent feature with the survivor behaving, speaking and feeling as if nothing has happened. Visual and auditory hallucinations are frequently experienced. The survivor's life is often continued as they perceive the deceased would have wished it – indeed the elderly bereaved person may talk of 'conversations' they have with the deceased, asking what they should do in various circumstances. We must also remember that, when an older person dies in residential or hospital care, others not commonly thought of as bereaved in fact are so – other residents or patients and the nursing or care staff who looked after them, perhaps over a long period of time. This is a point to which we will return later.

What implications do these factors have for us as we work with elderly people? As always in nursing care it is vital to recognise generalisations which have points to make, but to which we must not slavishly adhere. Sensitive assessment of individual situations is essential. Our aim must be to provide high quality nursing care appropriate to the specific needs of the dying person and her family; in the words of Cicely Saunders, that care must show that "you matter because you are you; you matter to the last moment of your life, and we will do all we can to help you die peacefully but also to live until you die" (Saunders, 1976).

Truly living until the moment of death, however, may not be easy in the face of the multiple assaults which the dying older person confronts. These are by no means all physical, although pain, immobility and incontinence may pose considerable problems and distress. Yet it has been said that it can be quite "easy and non-threatening to relieve the physical symptoms associated with dying, but to permit oneself to become involved in meaningful interpersonal relationships to support the aged dying is extremely difficult for most nurses and care givers" (Ebersole and Hess, 1981). Identifying and intervening to meet psychological needs has perhaps not been the forte of many of us; all too often stock phrases such as 'relieve anxiety' appear on our care plans, and we see the more 'spiritual' needs of the patient as the domain of other specialists, ministers of religion perhaps. But in holistic care we cannot make such assumptions, in that *we* must be the specialists.

One model of human needs which can help us to identify potential problems is that of Maslow (1962). His hierarchy demonstrating the progression from basic physiological needs to self-actualisation or transcendence can serve to remind us of the several levels at which we may need to intervene. It is interesting to note that Maslow felt that the peak of self-actualisation or fulfilment is not attainable by younger people, since it demands the wisdom and maturity that comes with age. But it also requires the older person to accept herself for what she is and to value herself for it, to accept and value others and to be able to rise above the limitations of her situation. To do this when faced with prolonged illness, failing energy and a shrinking environment (both physical and social), however, the older person may well need the support and help of those caring for her.

All too often an older person's self-esteem is threatened as death approaches – she perceives herself as having no social role, no self-determination left; the physical and mental changes can so easily lead to loss of dignity, perhaps to rejection by others. We need to be looking to the maintenance of self-esteem as a priority in our care.

In case all this should seem somewhat esoteric, let us spend a few minutes considering a very practical way in which it has been suggested that self-esteem may be elevated. In recent years the positive value of reminiscence has been acknowledged, and many nurses in elderly care units have gained some experience in its therapeutic use, particularly in group work. Perhaps fewer have explored its use at an individual level and as a vehicle in the preparation of legacies to leave after death.

We all have a need to leave a mark on the world as we pass through it. For a few, the great and the good, that mark may be bold and enduring through time and across continents; for most of us it is more modest in impression and recognition. But that need is in us all to know that our living has not been in vain, and in exploring with our elderly patients their achievements, great and small, we can help them find meaning in the last phase of life. And since, regardless of religious belief, there is life after death in that memories and other legacies survive the deceased, we can help to ensure a little immortality.

Legacies are often defined as financial or other tangible assets bestowed on following generations, but anything handed down from the past should correctly be placed in this category, for many of us the less tangible effects are often the most meaningful. In their discussion of legacies, Ebersole and Hess (1981) include features as diverse as oral histories, autobiographies, shared memories, taught skills, objects of significance, written histories, bestowed talents, traditions and myths perpetuated, indeed children and grandchildren themselves. Such legacies obviously have a personal significance for the older person, and the process of giving them, passing them on, prepares them to leave the world with a sense of meaning and a transcendent feeling of continuation, of ties with those who will survive them. Through them the generations who follow learn of their origins, their place in history, something of their own significance.

Nurses can encourage their older patients to talk, to write, to express the meaning of their lives in other ways. Whilst a little time and a genuine, compassionate interest are necessary pre-requisites, the preparation of legacies does not have to be elaborate or sophisticated. Obviously the condition of the patient and her resources, both physical and mental, must be taken into account. Family members, volunteers and other personnel can be enlisted to help if necessary in the compilation of photograph albums, scrap books, taped memoirs, family trees or written materials, but many older people will put in enormous personal effort, however laboriously, when the project is of significance for them.

I have in mind a man who was valley Welsh, and characteristically had a life-long interest in choral and church music. In the three years of the illness that preceded his death he worked on his hymns project, an investigation into the background of his favourite hymns, their composers, their histories, and their liturgical uses. In a black ring binder, on a mixture of hand and typewritten sheets, he put together his work during those months, spasmodically as his fluctuating condition allowed. That man was my father, and his hymn book was the legacy he left us.

So far we have looked at the elderly person who is dying, but in the well-known words "No man is an island entire of itself; every man is a piece of the continent, a piece of the main". That quotation goes on "Any man's death diminishes me, because I am involved in mankind": it is to the social context of death that we now turn as we look at bereavement. Here, however, we shall consider not partner or family reactions, which usually receive most attention and about which most is written; but rather the situation of other patients or residents when an elderly person dies in hospital or residential care.

In Maslow's hierarchy the third category of need covers love and belonging – the need human beings have to communicate with each other, to relate to each other in different ways. We must remember that our ward or residential home community is the one in which many elderly people must fulfil that need as the end of their life approaches. Their everyday relationships with each other and with staff assume an importance which must not be underestimated.

Most of us who work professionally with older people are considerably younger than our clients, a point of some significance when we look at attitudes to death and bereavement. We cannot assume that their feelings in any way correspond to our own; they have been shaped by their life experience which by its very chronology differs markedly from ours. They lost fathers and brothers in the Great War, they grew up in a world of much higher maternal and infant mortality, a pre-antibiotic era when friends succumbed to TB and childhood infectious diseases, when medical care was costly and not readily available, when family members were nursed and died at home. They are the survivors of many bereavements; bereavements marked very often by customs and practices which may seem outmoded to our younger generation, but which remain meaningful to them. With some of our ethnic minority elders, their valued customs may quite literally be foreign to us.

In most care situations the control and direction of activity remain in the hands of the professionals, whatever lip service we pay to the concept of patient or client-centred care. Thus dying and death are frequently managed in the way we feel appropriate – which is quite often quietly, with the minimum of intrusion on other patients' or residents' lives. Often in the name of privacy the dying person is moved to a secluded area, with little said to other residents, and after the event the body is removed unobtrusively, often secretly. The deceased's room or bedspace is allocated to someone else, and life in the ward or home goes on.

We need to remember that, in this situation, other patients or residents are not just passive figures, they are participants in a scenario in which they will one day centre. They see foreshadowed in the situation how their own death will one day be managed. In their own former communities, when a friend or neighbour was dying, they would have visited, perhaps sat with them; they would have given their condolences to the family, perhaps viewed the body to pay their respects, gone to the funeral or sent flowers. By stage-managing a death in care and excluding them from participating in such ways, we deny them the opportunity to behave in the normal, everyday way they would outside an institution.

A death in a small residential community means not only grief for individuals who have been close to the deceased, but also alters group dynamics. As nurses we must be ready to recognise and respond appropriately to grief and to changed and changing relationships. Some of the clients with whom we deal may appear unaware because of mental incapacity, but often these people too may show behavioural changes indicative of a perception with which we had not credited them. The role of nurse as supporter and counsellor is crucial providing time and opportunity to grieve, the chance to identify and talk through feelings, to look at other residents' shortening futures with them, and to plan accordingly.

But in these situation the nurse too is often bereaved. Especially where an elderly person has no family of her own, she may adopt a carer in a surrogate daughter or grand-daughter role, and a real closeness may develop. The acceptance of such a role should not be dismissed out of hand as undesirable or unprofessional, it is a privilege that the elderly person grants us, and that we should use to their advantage. But by their very nature such relationships are finite, and they take their emotional toll of the nurse on their conclusion, yet she has to remain supportive to others in the situation, and to continue to function normally with others in her wider care. Here understanding colleagues and the opportunity to talk through distressing situations and to recharge batteries can lighten the burden considerably.

Working with older people is challenging in many ways, but perhaps for the nurse the care of the dying and the bereaved is the most demanding aspect of all. It requires of her technical expertise and knowledge certainly, and also interpersonal skills of a very high level; but these must be underpinned by a maturity of outlook, a personal philosophy, an openness and a flexibility not found in us all. In the past nurse training has concentrated on that technical expertise and knowledge; of late it has given more credence to interpersonal skills. Yet it remains to be seen whether the new educational programmes now beginning are able to give the student the experiences and opportunities to develop these less tangible qualities, without which she cannot hope to meet total needs.

The constraints of space have meant that we have looked here at only two aspects of a multi-faceted care situation. However, it is a situation which merits far more emphasis than we have given it in the past. Although a personally and professionally very demanding one, it can be a very positive and creative area in which to work. At the point where some would say there is nothing more to be done, we know that there is so much *we* can do and we owe it to the elderly people for whom we care to ensure that it is done.

References
Ebersole, P. and Hess, P. (1981) *Towards Healthy Ageing: Human Needs and Nursing Response.* 579–80, chapter 5. C V Mosby, St Louis.
Maslow, A. (1962) *Towards a Psychology of Being.* Van Nostrand, New York.
Saunders, C. (1976) Care of the dying. *Nursing Times* **72**. Quoted in Carver, V. and Liddiard, P. (eds) *An Ageing Population.* Open University Press, Milton Keynes.

Health Problems in Old Age

For those who adhere to the World Health Organisation definition of health: "a state of complete physical, mental and social wellbeing and not simply the absence of disease or infirmity", it may seem odd, that in a book entitled Healthy Ageing a large section should be devoted to the consideration of health problems! Perhaps this anomaly makes more sense if Ivan Illich's view of health is applied: "the ability to adapt to changing environments, to growing and ageing, to healing when damaged, to suffering and to the peaceful expectation of death" (Illich, 1975).

Whilst current health care trends aim to encourage those approaching later life to do so in conventionally understood 'good health', many of those presently in old age manage their lives effectively and constructively even in the presence of chronic disabling conditions. Nurses may not be able to ensure the 'state of complete wellbeing' but they can certainly encourage, motivate and assist with the adaptation that allows older people to cope with life and its demands following illness or the onset of frailty.

In this section one or two specific disorders are discussed (eg, hypothermia, leg ulcers) but for the most part the effects upon older people of pathological processes are considered: limitation of mobility, incontinence, confusion. These in themselves are not diagnoses of course but symptoms of underlying disorders. Promptly and thoroughly investigated and appropriately managed, there is no reason why they should not be largely resolved or the distress and discomfort at least alleviated. Far from the old notion of a 'lost cause' there is no reason why health problems in old age should not be optimistically, vigorously challenged.

Reference
Illich, I. (1975) *Medical Nemesis. The Exploration of Health*. Marion Boyars, London.

12

Hypothermia in elderly people

Gill Garrett, BA, RGN, RCNT, DN (London), Cert Ed(FE), RNT, FP Cert
Freelance Lecturer, Bristol

Every year in Great Britain some 500 deaths are officially attributed to hypothermia; there is widespread belief amongst health professionals however that this is a gross underestimate. The true incidence of the condition remains unknown; the mortality figures are probably highly inaccurate partly because hypothermia may not be recognised post-mortem and partly because death certificates may only record other pathologies with which it is associated and from which individuals are known to have suffered. It has been suggested that a truer figure may be 500 deaths weekly in the Winter months rather than that figure annually.

The condition has been defined as one in which there is "a deep body or core temperature of below 35 degrees Centigrade (measured rectally or in freshly passed urine)" (Royal College of Physicians and BMA, 1966). This may be seen as a somewhat arbitrary figure however as one study discovered 10% of elderly people in their own homes with core temperatures only just above this (Fox, 1973). The elderly person is especially at risk because of several intrinsic factors, such as impaired temperature perception and discrimination and decreased hypothalamic thermostat sensitivity secondary to senescence or concomitant disease, and they may be tipped over into hypothermia even without the influence of extrinsic factors as described below.

The factors affecting the elderly person's ability to maintain a normal body temperature can usefully be described under five headings: physical, psychological, socio-cultural, environmental and politico-economic.

Physical
Several disease processes may precipitate hypothermia either because of a direct effect upon the temperature regulating mechanism or because they inhibit mobility; these include endocrine disorders such as myxoedema and hypopituitarism and neurological conditions such as Parkinsons disease and cerebro-vascular accident. Severe infections such as bronchitis and pneumonia are similarly culprits.

Many drugs have been implicated in the development of the hypothermic state. Phenothiazines have a central effect; sedatives and hypnotics may cause drowsiness and inertia, limiting mobility and increasing the likelihood of falls; hypotensives and drugs which affect balance (such as L Dopa and alcohol) may have this latter effect too. If an elderly person who had fallen is unable to get up or summon help, lying immobile on a cold floor for hours or days before discovery is highly likely to lead to hypothermia.

Psychological

Any situation which leads an elderly person to neglect their own needs, such as depression or bereavement, renders them at risk of hypothermia. Living accommodation may be inadequately heated, insufficient clothing worn and an inadequate diet consumed. Dementing elderly people who may wander outside inappropriately dressed in all weathers are at high risk of exposure as are elderly alcohol and substance abusers who may be living rough.

Socio-cultural

Many UK elderly appear to have a particularly spartan attitude to heating. Perhaps from an upbringing in the days which heavily stressed the 'fresh air is good for you' philosophy, this has translated into the 'a cold bedroom is good for you' syndrome with windows left open even in mid winter and room temperatures sometimes at freezing. Clothing and bedding habits may reflect equally erroneous thinking, with one thick layer often preferred to several lighter, more effectively insulating ones.

Environmental

Whilst hypothermia is a condition seen throughout the temperate and polar regions of the world, the UK suffers far more than other countries where lower overall temperatures are often the norm. This may be due to humidity and wind variations giving a high chill factor; it may also reflect the low priority given to environmental planning for at risk groups (see below).

Politico-economic

The UK has a high residue of low quality housing, in poor repair and thermally inefficient, much of which is inhabited by elderly people. In many areas there has been insufficient or ineffective local authority expenditure on such properties to render their occupants safe. Pensions and benefits for older people, decided at central government level, often do not meet the needs of those with little or no other financial income and their heating, clothing and food expenditure may be severely limited because of this. It has been estimated that 50% of the elderly at risk of hypothermia are in receipt of income support.

Recognition of hypothermia

Recognition of the condition is not always easy, especially in the early stages. All health professionals working with older people should have low reading thermometers, extending down to at least 25 degrees Centigrade. These should be used for oral or axillary temperatures in all ill old people and, if a peripheral reading is less than 35 degrees, the core temperature should be checked, either rectally or using the Uritemp technique with freshly passed urine.

As body temperature drops the organs of the body progressively fail to function. Often the hypothermic patient's face appears puffy and the skin, especially of the abdomen, is cold and waxy to the touch. Once the core temperature has reached 35 degrees, metabolism slows and respirations become wheezy and shallower; a drop of a further degree sees bradycaria and hypotension. At 33 degrees the patient becomes confused and the conscious level decreases; convulsions follow as the temperature goes down further and by 30 degrees the patient is unconscious with dilated pupils and irregular respirations and heart beat. At 28 degrees respirations cease and fatal cardiac dysrhythmias, ventricular fibrillation or asysole ensue.

The management of hypothermia

Given that an elderly person's environmental surroundings are often instrumental in bringing about hypothermia, home management of the condition is rarely practical. In mild cases where social conditions are reasonable and adequate care is available it may occasionally be feasible however. The patient should be nursed at rest in bed in a room temperature of 25 degrees Centigrade with the whole body, including the head, insulated by suitable clothing and bedding. Warm fluids are given by mouth and a search is made to ascertain the cause of the problem. Specific treatment (eg, for myxoedema) can then be commenced or inappropriate drug therapy discontinued or altered.

Transfer to hospital is mandatory in most cases however and further heat loss must be avoided whilst this is effected. 'Space blankets' (highly reflective foil wrappings carried by most community nurses in the Winter months) may be used but if the patient does not start to recover and generate body heat these simply insulate a cold body; ordinary blankets or duvets may be more effective.

On admission the patient should preferably be nursed in a side room warmed to 25 degrees. Passive rewarming only should take place with the application of no direct heat; ideally a temperature rise of 0.5 degree hourly should be attempted. Too fast a rise will lead to surface vasodilatation with hypotension and rapid electrolyte changes. Temperature recording should be by rectal probe and the use of electronic monitoring such as by Dynamap gives pulse and blood pressure readings without having to expose or disturb the patient. Cardiac monitoring should be instituted to facilitate the early detection of dysrhythmias.

Other supportive measures will be required and these include the

administration of humidified oxygen mask or nasal cannulae
(endotracheal intubation is avoided if at all possible as it may stimulate
ventricular fibrillation), and intravenous access should be available to
ensure ready administration of drugs. Anti-dysrhythmic agents may be
required as may dextrose if hypoglycaemia develops as the temperature
rises. Broad spectrum antibiotics are generally given and any co-existing
disease is appropriately treated.

Whilst general nursing measures are obviously important in the
unconscious, immobile patient it is important to ensure that handling
and exposure for procedures is kept to a minimum. Urinary
catheterisation is avoided if possible, again because of the likelihood of
stimulating dysrhythmias, but incontinence requires rapid attention to
prevent further heat loss by evaporation.

The outcome of the hypothermic episode depends upon the severity
of the condition, the patient's age and the presence or absence of other
precipitating or consequent diseases. When an elderly person recovers
and goes home however an essential component of care is adequate
discharge planning and follow up support. Thorough investigation of
the circumstances surrounding the episode is mandatory with medical,
functional, social and environmental problems identified and suitable
strategies for their management instituted. A multidisciplinary approach
with effective hospital/community liaison is vital if this is to be
achieved.

Prevention of hypothermia

Deaths from hypothermia are tragedies indeed in that they are for the
most part avoidable. Prevention however is not only dependent upon
health education and the close surveillance of at risk groups, it demands
political and economic commitment to the provision of a safe
environment. This latter may be far more difficult to ensure than the
former.

To begin though with the preventive measures in the hands of most
health care practitioners: the very real risk of hypothermia in old age
and the necessary avoiding steps must be made clear to the general
public and to the elderly population especially. There are many
opportunities for this on Retirement Planning Courses, at Day Centres,
on one to one bases whenever members of the Primary Health Care
Team interact with older patients in surgeries or in home situations.

The need for a temperature of 21 degrees Centigrade in all rooms used
should be stressed; where economic factors make heating several rooms
impractical, the use of one room for Winter living (with a bed brought
into the living room for example) should be suggested. Several layers of
thinner clothing provide more insulation than one thick one and the
head, through which a high proportion of heat is lost, should be covered
indoors as well as out. The bed should be heated before getting in to
prevent body heat being lost to cold bedding. Electric overblankets are

much cheaper to run than many elderly people think and can be left on overnight. Hot drinks at regular intervals and a nutritious diet are also important; mobility, to generate body heat, should be encouraged.

'At risk' elderly people may be identified by health or social services personnel and appropriate input planned. This may involve social work support to assist with application for additional pension or benefits, the organisation of Meals on Wheels where food preparation is a problem, medical or nursing treatment for underlying pathological conditions; it is totally dependent upon individual needs having been individually assessed. Informal carers, friends, neighbours, volunteers from groups such as Age Concern, are often invaluable in general surveillance and everyday support further to such assessment.

Volunteer groups have also become active in recent years in assisting with loft insulation and the provision of wall thermometers which can alert older people to falling temperatures. The ability to pay fuel bills remains a prime concern for many old people however and it is essential that they should be made familiar with the Gas and Electricity authorities information services which explain special payment facilities for those with difficulties.

Whilst the above measures can all be effective at a more individual level, the government's responsibility to the vulnerable elderly nationwide cannot be overlooked. In ensuring safe environments and in providing adequate financial income for all older people both current local and national government may be found sadly lacking. With demographic changes now occurring resulting in an elderly electorate who will make their particular needs more clearly known and who will demand that they are met, however, it is to be hoped that this situation will not persist. Until such changes are effected much unnecessary suffering and associated mortalities continue to take place.

References

Fox, R.H., McGibbon, R., Davis, L. and Woodward, P.M. (1973) Problems of the old and the cold, *British Medical Journal*, **1**, 21-4.

Royal College of Physicians (1966) *Report of the Committee on Accidental Hypothermia*. Royal College of Physicians, London.

13

Falls in the elderly

Karen A. Webb, RGN
Ward Sister, Elderly Care Unit, Whittington Hospital, London

For many older people, the experience of falling signals an end to independence, leading to limitation of activities through fear of further falls (Craven and Bruno, 1986), and of being labelled a 'faller' by their families and carers or by outside organisations. To admit to falling is synonymous with admitting failure, resulting in loss of confidence and dignity. Perhaps for these reasons some elderly people initially deny falling when interviewed (Campbell *et al*, 1990).

Older people fall for numerous reasons, threatening their physical well-being, social integrity, and psychological health. Nurses in all settings have an important role to play in assessing the causes of falls, and in planning with clients the means to minimize future risks.

Mortality and morbidity due to of falls

Mortality rates increase with age as a result of falls. In the 65–74 age group, men and women show similar mortality rates due to falls. In the over 75s however, the rate trebles among men, and is over six times higher in women who fall. (OPCS, 1989).

Similarly, deaths as a result of fracture increase with age (OPCS, 1989). A growing population of over 75s with higher incidence of falls has implications for both hospital and community facilities, in terms of bed occupancy, length of stay, frequency of admission and manpower costs.

There has been debate as to whether falls can be used as a precursor of death. Gryfe *et al* (1977) discovered that falls appeared to 'cluster' prior to the deaths of some of the elderly people they studied. Wild *et al* (1981) reported that those who fell during their research had a higher incidence of mortality at the end of one year than those who had not fallen.

Evans (1988) points out that caution should be exercised when regarding such findings, as often the elderly people being studied are either in residential care or are reliant on the health or social services for support. He argues these previous samples may be more frail than a random selection of older people. However Campbell *et al* (1990) suggest that although the elderly in institutions are more frail, they do not have to cope with housework and other physical activities, and are more likely to live in an environment designed for safety. The question of whether falls can be used to predict imminent death will continue to be researched, but there is no doubt that their incidence increases with age, and that they are often a symptom of underlying deterioration in the physical or mental health of an aged individual.

Causes of falls in older people

Impaired vision or hearing   Balance is maintained by continuous adjustments of the body to sensory inputs. Gerson (1989) studied the effects of impaired sight or hearing on balance, in a sample of people over 65. Poor eyesight and hearing were problems. Despite spectacles or hearing-aids, 27% of the sample reported vision difficulties, and 30% hearing problems. A fifth of those studied reported balance problems, and this deterioration appeared to increase with age. Women reported slightly more balance difficulties than men. Those people with impaired hearing were more likely to admit to imbalance regardless of age, while the effect of impaired vision appeared to be limited to the younger 65–69 age group, no increased risk of imbalance being evident in those aged over 85. Gerson asserts that this may be because of accommodation to visual deterioration. On the basis of the results, impaired hearing or vision seemed to be precursors for imbalance and falls.

Neurological disease   Exton Smith and Weksler (1985) state that most falls occur while walking. Locomotion is normally a sequence of regularly repeated and predictable movements which are modified slightly to conform to the perceived variations in the environment. In the presence of many neurological diseases the rhythmicity and regularity of stepping is affected such that the legs make unplanned contact with one another or with the ground, thus disturbing the centre of gravity, causing instability. People who have suffered a stroke are prone to falls, especially when there is foot-drop deformity as a result of immobility, or where perception is altered. Mion *et al* (1989), in their study of falls in the rehabilitation setting, found that 41% of those people who fell had an admitting diagnosis of left cerebrovascular accident.

Where the older individual suffers from peripheral neuropathy or multiple sclerosis, this leads to weakening of leg muscles and failure to raise the feet when walking, both symptoms rendering the person less able to correct movement. In Parkinson's disease the whole stepping mechanism is affected. Older people with this disorder characteristically have hesitancy in beginning to walk, leading to stumbling, and often will unexpectedly stop in mid-stride, causing a high risk of falls.

Elimination   Changes in elimination are contributing factors to falls in the elderly (Spellbring *et al*, 1988, Berryman *et al*, 1989). Garcia *et al* (1988) analysed the relationship between falls and patient attempts to satisfy elimination needs, and concluded that patients at risk of falling were those who still responded to the strong need for elimination control, but required assistance to reach the toilet. Those patients who had not the urge sensation to eliminate did not display a high risk of falls, nor did patients who were fully mobile.

Elimination is a private process, and there may be some urgency, so many patients who fell did not wait for assistance from nursing staff. Kustaborder and Rigney (1983), state that the desire to maintain independence make many older patients reluctant to ask for assistance. In the Garcia study this led to some patients also refusing to use walking aids.

Drugs   Older people are often prescribed a number of drugs because of multiple physical or mental health problems. Some, such as hypnotics, sedatives, anti-Parkinsonians and tranquilizers affect central conduction in the nervous system, slowing reaction time to imbalance. Other drugs cited by Berryman *et al* (1989) and Spellbring *et al* (1988) as predisposing to risk of falls have included:

- alcohol
- anaesthetic
- antihistamines
- antihypertensives
- antiepileptics
- diuretics
- laxatives
- hypoglycemics
- psychotropics

either because they also slow reaction time, or because they can cause urgency to eliminate, changes in postural blood pressure or in mental state such as drowsiness or confusion.

Mental health problems   Mion *et al* (1989) in their study of falls in the rehabilitation setting found that the incidence of falls was high in those people who failed to understand or follow direction, and in those who suffered from impaired memory or judgment. Decrease in cognitive or perceptual skills was identified as a predisposing factor in falls.

Hospitalization or change in environment   Mion *et al* (1989), Lund and Sheafor (1985) and Berryman *et al* (1989) report falls occurring soon after admission to hospital. These could be due to physical illness, but also to anxiety about hospitalization, failure to remember directions or the desire to be independent, despite their physical frailness as a result of illness. Barbieri (1983) suggested that some falls may occur due to the individual being preoccupied with a perceived life crisis, not paying attention to safety as a result.

Falls in hospital also seemed to occur more often as patients became independent and were anticipating discharge (DeVincenzo and Watkins, 1987). These researchers all studied falls in hospital, however nurses n the community may find that rehousing or discharge from hospital may incur similar risks.

Effects of falls

At the start of this chapter we saw that falls can have a profound affect psychologically on the older individual, leading to fear of further falls, feelings of failure, and anxiety about coping alone or placing pressure on others to give assistance. Depression about perceived loss of independence is common, as is increased awareness of physical deterioration, and acknowledgement of mortality.

Social integrity is also threatened. the individual may feel that following the fall their role has changed, for example from Grandmother to Invalid, resulting in expressions of 'loss' of role within the community. Although the effects of being diagnosed a faller by GP or hospital health professionals have not been measured, it may be worth considering that being labelled in this way could lead to a self-fulfilling prophecy in some instances, with the individual seeing the label as a negative one, losing confidence, and beginning to fall in consequence.

Evans (1988) discusses age related increase in fractured femur, and the increase in mortality as a result, the older one is. Along with risks of serous injury, individuals who fall often suffer bruising and abrasions, and complain of pain.

There are numerous results of lying on the floor waiting for help to arrive; stasis in the lungs and peripheral circulation, potential hypothermia and dehydration, and disturbance of the microcirculation, aiding development of pressure sores.

The nursing role in care

In all cases, an older person falls as a result of an underlying problem, whether it is physical, mental or psychological. For this reason a diagnosis of 'falls' is unhelpful, and can lead to failure to recognise the more important causal factors.

Nurse/client relationship As in all nurse/client relationships, whether in the hospital or community environment, mutual trust is of prime importance, if confidences and information are to be freely given. For this reason the relationship will be strengthened if the older individual works with one named nurse in partnership towards the achievement of mutually agreed goals of rehabilitation. This is not possible in all areas; however by limiting the group of nurses working with the client to the smallest number that the demands of the clinical environment will permit, a mutually trusting relationship can be built.

Clinical observations The nurse's role in the care of a client who has suffered a fall begins with an assessment of the clients' physical, psychological and mental health. This will include physical examination, observing bruises, lacerations, pressure areas, respirations, temperature, postural blood pressure, continence of urine and faeces, and urinalysis to detect possible urinary tract infection or the presence of glucose or ketones. If ketones are present in a client who has been lying on the floor for some time prior to being discovered, some degree of malnutrition is indicated. The overall appearance of the person should be regarded for evidence of dehydration, weight loss or jaundice. Signs of weakness in limbs may lead to diagnosis of old or recent strokes.

Asking the client about their condition will indicate their psychological or mental health. Confusion may be present, indicative of infection, drug interaction, or underlying deterioration in mental health as in dementia. The client's conscious level should also be observed. If the client is drowsy or unconscious the fall may have been related to excessive sedation, other drug interactions, stroke or epilepsy.

The client may talk of the hopelessness of their state, appear disinterested in their condition, their surroundings, or in eating or drinking, which could suggest depression. Proposing a walk to the client may bring on signs of anxiety or excessive fear, indicative of the individual needing a high level of support and counselling to overcome what will otherwise become a tremendous psychological problem for them.

Standing the client and asking them to walk a few paces will also aid assessment. Do they get out of a chair safely? Are the muscles in their lower limbs too weak to support them? Do they remember their walking aid if they have one? Can they see obstacles in their path? Do they have weakness on one side? Do they topple forwards or backwards? Do they grab at surrounding objects for support? Can they turn and sit down safely? Observing movement, and the clients' posture, balance, gait and verbal and non-verbal communication help the nurse to assess the reason for falls, along with questioning and examining the client, or interviewing carers.

Information giving and education   The nurse is ideally placed to discuss with the client, after assessment, the reasons for the fall. If one explains, for instance, that the fall was a result of feeling unwell due to an infection which can be treated, the individual may feel more positive about their situation. Through education about underlying conditions, for example hypertension, the client can be taught ways of minimizing the risk of future falls, thus gaining confidence, and utilizing the nurses' skill as informer and educator.

It is not possible to eradicate risk, indeed it could be argued that to do so would belittle the status of older people. But to work in partnership with the client and carers towards overcoming or adapting to health needs in order to minimize risk and encourage what the client deems to be a good 'quality of life', should be the aim of all nurses working with older people.

References
Barbieri, E.B. (1983) Patient falls are not patient accidents. *Journal Of Gerontological Nursing,*
    9, 1, 165–73.

Berryman, E., Gaskin, D., Jones, A., Tolley, F., Mac Mullen, J. (1989) Point by point: predicting elders' falls. *Geriatric Nursing*, **10**, (4), 199–201.

Campbell, A.J., Borrie, M.J., Spears, G.F., Jackson, S.L., Brown, J.S., Fitzgerald, J.L. (1990) Circumstances and consequences of falls experienced by a community population 70 years and over during a prospective study. *Age and Ageing*, **19** (2), 136–41.

Craven, R. and Bruno, P. (1986) Teach the elderly to prevent falls. *Journal of Gerontological Nursing*, **12**, (8), 27–33.

DeVincenzo, D.K. and Watkins, S. (1987) Accidental falls in a rehabilitation setting. *Rehabilitation Nursing*, **12**, 248–52.

Evans, J.G. (1988) Falls and Fractures. *Age and Ageing*, **17** (6), 361–64.

Isaacs, B. (1985) In Exton Smith, A.N. and Weskler, M.E. (eds) (1985) *Practical Geriatric Medicine*, Churchill Livingstone.

Garcia, R.M., Cruz, M., Reed, M., Taylor, P.V., Sloan, G. and Bevan, N. (1988) Relationship between falls and patient attempts to satisfy elimination needs, *Nursing Management*, **19**, (7), 80 V, 80 W, 80 X.

Gerson, L.W. (1989) Falls in the elderly. *Nursing Times*, **85**, (31) 63.

Gryfe, C,I., Amies, A. and Ashley, M.J. (1977) A longitudinal study of falls in an elderly population 1: incidence and morbidity. *Age and Ageing*, **6**, 201–10.

Kustaborder, M.J. and Rigney, M. (1983) Interventions for safety. *Journal of Gerontological Nursing*, **9**, 159–62, 172–3.

Lund, C. and Shaefer, M.L. (1985) Is your patient about to fall? *Journal of Gerontological Nursing*, **11**, 37-41.

Mion, L.C., Gregor, S., Buettner, M., Chwirchak, D., Lee, O. and Paras, W. (1989) Falls in the rehabilitation setting: incidence and characteristics. *Rehabilitation Nursing*, **14**, (1), 17–21.

OPCS (1989) *DH2 90/2*. HMSO, London.

Spellbring, A.M., Gannon, M.E., Kleckner, T. and Conway, K. (1988) Improving safety for hospitalized elderly. *Journal of Gerontological Nursing*, **14** (2), 31–7.

Wild, D., Nayak, U.S.L. and Isaacs, B. (1981) Prognosis of falls in old people at home. *Journal of Epidemiological Community Health*, **35**, 200–4.

14

Pain and its management in later life

Jane Latham, SRN, DN
Freelance Nurse Consultant in Pain Management, London

The elderly present with the same pain syndromes as any other age group whilst also being at greater risk of suffering pain as a result of diseases associated with the ageing process. A higher incidence of concurrent medical problems in the elderly can also exaggerate and/or complicate the presenting pain syndrome. This can also influence the fact that successful treatment may be measured in total pain relief or a percentage of relief that improves life style. Factors related to these issues can contribute towards the problem of being able to offer treatment that is not only appropriate but also acceptable for both the patient and the clinician. Despite the increasing elderly population there has been relatively little research in this field.

Pain assessment in the elderly
Physical, psychological, social and environmental factors all influence, positively or negatively, the way in which pain presents. (Walker *et al*, 1990; Latham, 1990).

Historical influences
It is important to remember that the elderly have experienced many life events such as two world wars and horse drawn carriages. Due to the lack of medical insight and expertise available in the field of pain when they were younger they may have been expected to just 'grin and bear it' because no treatment was available. 'Old remedies' they have come to trust are all too often overlooked, and even frowned upon by some clinicians today. They sometimes therefore have difficulty in coming to terms with modern day society and its inherent implications of what health care can offer.

Communication
Many of the ageing processes can make pain assessment and treatment more difficult in the elderly than in the younger population. However, without an accurate assessment of the pain it is difficult to decide on the most appropriate and feasible treatment. The key to accurate assessment

lies in a combination of time, patience and ingenuity.

Elderly people are sometimes reluctant to admit to problems such as deafness or blindness, and with some illnesses they may be unable to recognise that they are not communicating appropriately. It is therefore helpful before beginning pain assessment and treatment to take factors such as these into consideration, for example:

1. Patients who have hearing difficulties may prefer written questions, lip reading or sign language.

2. Patients who have difficulties with their sight may need more time to verbalise about their pain or depend on touch methods of communication such as braille.

3. Clinical problems such as a cerebro-vascular accident may mean that the patient can communicate in one way but not another, for example aphasics may still be able to write down how they feel.

4. Patients with failing mental faculties may portray facial expressions, actions or movements as indicators of pain.

5. Knowledge of any memory loss, either short or long-term, is helpful when formulating assessment questions and planning treatments.

6. The elderly who do not speak English as their first language may revert to their primary language when they are in pain.

Social and environmental factors
Checklist of key issues to consider:
- What family, friend or carer support is available?
- Have there been any major life-style changes, eg loss?
- Have they become more socially isolated?
- Have they become more dependent on others?
- What interests have been pursued during retirement?
- Are they happy or unhappy in their present situation?
- Are they able to cope in their present accommodation?
- Are they able to get out of their home?
- Do they want to go out of their home?
- How easy is it to use local facilities, eg shops or transport?

Physical factors
1. Initial onset of pain: eg trauma, illness, surgery or unknown. *Hint:* the patient's perception of the initial onset of pain may be different to the assessor's.

2. Anatomical position of the pain: *Hints:* remember there may be more than one site of pain in the elderly due to different disease processes. Body diagrams may be helpful.

3. Descriptions of the pain: *Hints:* which pain are they describing? Do they have different terms of description?

4. Factors affecting the pain: eg activity, position, stress, isolation, food, heat, cold. *Hint:* both informal observation and formal assessment may be helpful.

5. Previous treatment: eg drugs, non-invasive and invasive techniques, alternative therapies. *Hints:* how good is their memory? Do not just find out the drug(s) or treatment(s), but also how they were administered, how long the course was, and (if appropriate), what co-adjuvants were given. Did the patient feel helped or not? Were there any side effects?

6. Other medical history: eg gastric ulceration, constipation, diabetes, heart disease, depression etc. *Hints:* how good is their memory? Do these other problems contra-indicate any potential treatments?

Observation

Because of the many potential problems that can be encountered when assessing the elderly in pain the key to gaining a useful assessment may often be that of informal observation. It is this situation that the most natural reactions are seen, for example:

- physical movement, eg mobility or positional changes.
- facial expressions eg relaxed or screwed up in pain.
- mood, eg depressed, stoical or happy.

Interactions of the patient with different people may be varied. It is equally as important, therefore, to have an overview of all the individual responses that are observed.

Formal record keeping and measurement

Pain assessment charts can be a very useful formal documentation tool. According to the abilities and/or disabilities of the patient a chart can be filled in by the patient, the patient with the nurse or the nurse on behalf of the patient. Body diagrams, pain patterns, pain descriptions and nursing care plans can be included in the chart as appropriate.

Pain diaries kept on either an out-patient or in-patient basis are another useful way of combining the patient and/or carer's description of the pain with regular measurements over a continuous period of time.

If a formal measurement of pain is required various scales are available, these include:

1. Visual analogue scales or numerical rating scales. These can be adapted, if required, to indicators that the individual can interpret.

2. Verbal rating scales use descriptive terms to measure pain.

3. Colour rating scales use either different colours or the same colour in different intensities to measure pain.

For further information on assessment and measurement of pain see *Pain Control, 2nd edn,* p. 24–37, 1990, J. Latham.

Syndromes associated with pain in the elderly

Syndrome	*Location of pain*
Arthritis, Osteoporosis	Back and/or localised joint pains, fractures, contractures.
Carcinoma	Depending on the sites of the disease: visceral, bone, neurogenic, central pain.

Peripheral vascular disease	Ischaemia, gangrene, amputation.
Diabetes	Neuropathy, vascular ischaemia, infection, amputation.
Cerebro-vascular accident	Thalamic pain, contractures.
Cardio-vascular disease	Angina.
Chronic obstructive airways disease	Chest pain, secondary osteoporosis.
Herpes Zoster	Post-herpetic neuralgia.
Falls/trauma	Myofascial pain, fractures, resultant secondary pain syndromes eg colles fracture→reflex sympathetic dystophy.
Life-style changes, eg isolation, dependence etc, depression	Exaggeration of other physical pain symptoms, lack of success in treatment, 'total body pain' etc

(Walker *et al*, 1990; McCaffery and Beebe, 1989).

Drug therapy

As with any other age group, the elderly patient in pain should be offered specific drug therapies for specific types of pain.

Examples of these include:

visceral pain/potentially } → non-steroidal anti-inflammatories
opiate responsive pain   }   (NSAIDs)
                           }   ± simple analgesics
                                 ↓
                                 mild narcotics
                                 ↓
                                 moderate narcotics
                                 ↓
                                 strong narcotics

bone pain → NSAIDs

neurogenic pain → central acting drugs, steriods

central pain → central acting drugs

For details of specific drug groups, individual drug actions, side-effects and interactions see *Pain Control* 2nd edn, p. 55–82, 1990, J. Latham.

Certain factors should be taken into special consideration when deciding on the appropriate analgesic regime for the elderly. These factors may lead to modifying drug dosages, time intervals and combination therapies. They may sometimes even prohibit the optimal treatment regime for the presenting symptoms. Examples of these factors include: (McCaffery and Beebe, 1989.)

Distribution of drugs   1. Changes in body composition. An increase in the proportion of body fat may contribute towards drugs that are fat soluble having a delayed onset of action. Repeated doses of such drugs may also lead to accumulation.

Heart, kidney and muscle mass decrease with age, therefore drug doses may need to be reduced to avoid toxic levels in the blood and tissue.

2. Serum proteins. Many drugs bind to proteins leaving a percentage of each drug circulating unbound, ie free for pharmacological activity. Chronic disease in the elderly may contribute to less serum proteins and therefore higher levels of unbound drug, thus increasing the risk of toxic effects (Lamy, 1983). Many NSAIDs are protein bound (Flower, Moncada and Vane, 1985).

Metabolism   Whilst a much under-researched area, metabolism of drugs by the liver is not thought to be uniformly affected in the elderly. However, it should be remembered that it may be decreased with specific drugs (Pagliaro and Pagliaro, 1986), and in these cases a longer time interval may be required between doses.

Excretion   Drugs, or the active metabolites of drugs that are excreted by the kidney may remain in the body longer resulting in prolonged therapeutic and/or toxic effects. This can be due to factors such as decreased renal mass, renal blood flow, glomerular filtration rate and tubular secretion. Dehydration and heart failure in the elderly can also affect renal function (Pagliaro and Pagliaro, 1983).

Clearance   Morphine clearance from the plasma is thought to be reduced with age, therefore it may remain in the body longer, and at higher concentrations. Thus lower doses of narcotics may be required less frequently.

Drug receptors   There is at present unresolved debate about whether or not there is a decrease in the number of drug receptors and/or their responsiveness in the elderly which may contribute towards raised drug sensitivity (Pagliaro and Pagliaro, 1986).

Neural blockade

Neural blockade is an important treatment to consider when pain is found to be due to nerve irritation or invasion. It is particularly important to consider this option in the elderly if drug therapy is likely to cause, or is already causing, unwanted side-effects or management problems.

Some of the procedures available and their indications include:

Sacral intrathecal block   Perineal pain due to carcinoma, eg of the rectum/pelvis with sacral nerve root involvement.

Single epidural injection Back pain and/or referred nerve root pain due to either benign disease, eg osteoarthritis/porosis or malignant disease, eg spinal tumour.

Epidural catheter As single epidural injection + malignant disease, end stage peripheral vascular disease, post-operative pain or trauma requiring an infusion of local anaesthetic ± opiates via the epidural route.

Coelic plexus block Upper abdominal pain due to carcinoma of, eg the stomach, liver, pancreas, gall-bladder.

Lumbar sympathetic block Painful peripheral vascular disease of the lower limbs.

Thoracic somatic paravertebral block or catheter Pain due to carcinoma of the lung/bronchus pressing on the chest wall, malignant/benign bone disease, thoracotomy scar pain, trauma, eg fractured ribs.

Lumbar psoas block or catheter Painful hip or knee due to malignant or benign bone disease including fractures.

Stellate ganglion block Facial/opthalmic pain (C5-T1 distribution) due to, eg postherpetic neuralgia.

For further information on specific procedures and their nursing rationale see *Pain Control* 2nd edn, p. 96–111, 1990, J. Latham.

Transcutaneous nerve stimulation (TCNS)

TCNS is a form of electrical stimulation using electrode pads usually aligned over the course of a peripheral nerve innervating the painful area. The original concept underlying its use was the gate control theory (Melzack and Wall, 1965). More recently it has been found to be involved in the stimulation of endogenous opiate release in the dorsal horn. Due to the fact that TCNS is both non-pharmacological and non-invasive with very few side effects it is a useful treatment to consider when deciding on treatment options for the elderly in pain.

Clinical indications include Peripheral nerve injury, causalgia, phantom limb pain, amputation post-herpetic neuralgia, nerve compression syndromes, chronic back pain, joint pains associated with arthritis, post-operative pain and trauma.

Complications and contra-indications

1. Allergic dermatitis due to some electrode gels or tapes. (Hypo-allergenic alternatives are available.)

2. Electrodes should not be placed close to vital body areas eg the carotid artery.

3. Implanted electrical devices such as pacemakers may be affected by the stimulator.

4. Patients with mental impairment should not use a machine unless under constant supervision.

Practical issues to consider with the elderly include the cost of buying and maintaining the machine, the size of the machine, whether the patient can change the control dials, if the patient cannot apply the pads is there someone who can?

For more details on TCNS see *Pain Control* 2 nd edn, p. 112–119, 1990, J. Latham.

Other therapies

It is important when planning pain treatments to consider all approaches that the patient will find both helpful and acceptable. Other therapies that the elderly may find beneficial include: topical preparations, cold/heat, water, acupuncture, aromatherapy, massage, reflexology, relaxation, distraction, imagery and socialization.

Striking the balance between offering the elderly patient in pain not only the treatments that we feel will help, but also finding out and offering options that they feel will help is the key to good pain management.

References

Flower, R.J., Moncada, S. and Vane, J.R. (1985) Drug therapy of inflammation. In Gilman, A.G., *et al*, eds: Goodman and Gilman's *The Pharmacological Basis of Therapeutics, 7th edn*, p. 674–715, Macmillan Publishing, New York.

Lamy, P.P., (1983) The elderly, undernutrition, and pharmacokinetics. *Journal American Geriatric Society* **31** 560–2.

Latham, J. (1990) *Pain Control 2nd edn*, Austen Cornish Publishers/Lisa Sainsbury Foundation, London.

McCaffery, M. and Beebe, A. (1989) *Pain: Clinical Manual For Nursing Practice*, The C.V. Mosby Co, St Louis.

Melzack, R. and Wall, P.D. (1965) Pain mechanisms: a new theory. *Science*, **150**, 971–9.

Melzack, R. and Wall, P.D. (1965) *The Challenge of Pain*, Penguin, Harmondsworth.

Pagliaro, L.A. and Pagliaro, A.M. (1983) *Pharmacological Aspects of Ageing*, p. 1–6, The C.V. Mosby Co, St Louis.

Walker, J.M., Akinsanya, J.A., Davis, B.D. and Marcer, D. (1990) The nursing management of elderly patients with pain in the community: study and recommendations.

15

Mobility problems of the new stroke victim: supporting the carer

Elizabeth M. Horne, MA
Publishing Director, Professional Nurse

Patients and relatives will vary considerably in their levels of awareness of the nature of a stroke and its effect on mobility, in their understanding of its effects on different faculties and the contribution they can make in helping the stroke victim regain mobility. The nurse's level of language and detail when explaining the nature and effects of the stroke will therefore need to be carefully chosen for each person. It is essential for the carer to have some understanding of the complexity of mobility problems, including all the factors outlined in Table 1.

Motivation

A major source of concern for a new stroke victim's carers is the uncertainty over the degree to which mobility will be regained and the length of time that rehabilitation will take. Both will vary considerably between patients, depending on age, severity of stroke and personality, but the carers should be given plenty of opportunity to express their anxieties, and as much information as possible about the likely pattern of rehabilitation for that person.

Rehabilitation may be very slow, and the degree of disability will probably vary from day to day, causing frustration and uncertainty and undermining the patient's self-confidence.

Perceptual problems, and poor memory or concentration span may make the patient appear to lack motivation about rehabilitation. An understanding of these by the carer may ease the frustrations of rehabilitation.

The stroke victim may be reluctant to use aids, feeling they represent an admission of disability. By encouraging discussion of this issue with the stroke victim and the carers, the nurse can help the stroke victim to come to terms with the new situation, and the carer to understand the patient's feelings more fully.

Basic points in assisting mobility

The carer may need a considerable amount of detailed practical help and advice from the doctor, physiotherapist, and occupational therapist on the correct positioning, methods of lifting and moving the patient, on exercises to promote rehabilitation and on the availability and use of appropriate aids, furniture and appliances in the home.

Table 1: Factors affecting mobility in the stroke patient

Impairment	Effect on mobility
Hemiparesis or hemiplegia	Innervation of muscles of legs, trunk and arms may be lost, causing paralysis.
Visual disturbances Perceptual difficulties Balance problems (if cerebellum has been affected)	Balance will be affected if vision, or the processing by the brain of visual information, or the balancing functions of the cerebellum are affected.
Communication	Impairment of speech, or of cognitive or reasoning functions may indirectly affect mobility if the stroke victim is unable to communicate his or her plans, intentions or wishes related to movement. Embarrassment over impaired ability to communicate may inhibit the person's progress toward mobility.
Psychological and social	Fear, anxiety and depression associated with the patient's changed body image will result in some loss of self-confidence which could affect the person's confidence in mobility. The initial uncertainty about the nature of the new patterns of mobility will also knock this self confidence.
Environmental	A once-familiar home may have become an obstacle-course for the new stroke victim, with steps and stairways and narrow doorways which may present insuperable barriers to reasonable mobility.

This advice and information should be followed up by the nurse, to ensure that the carer knows how to use the aids, and is confident about using them. The future carer should be fully involved with moving the stroke victim while still in hospital: watching the nurses, and then actually manoeuvering the patient under nursing supervision. Encouragement from the nurses can be invaluable in building up the future carer's self-confidence.

While encouraging the patient to be independent in hospital, the nurse will also need to recognise the patient's areas of difficulty and try to prevent him or her becoming tired and discouraged. Future carers should also be encouraged to follow this pattern. If the patient becomes too dependent on others, there may be less incentive to acquire the skills he or she will need to fully develop their mobility.

Importance of individual assessment

The new stroke victim and carers should be involved in assessing present skills and setting realistic goals in rehabilitation (Figure 1). The assessment of the home environment is also essential and must involve all relevant members of the household in conjunction with all members of the community-based caring team, including nurses, the GP, community physiotherapist and community occupational therapist, the speech therapist and also social services. Mobility aids, and adaptations required to a bathroom or kitchen may be available from social services, but could take some considerable time to arrange. Information about commercially available aids and furniture may be helpful.

Continuing support

Carers should be encouraged to remember their own health and strength over the coming months. They may welcome information on locally or nationally organized support groups, and may benefit from meeting people in similar situations. The social services should be able to provide information about local schemes to enable the carer to take a holiday.

Where further day hospital or outpatient care is envisaged, the patient and carers could be introduced to the relevant staff before discharge from hospital.

Regular contact with the community care team should involve the continuing assessment and setting of new goals in the rehabilitation programme.

Useful contacts:
District nurse:
Community occupational therapist:
Community physiotherapist:
Speech therapist:
Day hospital or outpatients:
Social worker:
Local stroke club:
Local transport scheme:

The Chest, Heart & Stroke Association (CHSA), CHSA House, White Cross Street, London EC1Y 8SS. Tel: 071-490 7999.
Scotland: 65 North Castle Street, Edinburgh EH2 3LT. Tel: 031-225 6963.
Northern Ireland: 21 Dublin Road, Belfast BT2 7FJ. Tel: 0232 320184.

The CHSA works for the prevention of chest, heart and stroke illnesses and to help those who suffer from them. They publish a number of useful publications.

The Disabled Living Foundation (DLF), 380–384 Harrow Road, London W9 2HU. Tel: 071-289 6111.

The DLF is concerned with those aspects of ordinary life which present particular problems to disabled people of any age. They have set up an aids and equipment cnetre displaying aids for disabled people and run a valuable information service. They publish a number of useful publications.

Action for Dysphasic Adults, 1 Royal Street, London SE1 7LN. Tel: 071-261 9572.

ADA published leaflets for adults with speech impairment and their carers and campaigns to get speech therapy for stroke victims.

Disability Alliance Education & Research Association, 1st Floor, Universal House, 88–94 Wentworth Street, London E1 7SA.

The Alliance provides a service to disabled people and their carers on disability benefits available. They publish the Disability Rights Handbook (price £4.50).

Handout: The care of the new stroke victim

Mobility   Complete this form with the help of your nurse:
Patient assessment   The stroke caused particular problems because it affected:
Movement: Vision:
Balance: Perception:
Objectives   We aim to be able to do the following tasks by ....

....
Carer   **Patient**

Some points for the carer to bear in mind
- Make sure you are confident about moving and positioning the patient correctly. Ask the nurse or physiotherapist to show you the correct way to work with the patient while he or she is still in hospital, and to let you try with their supervision. Always ask if you are not sure, or if you would like more help. There is an excellent booklet called 'Home care for the stroke patient in the early days' available from the Chest, Heart & Stroke Association, price 50p (or £4.50 for 10), which gives clear details on positioning and moving the patient, and on the exercises they may need to do.
- Make sure that the patient wears appropriate clothing and footwear. Avoid slippers or loose shoes, and very loose clothing. Your own footwear is important, too, if you are involved in lifting or helping the patient to move.
- Work out, with your district nurse and communicty occupational therapist, what would be the most valuable aids and appliances in the home. Are there are adaptations (such as grip-rails near the bath, or replacement of soft carpeting with firmer floor coverings) which you could see to yourself, or ask a friend or relative to fix? Ask your community occupational therapist about the best kind of chairs and beds and their availability.
- Make sure you know how to use all the aids and appliances fully and correctly. Ask your district nurse or community occupational therapist if you are not sure.
- Check regularly that all the aids are safe: look for worn ferrules on walking sticks and check the heels of shoes for uneven wear.
- Try not to let the patient become discouraged when he or she is tired, or frustrated. Rehabilitation may be slow, and his or her apparent degree of disability may vary from day to day. It may also take him or her some time to come to terms with the new situation.
- Don't lose sight of your *own* health. Caring for a stroke victim may be hard work both physically and emotionally, and your own good health is an essential requirement.
- Make contact with your local stroke association and national organizations. Your district nurse should be able to help you here.
- Find out about local transport schemes, exemption from vehicle excise duty, and mobility allowance, and the orange badge scheme. Information should be available from Social Services.

16

Leg ulcers: the nursing assessment

Jacqueline Dale, MSc, SRN, RCNT, DipN
Area Nursing Officer, Lothian Health Board, Edinburgh

Barbara Gibson, SRN, SCM
Liaison/Leg Ulcer Specialist Sister, Falkirk and District Royal Infirmary

Sometimes even the most experienced practitioners are puzzled by the cause of an ulcer which fails to respond to carefully chosen treatments. Poor diagnosis may lead to inappropriate treatment which, at best, does little to help and, at worst, may be positively harmful. In order to assess ulcers nurses should be able to distinguish between *venous ulcers,* which can be treated by relatively simple conservative measures, and those in which *ischaemia* is involved. In a poorly perfused leg, compression bandaging, the mainstay of treatment for venous ulcers, must obviously be avoided.

Ulcers which may be ischaemic can be identified by considering the patient's medical history, by careful observation and a few simple tests. These methods will not result in a final, definitive diagnosis but they will enable the nurse who applies them to alert the doctor to the possibility that a patient may have significant arterial disease needing further investigation.

Consider the patient

Before concentrating on the ulcer itself, first consider the patient. Is anything known which indicates that there may be generalised arterial disease? There may be pointers such as a history of stroke, transient ischaemic attacks, intermittent claudication or hypertension. Some information may be gleaned from patients' notes, they might volunteer it, or you might have to ask. Figure 1 shows the incidence of leg ulcers linked with a history of arterial disease in the Lothian and Forth Valley Leg Ulcer Study.

Other relevant conditions are diabetes and rheumatoid arthritis because they are associated with small vessel disease (arteritis). The patient may be a known diabetic but, if not, it is worth testing the urine for sugar as this occasionally reveals unsuspected diabetes. Rheumatoid ulcers are some of the most intractable. The condition is usually obvious from the characteristic deformities of the finger joints. Immobility and dependency of the legs for long periods may cause severe oedema in these patients and exacerbate the ulcer. Prolonged steroid therapy further predisposes them to ulcers because they develop paper-thin skin which breaks easily and heals slowly.

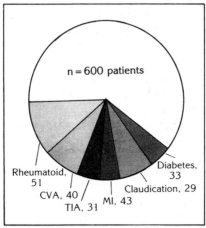

n = 600 patients

Rheumatoid, 51

CVA, 40

TIA, 31

MI, 43

Claudication, 29

Diabetes, 33

Figure 1. History of arterial disease.

Then consider the whole leg

Next examine the leg and foot. To assess whether the blood supply is good, stroke the leg gently downwards with the back of your hand. Is it warm and does it look a healthy pink? If the foot is cold and blue or white and if pain is worse when the leg is elevated, it may be ischaemic. Another test of perfusion is the rate of capillary filling. To assess this, press gently on the big toenail with your own thumbnail. The nailbed will turn white. Normally the colour returns to the nailbed immediately the pressure is removed (try this on yourself). It may be quite slow if the leg is ischaemic. Remember though, that both colour and capillary filling may be affected by cold weather.

Foot pulses

The presence of easily palpable foot pulses is the most reassuring sign of all. Check the dorsalis pedis pulse in the midline in the front of the ankle joint, and the posterior tibial pulse behind the medial malleolus (Figure 2).

The foot pulses may be difficult to find if the leg is oedematous or indurated but nurses should practise and improve their skills in this technique. In some clinics nurses have been trained to measure ankle systolic blood pressures accurately using a continuous wave ultrasound probe instead of a stethoscope (Cornwall, 1985). Eventually these probes may become more widely available, but we are concerned, here, with simple assessment techniques which can be applied by any nurse without special training or equipment. If neither the dorsalis pedis nor the posterior tibial pulse can be easily felt the doctor should be asked to

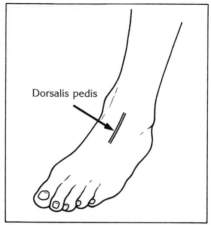

Figure 2. Foot pulses.

examine the patient to exclude arterial disease before a compression bandage is applied. Most of the factors discussed so far are those which indicate a non-venous ulcer but there are clues which help to confirm that the ulcer is venous. The patient may be able to tell you of an episode of deep venous thrombosis or some other thrombogenic event (Table 1).

Thrombogenic events		
None	:	424
Known DVT	:	207
Leg Fracture	:	78
Neuropathy	:	52
Infection	:	51
IV Infusion	:	15

Table 1. Legs affected by thrombogenic events.

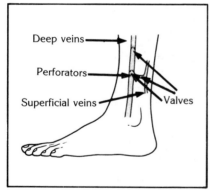

Figure 3. Venous system – normal.

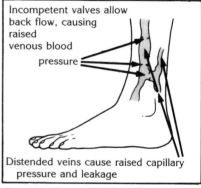

Figure 4. Venous system – after thrombosis.

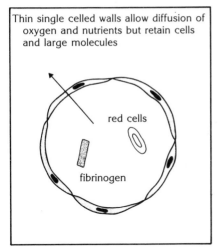

Thin single celled walls allow diffusion of oxygen and nutrients but retain cells and large molecules

red cells

fibrinogen

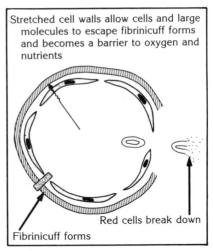

Stretched cell walls allow cells and large molecules to escape fibrinicuff forms and becomes a barrier to oxygen and nutrients

Red cells break down

Fibrinicuff forms

Figure 5. Normal capillary.

Figure 6. Distended capillary – venous hypertension.

Two sure signs of chronic venous insufficiency and therefore of a venous ulcer are "ankle flare" and pigmentation of the skin above and around the ulcer.

The sequence of events beginning with a deep venous thrombosis and destruction of the valves in the deep veins was briefly described in a previous article (Dale and Gibson, 1986) and is recapitulated in Figures 3-6. The outward manifestations of this process are staining of the skin as a result of the breakdown of the red cells and distension of the network of tiny veins on the medial aspect of the foot just below the malleolus

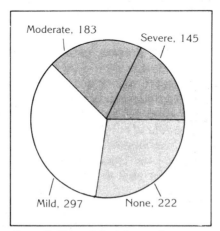

Moderate, 183

Severe, 145

Mild, 297

None, 222

Figure 7. Pigmentation observed.
Lothian and Forth Valley Leg Ulcer Study.
n = 827 ulcerated legs (600 patients).

known as "ankle flare" (Figure 8). Look for this when the patient is standing barefoot. When present, ankle flare is a sure sign of well established venous insufficiency. Pigmentation is almost always visible as well but it may be mild and not easily seen by an inexperienced observer (Figure 7). Oedema is much more likely if the cause is venous but its presence or absence does not necessarily help in discriminating between a venous and an arterial ulcer.

Lastly, the ulcer

Finally look at the ulcer itself. Where is it? Most venous ulcers occur in the lower third of the leg (the gaiter area) above the medial malleolus. Ulcers outside the gaiter area should always be treated with caution but unfortunately those within the gaiter area are sometimes ischaemic. Foot ulcers are almost always arterial. Ulcers that look punched out and deep are arterial. Those with a rolled edge may be malignant. This simple guide to ulcer assessment is summarised in Figure 8.

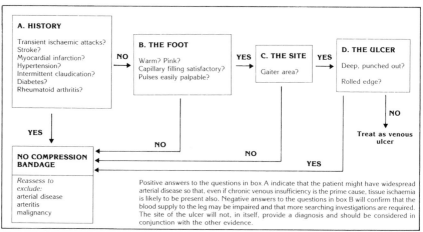

Figure 8. What kind of ulcer?

Leg ulcers may have several contributing causes. Many legs have both venous and arterial disease present at the same time. The severity of the arterial disease must be carefully investigated in order to select the most appropriate treatment for an ulcer of mixed aetiology.

If the leg is warm, well perfused and foot pulses are present, a nurse can confidently treat the ulcer with firm graduated compression and a moist non-adherent dressing. If, however, the patient has absent or weak foot pulses, suspected or known diabetes, rheumatoid arthritis, suspected arterial disease or foot ulcers, the nurse should refer the patient back to the doctor for further assessment. If this advice is followed some patients may be referred unnecessarily but it is preferable to err on the side of caution when a patient's leg may be at stake.

References
Cornwall, J. (1985) Diagnosis of leg ulcers. *Journal of District Nursing* **4**, 3, 4–11.
Dale, J. and Gibson, B. (1986) Leg ulcers: a disease affecting all ages. *The Professional Nurse*, **1**, 8, 213–214.

17

Treatment of leg ulcers

Jacqueline Dale, MSc, SRN, RCNT, DipN
Area Nursing Officer, Lothian Health Board, Edinburgh

Barbara Gibson, SRN, SCM
Liaison/Leg Ulcer Specialist Sister, Falkirk and District Royal Infirmary

To borrow Florence Nightingale's famous dictum, the first rule in treating leg ulcers is that the nurse should do the ulcer no harm. This may sound obvious, but some preparations used on ulcers have been shown to have a detrimental effect upon healing (Leaper, 1986). We have already discussed the importance of accurate diagnosis before embarking upon treatment. When assessing the cause of an ulcer we recommended that you should first consider the patient as a whole. This also applies to treatment.

Venous ulcers
Even when the underlying cause of an ulcer can be attributed to chronic venous insufficiency, other conditions may be present which exacerbate the ulcer.

Oedema   Severe oedema is a common problem, usually reduced by a few days bed rest with the foot of the bed raised by about eight inches. Bed blocks are the best thing to use if they are available, but heavy books are a good substitute. We are not suggesting that you commandeer the family Bible, but have you thought of using telephone directories? With their five directories Londoners have an advantage here! Patients who cannot take to their beds should be advised to sit on a sofa with their legs raised on cushions above the level of their hips at every possible opportunity. Some nurses use a 'legs up chart' to encourage their patients in leg drainage.

Leg elevation should not be used indiscriminately. A sudden return of tissue fluid to the vascular circulation might precipitate cardiac failure in frail elderly patients. If in doubt seek medical advice.

Never try to reduce oedema with a bandage, but once swelling has been reduced, applying a compression bandage and encouraging the patient to take exercise will prevent the recurrence of oedema by improving the venous return. Walking about two miles a day is excellent therapy. Housebound patients (or the elderly during bad weather) can be taught to walk on the spot and for the chairbound, ankle extension, flexion and rotation at frequent intervals are a useful substitute for walking. Standing still for long periods should be avoided. Many household chores such as ironing can be done equally well when sitting, and simple ankle exercises can be done while waiting at the bus stop. If those who are mobile enough can be persuaded to attend clinics for their treatment, this in itself will provide some of the exercise required.

Weight reduction, if it can be achieved, will improve mobility in the obese and advice on eating a well balanced diet might help to improve general nutrition which may in turn contribute to faster healing. Any other untreated conditions which you may observe should, of course, be brought to the doctor's attention.

Some patients who have suffered from a chronic ulcer for many years become depressed. It is important to give them hope. If you can convince them that with their co-operation the ulcer will heal, the battle is half won. Some nurses have found that ulcer clinics where sufferers can meet others in the same plight can be a useful morale booster. Often a club-like atmosphere prevails and the patients look forward to their visits. Some are known to call in occasionally even when their ulcers are healed just to keep in touch with their friends (*Community Outlook*, 1980).

Local treatment
Before thinking about what to put on the ulcer, first consider the health of the leg.

Cleansing Many ulcer patients have not had a bath for years because they have been told not to put their leg in water. Unless eczema is very severe there is no reason why they should not, and a bath gives a sense of wellbeing. In clinics the legs can be immersed up to the knees in warm water using a leg bath lined with a polythene bag (to prevent any risk of cross infection). Where baths are not possible, gently swab the ulcer with hypertonic saline and wash the leg with warm water. Exceptionally dry or eczematous skin should be cleansed with olive or arachis oil.

Sometimes the eczema presents more of a problem than the ulcer itself. In severe cases the advice of a dermatologist should be sought, sooner rather than later. Steroid preparations are usually prescribed in these circumstances but it is most important to seek specialist advice first.

Support It is essential to improve the venous return from the leg if the ulcer is to heal. A compression bandage or elastic stocking is applied for this purpose. Research has shown (Jones et al, 1980) that blood flow is faster if the pressure applied is graduated from ankle to knee. There is still some debate about the optimum levels but it is generally agreed that a pressure of about 30-40mmHg at the ankle reducing to about 15-20mmHg at the calf is enough. Few patients can tolerate pressures much above these levels for very long. Choice of bandage and techniques used are most important and will be dealt with in the next chapter.

Choice of dressing

Turner (1985) summarises many years of research into the aims of the ideal wound dressing as follows: –

- To maintain a high humidity between wound and dressing;
- To remove excess exudate and toxic compounds;
- To allow gaseous exchange;
- To provide thermal insulation to the wound surface;
- To be impermeable to bacteria;
- To be free from particles and toxic wound contaminants;
- To allow removal without causing trauma during dressing change.

In addition, as far as leg ulcers are concerned, the substance should not cause skin reactions. During our survey we found this to be a common problem. In 1981 when the Lothian and Forth Valley district nurses reported on 377 patients currently in their care, 95 (25 per cent) were known to have had an adverse skin reaction to substances used to treat their ulcers. Paste bandages appear to be the most common culprits but Viscopaste PB7 was less often cited than would be expected from the proportions used. Almost any product might cause trouble in this way, therefore the ulcer should be inspected if the patient complains of increased irritation or discomfort (Table 1).

	No. of reports	% (n = 95)	% in use (n = 377)
Paste bandages			
Ichthopaste	31	33	9
Viscopaste PB7	24	25	16
*Other	15	16	6
Sofratulle	11	12	12
Bactigras	4	4	9
Cetrimide	6	6	14
Melolin	9	9	5
Opsite	3	3	0
Adhesive bandages	3	3	3
*Quinaband, Calaband, Icthaband, Coltapaste			

Table 1. Products reported to have caused skin reactions in 95 out of 377 leg ulcer patients (District Nurse Survey).

The guiding principle should be to keep the treatment simple, disturb the ulcer as little as possible and avoid trauma during dressing changes.

One of the best all-purpose treatments is the paste bandage, which can be left in position for a week or longer without a change. There is no need to apply de-sloughing preparations, the paste bandage will be sufficient. Apply the bandage from toe to knee next to the skin. The paste bandage should not be tight. Folding the bandage back on itself and reversing the direction over the sharp edge of the tibia prevents it being applied too tightly and gives extra protection over the bone, especially on a thin leg. A few extra layers should be applied over the ulcer itself to keep it moist. A cotton-stretch bandage should be applied over this to provide support. This combination has been shown to achieve and sustain satisfactory pressures (Dale et al, 1983).

The paste bandage may be covered, if necessary, with Tubegauze and padding to absorb excess exudate and a compression bandage such as a 10cm Elastocrepe should be applied to cover it from toe to knee. If the patient has not worn a paste bandage before, a visit should be paid the following day to check that there has been no discomfort or allergic reaction. Patients who react to paste bandages may be patch-tested to discover the cause, but it is not always possible, even with patch-testing, to demonstrate an allergy. The cause of the reaction might be occlusion rather than an allergic response to substances used in the bandage.

The hydrocolloids are a very useful alternative to a paste bandage, they may be left undisturbed for a week or longer if the exudate is not excessive. They can be used successfully under compression stockings or tapered Tubigrip and the patients can bathe without disturbing the dressing. This regimen is most acceptable, especially to patients who are very active. As a general rule the dressing should be as simple as possible. In the absence of a paste bandage a stronger support bandage is needed. An elastic web bandage such as the Blue Line (Seton) or Elastoweb (Smith and Nephew) gives well sustained support but it should be removed before going to bed and re-applied each morning before getting up. For this reason the bandage is best suited for patients who are able to apply it themselves and they must be taught how to apply it correctly. Some patients can be taught to carry out their own treatment; this, with periodic supervision, can be very successful. It reduces the number of home and treatment room visits, places less restrictions on the patient and is cost effective.

Tubigrip SSB is useful as it provides graduated compression. A single layer is not powerful enough but, over another bandage like Elastocrepe, or as a double layer, it will give sustained graduated compression.

Removing slough If the slough is dry and dark coloured in appearance it should be left to separate spontaneously, unless there are signs of infection underneath. In this case Varidase might be required to remove it more quickly. In these circumstances seek medical advice. Soft, moist slough may be carefully trimmed away with scissors at dressing changes.

The infected ulcer

Persistent pain in the ulcer site may be an indication that infection is present. Although it is not essential to take wound swabs for culture from all leg ulcers, wound swabbing is indicated when cellulitis is present in the surrounding area and when there is persistent pain. In these circumstances systemic antibiotics may be prescribed but topical antibiotics should be avoided because they tend to cause allergies. The use of topical antiseptics is controversial (Leaper, 1986) and should only be resorted to in exceptional circumstances.

Exudate   If the discharge is copious, pad well, change the dressing as often as necessary until the exudate subsides then reduce dressing changes and disturb as infrequently as possible. Increased leg elevation will help to reduce the amount of exudate.

Painful ulcers   Ensure that oedema is reduced as this may be the problem. Infection may be the cause and should be treated. If an ulcer is persistently painful the diagnosis should be reassessed to ensure that the leg is not ischaemic. Certain of the new non-adherent materials and gels like Corethium, Granuflex or Sorbsan provide comfortable pain-free dressing for some patients. In difficult cases these are worth trying.

Arterial ulcers

The underlying disease must always be fully investigated and if possible treated (Dale and Gibson, 1986). The ulcers tend to be painful, sloughy, have a pale appearance and heal slowly. The aim is to keep the patient as comfortable as possible, to avoid deterioration of the ulcer and reduce pain. The new dressings already mentioned have been reported to reduce pain and simple measures such as a bed cage and keeping the leg cool at night are helpful. Compression bandaging should never be used. Sometimes the circulation to the leg can be improved by reconstructive arterial surgery, so these patients should be referred to a vascular surgeon.

Mixed ulcers   Some ulcers are caused by a combination of both venous and arterial disease. Medical advice must be sought to determine which condition is the most important cause in each case. Judgement regarding whether or not to apply compression can then be made. One layer of shaped Tubigrip or a very light crepe bandage to keep the dressing in place may be all that can be applied.

Assessing progress

To monitor the rate of healing, trace the outline of the ulcer at monthly intervals using a permanent marker pen and a small polythene bag. The polythene that has been in direct contact with the ulcer can then be cut away leaving a clean sheet which can be dated and attached to the patient's records. Mark the top with an arrow so that the tracings can be compared. The tracing can help the patient too when she can see how the ulcer is progressing.

There are no hard and fast rules as to which dressing to use but the general rules are — for venous ulcers provide graduated elastic compression and the simplest dressing possible. Do not change treatments once the ulcer is clean unless there is marked deterioration or an allergic reaction. For arterial ulcers apply no compression and find a dressing which will keep the patient as comfortable as possible.

Once a venous ulcer has healed patients must be fitted and supplied with elastic stockings and be shown how to get them on. Finally, do not abandon your patient. Recurrence is so common that it is well worthwhile investing time to encourage him or her to persist with exercises and compression therapy by arranging some follow-up appointments.

The Lothian and Forth Valley Leg Ulcer Study Group have made a video recording 'Bandaging for Leg Ulcers' which includes a section on paste bandaging. The programme received a BLAT award for educational merit in 1986. Enquiries to Dr C. McEwan, Department of Public Health Medicine, Forth Valley Health Board, Spittal Street, Stirling FK8 1DX.

References

Leaper, D. (1986) Antiseptics and their effect on tissue healing. *Nursing Times*, **82**, 22, 45–47.

Community Outlook (1980) Editorial Veins at Staines. *Nursing Times*, **76**, 231–2.

Turner, T.D. (1985) Which dressing and why? In: Westaby, S. (Ed), Wound Care, pp 58–59, Heinemann, London.

Dale, J.J., Callam, M.J. and Ruckley C.V. (1983). How efficient is a compression bandage? *Nursing Times*, **79**, 46, 49–51.

Jones, N.A.G., Webb, P.J., Rees, R.I. and Kakkar, V.V. (1980). A physiology of elastic compression stockings in venous disorders of the legs. *British Journal of Surgery*, **67**, 569–73.

18

Compression bandaging for venous ulcers

Jacqueline Dale, MSc, SRN, RCNT, DipN
Area Nursing Officer, Lothian Health Board, Edinburgh

Barbara Gibson, SRN, SCM
Liaison/Leg Ulcer Specialist Sister, Falkirk and District Royal Infirmary

Venous ulcers cannot be healed by dressings alone without at the same time taking steps to correct the abnormally high blood pressure in the superficial veins. This results from incompetent valves in the related deep and perforating veins of the leg and is the underlying cause of venous ulcers. The disease process has been described in previous articles (Dale and Gibson, 1986a and b).

No matter how carefully the dressing is chosen, successful treatment depends on improving the return of blood from the leg. The simplest way is to raise the legs above heart level and let the blood run downhill. Patients with leg ulcers are sometimes prescribed rest in bed and treated in this way, to reduce oedema, but sooner or later they have to get up and the benefits of improved leg drainage are lost.

A well applied compression bandage is needed at this stage to prevent pooling of blood in the capillaries and the resumption of leakage of fluid into the tissues which will eventually lead to recurrence of the ulcer.

Less emphasis is placed on teaching the art of bandaging in colleges of nursing than was the case before the development of a wide range of versatile, easily applied tubular bandages which can hold a dressing on almost any part of the body more comfortably than the most skilfully applied rolled bandage, but when dealing with venous ulcers, simply retaining the dressing is not enough. Compression bandaging should be recognised as a valuable skill which all nurses should learn *as a treatment in its own right.*

Graduated compression
The concept of graduated compression is illustrated in Figure 1. The arrow sizes indicate that the pressure should be greatest at the ankle gradually decreasing upwards towards the knee. Several research studies have shown that the blood flows much faster when this is achieved. (Lawrence and Kakkar, 1980; Horner et al, 1980).

Though there is some debate about exactly what pressures are required, it is generally accepted that about 30 — 40mm Hg at the ankle diminishing

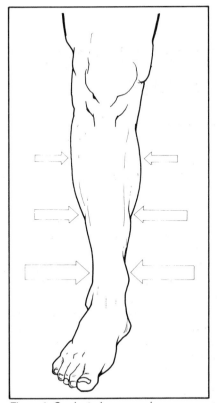

Figure 1. Graduated compression.

by about 50 per cent below the knee is sufficient. In practice, few patients can tolerate pressures much above these levels for any length of time. The problem for most of us is knowing what pressures we are achieving.

Measuring the pressures exerted by bandages and elastic stockings is, unfortunately, no simple exercise. Most manufacturers test their products in the laboratory by using pneumatic or wooden formers to simulate the leg, or they deduce the pressures achieved by measuring the force required to stretch standard samples of the material by a given amount. Laboratory experiments are useful but they are not an adequate substitute for testing on patients in the real situation, where the bandage might perform differently. A number of techniques have been developed, either to measure the effect on superficial venous pressures directly, by cannulating foot and calf veins, or indirectly, by using isotope clearance studies to measure the effect on blood velocity. These are invasive techniques and undesirable for patients who already have impaired veins. In the last few years, devices to measure the pressure exerted on the leg underneath elastic stockings have been developed. This is a great advance because they can also be used for bandages, but the equipment available so far is expensive and not suitable for trials lasting more than a few hours, so that the long-term effects cannot be ascertained.

Tension and pressure   The pressure exerted by a bandage depends partly on how much it has been stretched, that is to say, its tension, partly on the size of the leg and partly on the number of layers applied. The pressure can be calculated if the tension is known. Laplace's Law states that: Pressure = $\dfrac{\text{Tension}}{\text{Radius}}$

It follows that if a bandage is applied at a constant tension the pressure will be greatest at the ankle when the leg is narrowest and the desired gradient will be achieved naturally from the shape of the leg itself. It also follows that the pressure varies around the circumference of the leg and is greatest where the curves are sharpest over bony prominences.

Elasticity   The elasticity of a bandage determines how much tension is necessary to achieve the required pressures, how well the pressures are maintained and how comfortable it is to wear. A bandage which can exert satisfactory pressures when applied at 20 per cent extension, will recover more completely after movement and feel more comfortable than a less elastic one which is designed to operate at full extension. The elasticity of the bandage material depends on whether it contains an elastomer such as rubber, or whether it relies on crimped threads.

Stopping distance   Another useful concept when considering how bandages behave, is that of the 'stopping distance'. How far can the bandage be stretched before it is fully extended, or before it 'stops'? Experienced bandagers tend to recognise the feel of the bandages they use regularly and are able to keep the tension even. Lestreflex is an example of a bandage with a very short stopping distance and Elset of a long one. The choice depends on the circumstances, but it should be remembered, when using a short stop bandage, that a little more extension will produce much more bandage pressure, whereas there is considerably more leeway with a long stop bandage. It is, however, more difficult to judge and control the stretch of a bandage which has a very long stop because one has to work at arm's length. On the whole we find bandages with a shorter stopping distance more suitable.

Types of bandage   Extensible bandages are of two types:
● those which rely on crimped cotton, wool or rayon threads for their elasticity — known as 'crepe' bandages.
● those which incorporate an elastomer such as rubber or Lycra (some of these are woven onto an 'elastic web' from which they take their name).

Elastomers return to their original length after stretching and therefore maintain compression more effectively in use.

All bandages lose pressure after they are first applied. Thomas et al (1980) tested a number of extensible bandages in common use and showed that crepe bandages performed poorly in this respect, losing between 40 and 60 per cent of their tension in the first 20 minutes, whereas elastic web bandages lost only about 20 per cent.

Technique

The aim is to achieve graduated pressures with no tight bands — the golden rule is 'keep the tension even and rely on the shape of the leg to do the rest'. Normally the leg should be bandaged from the base of the toes to just below the knee; continuing further may produce a tight band of pressure behind the knee. The foot must be included or it will swell. A 10cm width is the most suitable for most legs but with heavy elastic web bandages a 7.5cm width conforms better around the ankle.

It is a good idea to practise on yourself or with a friend. To get some idea of how the required pressures feel, use a sphygmomanometer. Put on the cuff just above your ankle and inflate it to about 35mm Hg. How does that feel? Next move it up to your calf and inflate it to about 20mm Hg. It will feel pleasantly firm and supportive but not tight. That is the aim of the bandage.

Follow the manufacturer's instructions which might say 'apply at full extension' or 'apply at 20 per cent extension'. In the first case stretch the bandage until it stops and keep it like that as you put it on; in the second case do a little preliminary testing. Unroll a new bandage for about 1.5 metres and mark it at 10cm intervals. Re-roll it and apply it at what you judge to be the correct extension. Next measure the intervals between the marks. If the distance is now 12cm the bandage has been stretched by 2cm or about 20 per cent. Several intervals should be measured to see if the tension was consistent. It is important to concentrate on how much effort it takes to achieve the required extension and how tight the bandage is. With practice you will gradually develop a feel for what you are achieving and will be able to obtain the pressures you need, even with a bandage you have not used before.

Different methods of application are advised for different types of bandages. The foot and ankle turns are the most important.

Heavy high compression bandages Examples are Blue Line (Seton) or Secure Forte (Johnson and Johnson). With the foot at right angles, the bandage end is placed under the ball of the foot. The first turn encircles the base of the toes and secures the loose end. The second turn is carried from the ball of the foot to the point of the heel. The third turn comes down under the arch of the foot to fill the gap and then up to encircle the ankle. As the spiral continues up the leg, each turn should just cover the centre line. This keeps the layers even and avoids the formation of pockets of oedema between the turns. Heavy bandages of this type must be taken off at night and reapplied first thing the next morning.

Lighter bandages   For these, a slight modification of this method is needed to increase the pressure round the ankle and lower gaiter area. The first turn should start behind the leg and go once round the ankle. The second goes to the base of the toes and around the ball of the foot. Thereafter the method is as before. Pressures exerted by the lightest bandages can be increased by making figure of eight turns above the ankle. If the bandage is too long, cut if off when you reach the knee. Winding the superflous length around the leg will cause more pressure where it is least wanted and spoil the gradient.

Other factors may affect the performance of a bandage. Dale et al (1983) showed that a single wash reduced the pressures obtained by an Elastocrepe bandage by about 20 per cent, but applying an Elastocrepe over a paste bandage increased the pressures achieved and improved their maintenance over time. This may be a reason for the success of paste bandaging as a treatment for venous ulcers.

Always examine the toes and ask the patient if the bandage feels comfortable before you leave and advise those in the community to call you if it feels too tight.

Jarrett (1984) and Cornwall (1985) recommend the use of elastic stockings to provide support when treating leg ulcers. The pressure profile produced by the best stockings is known and, if they are properly applied, many of the problems discussed above can be avoided. There are, however, obstacles which prevent us from recommending them for widespread use: they are expensive; they are extremely difficult to put on; a size larger than the patient would normally wear is necessary to allow the stocking to be applied over bulky dressings.

Shaped Tubigrip, applied over another support bandage is sometimes recommended as a useful alternative. Research of our own suggests that using this product over Elastocrepe is helpful because, though the pressures achieved are only slightly higher, it completely eliminates slippage of the bandages.

Hazards

In the wrong circumstances compression bandaging is a very dangerous procedure, so it should only be used after a careful assessment and accurate diagnosis of the cause of the ulcer has been made. Applying a compression bandage to a leg with impaired arterial circulation could cause ischaemic ulcers over bony prominences and possibly damage the leg so severely that it might need amputation. We, therefore, make no apologies for repeating the advice given in previous articles (Dale and Gibson, 1986 b and c). Examine the leg, and if you cannot easily feel at least one of the foot pulses, or have any other reason to suspect that arterial disease might be present, apply only a light bandage to keep the dressing in place and refer the patient back to the doctor.

Even without arterial disease, over-tight bandaging on a thin leg can cause pressure sores over bony prominences and tendons. Velband padding can be used under the bandage to prevent this.

Slippage of the bandage turns with movement of the leg may result in rumpling and constriction. Preventing this with graduated Tubigrip has already been discussed. The objection to using straight Tubigrip for this purpose is that a size which fits about the ankle will be too tight at the calf. For this reason a size which fits easily about the calf should be selected. A single layer will have little effect on the pressure gradient but will help to keep the underlying bandage in place.

Choices

The range of compression bandages on the market is enormous. Most hospital departments keep a range of different types in stock, some of which are very costly and should be selected carefully. Unfortunately the choice for community nurses is much more limited. Only those which can produce moderate or high compression are suitable for venous ulcers. Bandages containing elastomer are sometimes more expensive than crepe but will continue to perform well after washing. Heavy compression bandages such as Blue Line, Red Line and Elastoweb may cause pain when the patient is inactive, therefore, they must be taken off at night and reapplied next morning. In the community, this is only practicable for patients who can be taught to do this for themselves (or who have a skilful relative).

For those who can obtain them, the elastic cohesive bandages, which stick to themselves but not to skin or hair are useful, as they give well sustained high pressures and do not slip. Coban and Secure Forte are examples). They can be dangerous, however, in inexperienced hands because they may cause tight bands around the ankle and damage over the tendons if they are wrongly applied. They are expensive and lose their cohesive properties if they are washed. There are some new, medium- and light-weight bandages containing the synthetic elastomer, Lycra, on the market (Tensopress, Smith and Nephew, Setopress, Seton are examples). They are comfortable and maintain their pressures adequately in wear and after washing. Some brands can now be prescribed on form FP10 and therefore will be available to community nurses.

References
Cornwall, J. (1985) Treating leg ulcers. *Journal of District Nursing*, **4**, 4, 4–6.
Dale, J. and Gibson, B. (1986a) Leg ulcers: a disease affecting all ages. *The Professional Nurse*, **1**, 8, 213–214.
    (1986b) Leg ulcers: the nursing assessment. *The Professional Nurse*, **1**, 9, 236–238.
    (1986c) Treatment of leg ulcers. *The Professional Nurse*, **1**, 12, 321–324.
Dale, J., Callam, M.J., Ruckley, C.V. (1983) How efficient is a compression bandage? *Nursing Times*, **79**, 46, 49–51.
Horner, J., Fernandes é Fernandes, J., Nicolaides, A.N. (1980) Value of graduated compression stockings in deep venous insufficiency. *British Medical Journal*, **1**, 820–821.

Jarret, P. (1984) Leg ulcers: a clinical update *Journal of District Nursing*, **2**, 7, 4–6.

Lawrence, D. and Kakkar, V.V. (1980) Graduated, static, external compression of the lower limb: a physiological assessment. *British Journal of Surgery*, **67**, 119–121.

Thomas, S., Dawes, C., Hay, P. (1980) A critical evaluation of some extensive bandages in current use. *Nursing Times*, **76**, 26, 1123–1126.

19
Prevention of venous ulcers

Jacqueline Dale, MSc, SRN, RCNT, DipN
Area Nursing Officer, Lothian Health Board, Edinburgh

Barbara Gibson, SRN, SCM
Liaison/Leg Ulcer Specialist Sister, Falkirk and District Royal Infirmary

Venous ulcers are those caused by raised venous pressure in the leg due to the incompetence of the valves of the saphenous and perforating veins. The damaged valves allow backflow of blood from the deep to the superficial veins, causing distension, capillary damage and oedema, eventually resulting in breakdown of the skin. The damage to the valves is usually the result of an episode of deep venous thrombosis (DVT), associated with pregnancy, surgical operations, prolonged immobility or leg injuries which may or may not have given rise to symptoms at the time (Figure 1). Bauer (1942) showed that, if there is persistent swelling of the leg, the incidence of ulcer increases with the length of time after DVT.

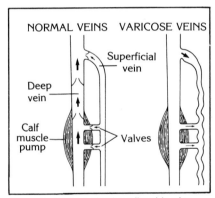

Figure 1. Damaged veins allow blood to flow back.

Venous ulcers have been described as ''one stage of a very chronic disease'' (Dodd and Cockett, 1976). All nurses are taught that post-operative patients are at risk of DVT and that this may be a cause of pulmonary embolism and sudden death but few are aware that the patient who survives these risks may eventually develop a condition which causes discomfort, misery and even depression and social isolation.

Prevention is a worthwhile goal, but both primary and secondary prevention must be considered. First priority is prevention of DVT, second to teach those who have had DVT how to look after their legs and finally to prevent recurrence after the ulcer has healed. The key to success lies in effective health education. The message must be clearly expressed, with follow-up sessions. Those who have had ulcers should be seen regularly and encouraged to continue their preventive exercises and treatment.

All teachers must know their subject. This applies equally to nurses in their role as health educators. A detailed knowledge of the causes of leg ulcer is essential (Dale and Gibson, 1986a, 1986b). A teacher must be able to present the information in a way which each individual recipient can understand. Nurses should draw on skills developed in normal practice and use them in teaching patients.

Primary prevention   During their training nurses are taught that immobility increases the risk of DVT and much emphasis is placed on how to prevent it. It is worth bearing in mind that it is not only when they are ill that people are immobilised. Travellers on long flights are at risk. Three cases of pulmonary embolism, which occurred when they left the plane, were diagnosed in 1983 at Hillingdon Hospital near Heathrow airport (Ledermann and Keshavarzian, 1983).

Once a DVT has occurred, the patient needs a different type of warning. In this situation the problem is to emphasise the long term effects of DVT without causing undue alarm. How does one convince a young fashion-conscious mother that she should wear an elastic stocking on all but social occasions for the rest of her life? Teaching aids and techniques must suit individuals. Imagine the contrast in the approaches required when treating a retired biology teacher and a middle aged office cleaner.

Secondary prevention   Someone who has had an ulcer knows what has to be prevented. Detailed knowledge of the disease process will enable the nurse to explain clearly the benefits of improving the venous return and how this can be done. We have made a video recording aimed at patient education and have developed advice leaflets for patients.

Handout: how to care for your legs

If you have had leg ulcers it is probably because of an injury to the veins in your leg which happened so long ago that you may have forgotten all about it. Veins carry the blood back to the heart, and in the legs it has to flow upwards most of the time. Your leg muscles help to pump it upwards every time they move, so exercising the legs is good for your veins.

There are valves in the veins which hold the blood where it is between muscle movements but if the valves have been damaged, the blood flows back down the veins when the muscles are not moving. If this goes on for years without treatment, the veins become stretched, the leg swells, the skin becomes discoloured and irritable and eventually an ulcer may appear. Once you understand how ulcers start, you can see how they could be prevented. The important things are to help the blood back to the heart and avoid anything which would slow it down.

Below is some simple advice, but for your own needs you should be guided by your doctor or community nurse. Unfortunately, other people can only do so much; **mostly it depends on you helping yourself**.

Wear a firm elastic support on the leg. An elastic stocking or bandage will be prescribed for you. Be sure to wear it always – good support helps your veins.

Elastic stockings. These must fit properly. Your leg will be measured when the stocking is first supplied. You should have two stockings so that you need never be without while one is washed. Follow the manufacturer's instructions carefully in this respect and go back to your doctor to ask him to prescribe new ones when the old ones become slack, usually after about six months. If you have difficulty in putting the stockings on, try sprinkling a little talcum powder on the leg.

Bandages. You will be shown how to apply your bandage. It must be smooth and firm, especially around the ankle and should cover the leg from the base of the toes to just below the knee. Remember not to leave out the heel. If the bandage works loose you should take it off and re-apply it. Bandages should be washed every time they are changed to keep them firm and should be replaced when they become slack. How long they last depends on the type. The nurse will be able to advise you about this.

Figure 1. Exercise is good for you.

Don't be afraid to exercise. If you are wearing elastic support, exercise is good for you, so walk two or three miles a day if you can. Otherwise, exercise by flexing your ankles up and down for five minutes every half hour while you are sitting in a chair. Avoid standing still. If you have to stand a lot, keep moving your toes inside your shoes, bend and straighten your knees from time to time and shift your weight from foot to foot. Use this exercise sheet to start a daily programme to help to maintain good circulation.

Rest   The important thing is to get your feet right up above your hips. Sitting with your feet hanging down is nearly as bad for your legs as standing still. At night, raise the foot of your bed by about nine inches. Use wooden blocks or bricks or large books to do this. When you are sitting in the evening, use a really high footstool and extra cushion to get your legs right up.

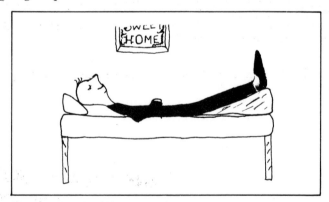

Figure 2. Keep legs elevated when resting.

Avoid obstruction to the veins   Do not wear garters or tight girdles. Don't fall asleep in an armchair and allow the edge to press into your legs.

Keep your weight down   This is good for your general health anyway, and it certainly helps your legs. Eat plenty of protein and fresh fruit and vegetables, and avoid fatty, sweet and starchy foods.

Protect your legs   Keep them warm and protect them from injury. People often say that a blow on the leg started their ulcers. If the skin is irritable don't scratch it; ulcers often start that way too. If the itching becomes too bad seek help from your doctor.

Ask for help early   Itching, any sign of a rash or eczema, or darkening of colour around the ankle may be warning signs that the ulcer is going to break down. Contact your doctor or nurse immediately.

Exercises for you to do   The following exercises should be done as often as possible, and at least three times a day.

Toes: Bend and stretch.
Ankles: bend and stretch, circle in both directions.
Walking: two or three miles a day if you can.
Avoid standing still, sitting still, scratching and household remedies.

References
Bauer, G. (1942) *Acta Chirurgica Scandinavica*, **26**, Supplement 74, 104.
Dale, J.J. and Gibson, B. (1986a) Leg ulcers: a disease affecting all ages. *The Professional Nurse*, **1**, 8, 213–216.
Dale, J.J. and Gibson, B. (1986b) Leg ulcers: the nursing assessment. *The Professional Nurse*, **1**, 236–238.
Dodd, H. and Cockett, F.B. (1976) *The Pathology and Surgery of Veins of the Lower Limb*, Churchill Livingstone, London.
Ledermann, J.A. and Keshavarzian, A. (1983) Acute pulmonary embolism following air travel. *Postgraduate Medical Journal*, **59**, 104–105.

Videorecording
Bandaging for leg ulcers, Dr C. McEwen, Forth Valley Health Board, 33 Spittal Street, Stirling.

20

Incontinence: who cares?

Marian Egan, RGN, Thelma M. Thomas, MB, MRCP,
T.W. Meade, DM, FRCP

Marian Egan was, until her retirement last year, Continence Adviser for Brent Health Authority. Thelma Thomas is in General Practice in Greenford, and Dr Meade is Director of the MRC Epidemiology and Medical Care Unit, Northwick Park Hospital, MIddlesex

A study was carried out by the Medical Research Council's Epidemiology and Medical Care Unit at Northwick Park Hospital over a four year period. (1976–1980).

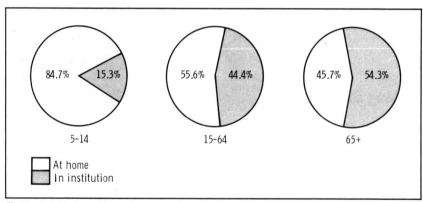

Figure 1. Location of incontinence sufferers by age category.

A survey of the prevalence of urinary incontinence was undertaken by studying the patients under the care of health and social services agencies in two London boroughs and by a postal questionnaire relating to the 22,430 people aged five years and over on the practice lists of 12 general practitioners based throughout the UK (Thomas, Plymat, Blannin and Meade, 1980). The results of these studies showed that:

- The prevalence of incontinence known to health and social service agencies was 0.2 per cent in women and 0.1 per cent in men aged 15-64 years and 2.5 per cent in women and 1.3 per cent in men aged 65 and over.
- The prevalence of urinary incontinence among those involved in the postal survey (to which 89 per cent of the people whose correct address was known replied) was 8.5 per cent in women and 1.6 per cent in men aged 15-64 and 11.6 per cent in women and 6.9 per cent in men aged 65 and over.
- Over 20 per cent of those who reported continence problems in the

postal survey were suffering moderate or severe incontinence, and less than 30 per cent of this group were receiving treatment or support for the condition from health or social services.

- Childless women had a lower prevalence of urinary incontinence, than those who had had one, two or three children; prevalence was appreciably increased among women who had had four or more children.

A common problem

These results indicate that urinary incontinence is a common problem, but one for which the majority of cases are unknown to and therefore unsupported by the health and social services networks. In the two London boroughs, 2,192 people known to be incontinent were referred to the study from agencies in the community (eg district nurses, pad delivery service, social services) and from long-stay institutions. Referrals from each source were for a period of one year.

Those living in the community (ie in their own homes) were then interviewed wherever possible, using a detailed questionnaire to determine problems faced by them and their carers and to establish what services were being provided for them. A total of 843 interviews were carried out by a team of research nurses. The figures summarise some of the findings of this study, and raise some important questions about the provision of services to incontinence sufferers and to friends and relatives involved in their care.

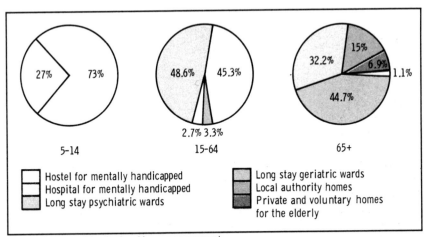

Figure 2. Type of institution (three age groups).

Location of incontinence sufferers   The majority of younger (under 65) incontinence sufferers live at home, as indeed do almost half of those aged 65 and over (Figure 1). Of those suffering incontinence in hospital or other institutions, the majority of young (under 65) people have mental handicaps, or are based in long-stay psychiatric wards. For the 65+

group, the majority of sufferers are based in long-stay geriatric wards (Figure 2).

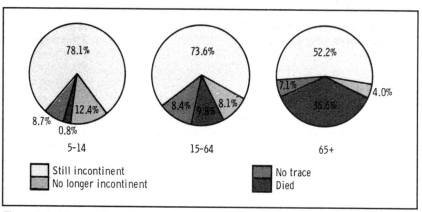

Figure 3. Incidence of incontinence after one year.

Nature of the problems   Figure 3 shows the incidence of incontinence amongst the 2,192 sufferers after one year. The majority in each group were still suffering incontinence. More than one third of those over 65 had died. Figures 4, 5 and 6 show some of the results from the 843 interview questionnaires, showing the most common diagnoses, the most difficult problems faced by sufferers and the duration of their incontinence.

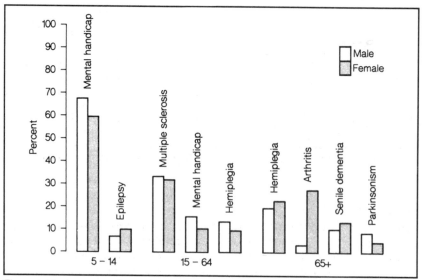

Figure 4. Most common diagnosis.

Among those people known by health and social services to be suffering from incontinence, there is a wide range of particular problems with mobility, personal and domestic hygiene and social activity. The duration of the condition tends to be longest among younger people – particularly where handicap has existed from birth, and for the majority of sufferers of all age groups, duration is over 12 months. For the majority of sufferers, frequency of the problem is once or more daily, both night and day. These statistics describe a problem of huge proportions, and are taken from that group of people whose incontinence is known to the health and social services. For the 70 per cent or so sufferers of moderate or severe incontinence, who are not in contact with these agencies, the nature of the problems is presumably similar. This represents years of human indignity and suffering from a wide range of problems resulting from incontinence. So what provision is there to help and treat these sufferers, and to support their carers, the majority of whom are relatives and friends?

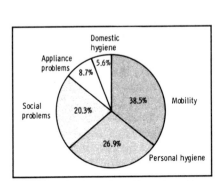

Figure 5. Most difficult problems faced by sufferers.

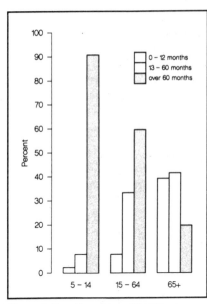

Figure 6. Duration of incontinence.

Treatment and care

The majority of cases (63.4 per cent) of incontinence known to health and social services are not referred to specialists for urological investigation, and a small minority (13.1 per cent) of sufferers are treated with the use of catheters or other appliances. A wide range of services are involved with incontinence sufferers in the community; it is not possible to tell from this survey whether these services are involved as a result of the incontinence or as a result of other health problems which may or may not be connected with the incontinence problems.

Most incontinence sufferers of all ages have one or two relatives or friends helping them, usually with some help every day and every night. These helpers provide support with domestic and personal hygiene, (especially with laundry) and with cooking, shopping, dressing, moving and lifting (Figure 7). Incontinence usually causes extra laundry, which for most sufferers in the survey is done by a resident friend or relative.

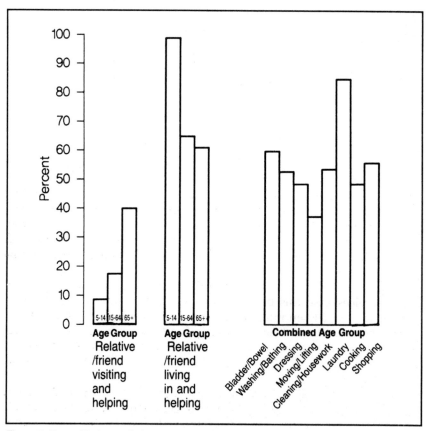

Figure 7. Type of help needed.

Over half of the known incontinence sufferers in each age group use incontinence pads, which most have delivered by either the district nurse or the local community pad service (Figure 8). Since this survey was conducted, incontinence pads have become more readily available directly to the general public, who can now purchase them in chemists.

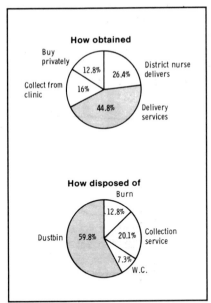

Figure 8. How pads are obtained and disposed of.

Implications for nursing services   The above statistics highlight some of the dimensions of a common, chronic problem, which, in the main remains undetected and untreated or self-treated. Even for the sufferers known to the health and social services, the major burden of care is taken on by friends and relatives, with relatively little support in some domestic tasks such as extra laundry.

Could more complete and appropriate provision by the health and social services ease this burden and reduce the extra domestic tasks, such as laundry? Even more important is the fact that incontinence is a degrading and demoralising condition for the sufferer. These statistics represent years of human indignity for incontinence sufferers, which are also shown by the numbers of sufferers who do not seek medical or other help.

Since the results of the above study were published, increased support and advice have become available to incontinence sufferers and their carers following the widespread appointment of full-time Continence Advisers by local health authorities.

Reference
Thomas, T.M., Plymat, K.R., Blannin, J. and Meade, T.W. (1980) Prevalance of urinary incontinence. *British Medical Journal*, **281**, 1243–1245.

21

Continence in later life

Lesley M. Irvine, RGN, H Ed Cert
Clinical Nurse Specialist/Continence Advisor, Singleton Hospital, Swansea

The ageing process, modified by external circumstances, can contribute to incontinence and psychological, social, environmental and physical factors must all be investigated. "Age changes in the central nervous system predispose to incontinence by diminishing the effectiveness of conscious control over the process of micturition" (Brocklehurst, 1984).

Consideration needs to be given to where the patient is living, be it their own home, with or without carers, sheltered accommodation, Part III residential home, nursing home, Elderly Mentally Infirm (EMI) Unit, long stay hospital – either psychogeriatric or physically handicapped, acute short term hospital or terminal care. This chapter seeks to put into context the problems of incontinence in later life but within these different locations. It offers practical advice not only for the patient's own physical causes of incontinence but for modifying the environment in which the patient is living.

To be fully continent requires the cortical ability to recognise the need to micturate or defaecate, reach a lavatory, to overcome the urge to void until it is appropriate so to do, adjust appropriate clothing satisfactorily and to adopt the appropriate position.

Those who are unable to achieve all or any of the above, require a full and meticulous assessment, diagnosis of the type of incontinence and treatment of the causes. This should involve assessment by the nurse and clinical examination by the nurse and the appropriate medical specialty. Assessment should include:

- incontinence history
- type of incontinence
- type and amount of fluid intake
- bowel habit and management/dysfunction
- aids/pads used
- medical history
- medication
- parity and difficult deliveries
- mobility/manual dexterity
- hearing and sight
- attitude to incontinence and mental alertness
- lifestyle
- independence or support services used or needed

- physical examination
- urinalysis, and examination of specimen of urine for culture and sensitivity
- baseline chart of voiding and incontinence episodes.

From this, treatment/management should be planned, implemented and followed up. There should be appropriate liaison with physiotherapists, occupational therapists and other paramedical services. *The primary aim is to cure.* If cure is not achievable the aim is optimum management with regard particularly to the patient's dignity and lifestyle.

The independent person

Screening by practice nurses and health visitors from the primary care team must alert carers to incontinence problems. The fit fully independent person, in later life, living at home, who is incontinent, must have first a full assessment to diagnose the type of incontinence and eliminate any treatable causes. It should be determined whether a curative diagnosis is possible or whether it is a management problem. Ignoring the problem can lead to isolation, depression and loss of motivation and mobility with associated problems.

Incontinence must not be regarded as inevitable in later life. Thomas *et al* (BMJ, 1980) revealed that 11.6% of women over the age of 65 and 6.9% of men over the age of 65 were incontinent. A recent Mori poll (March, 1991) indicates that the figure for incontinent people over the age of 30 could be as high as 10.5 million in the UK.

Those in later life can experience all types of incontinence but the most common are urge incontinence, genuine stress incontinence (GSI) (or both), overflow incontinence and lomomotor incontinence. The latter refers to such factors as poor mobility, inadequate toilet facilities, difficulties in adjusting clothing and environmental problems associated with difficulty in reaching the toilet and using it.

Urge incontinence can be treated with bladder drill in the mentally aware; with or without anticholinergic drugs. Pelvic floor exercises can improve significantly both GSI and detrusor instability. Removal, where possible, of outflow obstruction ie faecal impaction or prostatic hypertrophy should be undertaken, after appropriate assessment.

Many factors may predispose to incontinence as age change takes place, but the attitude prevalent in both those in later life and their carers, both professional and informal, is that incontinence is the expected norm. How sad this is, how defeatist, and how wrong. It leads to a negative attitude regarding continence promotion. "The great secret of help is encouragement" Octavia Hill (1948).

A positive, practical and informed approach will help patients to regain their confidence, self esteem and motivation. Patients should be involved wherever possible in the decisions regarding their treatment or management.

Those needing marginal support

Those who need marginal support in their daily living and who are incontinent will need further investigation into their needs. They may be living in sheltered or warden controlled accommodation, or with a carer at home. Besides assessment of physical causes of incontinence and treatment where applicable, assessment is needed of whether the toilet facilities need adjusting eg requiring the use of aids such as raised toilet seats, grab rails, footstool, better lighting, warmth and privacy. Make sure that if spectacles are needed they are worn and that the prescription is up to date for the patient's needs, and that a hearing aid is functioning and in use. These measures will help the patient to cope with recognising where the toilet is and to be able to see to undo and fasten clothing and hear any advice or instructions given.

Foot care by the chiropodist is important in keeping the feet pain free and therefore optimising mobility. Encouraging mobility with appropriate assistance, an adequate fluid intake and a high fibre diet will help to prevent constipation which is a contributory factor common to both urinary and faecal incontinence particularly in later age.

Monitoring the changing needs of the patient by health care professionals and responding to these changes will help to prevent unnecessary deterioration in independence. For example the provision of a commode, one suitable for the individual patient's needs, may enable continence to be re-established if temporarily impaired, due to problems of access to the toilet during the night.

In addition the adjustment of any necessary diuretic medication and the avoidance of all, non essential, especially smooth muscle affecting drugs, reducing the dose to the minimum therapeutic dose required in all cases will help to prevent or lessen their indirect contribution to incontinence.

The moderately dependent person

Where the patient becomes moderately dependent, because of decreased or impaired mobility or diminished manual dexterity the carers may play a significant but low key role in helping the patient with their daily living particularly with toiletting and dressing. Many of these patients will live in Part III or private residential homes, or if they are fortunate, be looked after by a carer or relative in their own home.

The attitude of the carers becomes more and more important as patient dependence becomes greater. In residential establishments it is easy for the patient to have his/her identity all too easily submerged in the institutionalisation of the surroundings. In consequence, loss of part or all motivation, self respect and interest may occur leading to institutional apathy with staff indifference. The patients need to be treated as individuals, to wear their own clothing, particularly with their own identifiable underwear and be involved wherever possible in the decisions regarding lifestyle generally, and the management of their incontinence specifically.

The patient's capabilities should be maximised. Where incontinence cannot be prevented or cured management should address that which is acceptable to the patient, is discreet, readily available and efficient. Incontinence odours are embarrassing for the patient and often repulsive for the carers. With good hygiene techniques they can be avoided or eliminated and certainly kept to a minimum. The use of modern carpet and furnishing fabrics designed to repel fluids and odour neutralising agents can help to reduce odours. The local authority may help with the provision and installation of toiletting aids.

Toilets for patients should be of the same high standard as we expect for ourselves – in fact there should be no distinction between staff and patient toilets with the exception of aids and adjustments for the disabled. The toilet itself must be in satisfactory mechanical condition. Problems arise where toilets are not easily identifiable or accessible either because of obstacles blocking the route, or because they are not adequately planned to allow those with walking aids or wheelchairs to enter, where there is no privacy, where they are cold, ill-lit or dirty. Such basics as a provision of toilet paper and washing facilities in the toilet are a necessity. No wonder constipation sometimes occurs so soon after a patient's admission to an institution. Add in the dietary changes, reduced mobility and reduced fluid intake and the vicious circle of constipation commences. Once started it often proves most refractory to correct – even if initially recognised, which too frequently it is not.

The fully dependent person

For those who are fully dependent on their carers more intensive attention needs to be given to their elimination needs and the psychological effects of their loss of independence. Wherever possible patients should be assisted to void privately and in as normal an environment as possible. The use of bedpans and the keeping of male urinals (bottles) permanently in situ in the bed or chair must be avoided. Individualised toiletting based on information from assessment and baseline charting may prevent many episodes of incontinence as will the nurse's or carer's prompt response to the patient's indication of the need to toilet. Where protection is required in between toiletting for management of untreatable incontinence the criteria for choosing the product should include the type of incontinence, the amount of urine loss, the size and weight of the patient, whether female or male the ease of fitting and the acceptability by the patient, the availability and disposal facilities. Excellent products to suit most needs are widely available. Most district health authorities make some provision for the issue of non-prescription items, eg, pads, pants and bed protection.

Where body worn pads and pants are not the system of choice, bed protection should be considered. There are a variety of one way 'stay dry' washable absorbent draw sheets and bed pads. In choosing suitable products the availability of laundry services must be taken into account, both 'in house' and local facilities.

When considering products and appliances an in-dwelling catheter should not be chosen as the first line of treatment for incontinence particularly as it may cause more problems than it solves. It implies that continence is not attainable. It should be used in cases of chronic retention if intermittent catheterisation is not appropriate. It can be especially useful in the terminally ill where incontinence and constant pad changes are exhausting and degrading for the patient and to prevent further breakdown of excoriated skin and pressure sores. In the latter case review of the need for the catheter and its earliest possible removal and the restoration to an appropriate toileting programme is desirable. Confused patients often interfere with or pull out the catheter causing urethral trauma and related further urinary problems. As always remember to use the smallest possible catheter size for adequate drainage with the smallest balloon.

Faecal incontinence or faecal staining is sometimes a problem in the ageing population. It must be assumed always until proved otherwise that an elderly person's occasional incontinence of faeces or faecal staining is faecal impaction with overflow 'spurious' diarrhoea. If the impaction is high in the colon a rectal examination may not reveal it and a plain X-ray may be necessary to determine the presence and extent of the problem. The approach to this may be daily enemas administered by the District Nursing Sister until the bowel is clear and then a maintenance dose of aperient titrated to suit the desired frequency of bowel action for that patient. The object is to keep the bowel empty, not to have recourse to continually strive to treat constipation.

The nurse must remember that a physically handicapped elderly person is not necessarily demented or senile, and needs to be treated as an adult, a human being with an active past, probably a caring family, who requires dignity and respect in the management of their incontinence.

"With every person he met he instinctively struck some point of contact, found something to appreciate, often it might be some information to ask for, which left the other cheered, self respected, raised for the moment above himself" (From Life of Charles Kingsley). Many elderly people have a wealth of experiences and if encouraged to share these benefit both themselves and their companions and carers.

An article in The Times newspaper in April 1986 draws attention to the fact that "people believe that incontinence is a physical problem, but a major factor is mental; lack of stimulation leads to incontinence and we aim to provide stimulus through this project". This project, supported by the charity Age Research, referred to a film made of a retired man's collection of memorabilia used to trigger the memories of old people and which requires active audience participation.

It should not be assumed that those who are mentally ill such as the

Alzheimer's sufferers, in fact any whose cortex is not intact, are a completely lost cause for continence promotion or incontinence management.

Recognising signs displayed by these patients indicating the need to void, providing a calm environment, a consistent approach, speaking the patient's name at the *start* of all communications, repeating reality 'clues' clearly and distinctly in all involvement and prompting patients to go to the toilet and adjust their clothing, help to achieve the correct response to the need to void. Painting of all toilet doors in the same bright colour plus large clear labelling, and encouraging the patient wherever possible to use the toilet rather than a commode at the bedside will help to reduce voiding in inappropriate places.

Review of drug therapy and possible interactions and side effects and the prescribing of only those essential and in the smallest possible doses will help to minimise their effect on incontinence, eg, sedatives, anti-depressants, analgesics and diuretics.

Acute illness: occurring in any of these environments

Those acutely ill may find that the onset or exacerbation of incontinence may occur with urinary tract infections, chest infections and in fact any febrile condition. These and constipation, polypharmacy and depression can cause acute confusion and if the cause is treated there is a good chance that continence will be restored and the confusion will disappear. Of course, degenerative cerebrovascular episodes are a frequent and common cause of acute incontinence in this age group, but a return to continence can progress commensurately with the general rehabilitation.

Good hygiene will help keep unpleasant odours to a minimum. The provision of community laundry facilities, appropriate lavatory adaptations and toileting aids will help to ensure that the independent can continue to live at home and be self caring. Regular review of their environmental, physical and psychological state will help to meet their changing needs and prevent the isolation and misery that incontinence can bring.

If discharge from hospital is a feasible outcome, it should be planned as soon as possible after admission and guidelines for the provision of nursing and social services after the patient's discharge from hospital should be drawn up (Williams and Fitton, 1991). The burden on carers of caring for an ageing dependent person can stretch their resources and goodwill to crisis level and the provision of short term respite care for the patient in hospitals, nursing homes or residential homes can do much to alleviate this and enable care to continue in the community – which conforms also to current government health care policies. Details of where to find information on financial benefits may be found under *Useful Addresses* at the end of this chapter.

In conclusion, it behoves *all* carers to keep in the forefront of their nursing practice Isaac's great maxim – "Incontinence can be sometimes cured, often relieved, always made more tolerable" (Isaac, 1986).

References

Brocklehurst, J. (1984) Urinary Incontinence in the elderly. *The Practitioner* **228**, 275–83.

Hill, O. (1948) *Being and Doing*, 44th Issue Young and Baxter, p117.

Isaacs, B. (1986) – *Incontinence 3rd Edn*, Smith and Nephew Medical, Hull.

Kingsley Charles (1948) *Being and Doing* 44th Issue Young and Baxter, p125.

Thomas, T.M. *et al* (1980) Prevalence of urinary incontinence. *British Medical Journal* **281**, 1243–5.

Williams *et al* (1991) Use of nursing and social services by elderly persons discharged from hospital. *British Journal of General Practice* **41**, 72–5.

Further reading, information

Association for Continence Advice (ACA) *Directory of Continence and Toiletting Aids*. A comprehensive directory of products to manage incontinence and assist with toiletting.

Burkitt *et al* (1989) *Constipation*. Geriatric Medicine Supplement.

Mares, P. (1990) *In Control* help with incontinence (self help and carers guide), Age Concern.

Norton, C. (1987) Continence and the Older Person series of articles, *Geriatric Nursing and Home Care*.

Norton, C. (1986) *Nursing for Continence*. Beaconsfield Publishing, Beaconsfield.

Useful addresses

Age Concern England, Astral House, 128b London Road, London SW16 4EJ.

Association for Continence Advice (ACA), 380–384 Harrow Road, London W9 2HU.

Carers' National Association, 29 Chilworth Mews, London W2 3RG.

Carers Unit, Kings Fund Centre, 12b Albert Street, London NW1 7NF.

DSS, Financial Benefits, eg Attendance Allowance, Invalid Care Allowance and the Social Fund – details available from local Social Security offices.

Disabled Living Foundation, 380–384, Harrow Road, London W9 2HU.

22

Care of the urinary incontinent patient

Janet Gooch, SRN, DN (London), RCNT
Ward Sister, Brighton General Hospital

In 1983 Josephs wrote that incontinence is a symptom, or a sign, rather than a diagnosis, that it is never normal and is frequently remediable. With those facts in mind it is possible to look afresh at this age old problem and try to deal with its cause rather than merely accepting its effects.

Technical aspects of voiding
The bladder should fill to a good capacity (about 500mls) and empty at a rate of 20mls per second or higher. Emptying should be under voluntary control and occur in such a way that ureteric reflux does not occur.

The bladder fills to a good capacity because the detrusor muscle does not contract until voluntary voiding begins. As a result the pressure in the bladder remains low at less than 15cm water. This is partly due to the inherent physical property of the bladder wall which allows it to be stretched without causing a rise in intra-vesical pressure, and partly because there is a neurological mechanism which prevents nervous impulses being transmitted to the bladder until a good capacity is achieved.

The patient is continent if the bladder neck stays closed and the urethral pressure is greater than the pressure in the bladder. These two criteria are achieved by two sphincter actions:

The proximal sphincter mechanism   This ensures that the bladder outlet only opens when the detrusor contracts, regardless of any rise in intra-abdominal pressure (eg caused by coughing or physical activity).

The distal sphincter mechanism   The high urethral pressure below the bladder neck is due to urethral smooth muscle, the striated muscle sphincter within the urethral walls, and the peri-urethral striated muscle, collectively called the distal sphincter mechanism.

When afferent impulses alert the brain to the fact that the bladder is full, and the circumstances for voiding are appropriate, voluntary voiding is initiated by impulses from the forebrain to the co-ordinating centre in the pons. Impulses from the pons cause relaxation of the distal sphincter mechanisms and contraction of the bladder. Bladder contraction opens the bladder neck and raises intra vesical pressure to about 50cms water. This causes the expulsion of urine (Mundy, 1983).

Reasons for incontinence

- Urinary control usually develops between the ages of 2-4½ years. The term urinary incontinence refers to the involuntary passing of urine after that time.
- Very rarely incontinence is caused by urine passing from an abnormal route that is not controlled by a sphincter, eg congenital ectopic bladder or acquired vesico colic fistula.
- Neuropathic incontinence is uncommon resulting always from some neurological lesion such as spinal cord injury, spina bifida, multiple sclerosis and diabetic autonomic neuropathy.
- In the most commonly seen type of incontinence the problem is not associated with any neurological disease but to some failure within the urinary system itself. Table 1.

Table 1. Failures of the urinary system:

Stress incontinence.
Urge — motor (secondary to obstruction or
           idiopathic).
       — sensory (stone, infection, tumour,
           idiopathic).
Overflow — usually secondary to obstruction
               in men and to overdistension in
               women.
Post micturition dribbling.
Reduced awareness.
Iatrogenic — from poor surgical technique.
           — from drugs such as tran-
               quillisers, hypnotics, diuretics,
               adrenergics.

- Stress incontinence refers to the involuntary loss of urine when intravesical pressure exceeds urethral closure pressure in the absence of detrusor activity. Thus the competence of the bladder neck and distal sphincter are reduced.
- Urge incontinence is the involuntary voiding of urine associated with a strong desire to micturate.
- Overflow incontinence occurs if the bladder pressure exceeds urethral pressure when the bladder is fully distended but is unable to contract.
- The loaded rectum of constipation can impinge on the bladder and reduce its capacity.
- For a patient with urgency the inability to get to, or use, a distant or unfamiliar toilet because of immobility or confusion can lead to incontinence.

Assessment

It is essential that incontinence is not passively accepted but that the cause is actively sought until a precise diagnosis has been made. A nursing assessment of the patient's physical and emotional state is a vital first step towards this. Table 2.

How long the problem has existed.
What time of day or night it is most troublesome.
Whether any action exacerbates the problem.
A description of the stream.
Details of any frequency, urgency or nocturia.
How the incontinence has affected normal lifestyle, work, marriage and sexual activity.
Any medication taken.
The emotional reactions to the problem and the coping mechanisms used to deal with these.
Any aids used and the success or otherwise of these.

Table 2. Information required to obtain the history of incontinence.

It must first be confirmed that the patient really is incontinent and has not merely had an accident due to some unusual circumstance. Physical assessment will determine whether there is any symptom requiring immediate treatment such as diabetes mellitus, distended bladder or severe constipation; whether there are any other signs that may indicate a cause for the incontinence such as uterine prolapse, neurological changes, confusion or difficulty with mobility.

The occupational therapist may be asked to assess the patient's ability to perform daily living activities in a more natural setting than the general ward.

Variability in the volume of urine voided can be a useful indicator of the possible cause of the incontinence. This parameter needs to be carefully assessed over a 48 hour period charting of the fluid intake, details of times, circumstances, and estimated or measured amounts of urine passed. This correlation of frequency to fluid intake will assess functional bladder capacity and show the exact form and degree of the incontinence.

Incontinence is an embarrassing problem for the patient and careful, tactful, questioning will be necessary to obtain the full history of the problem and the physical and emotional disturbance it causes. Once a diagnosis of the type of bladder dysfunction is made appropriate treatment can be instituted, whether this is medical, nursing or both.

Aspects of care

- By identifying and dealing with any exacerbating factors such as faecal impaction, drugs causing polyuria, and any urinary infection, it may be possible to prevent an impairment of bladder function giving rise to incontinence.

- Making the toilet more accessible, providing a bedside commode, making undressing easier, and improving the patient's ability to get about, are all examples of measures that can sometimes minimise incontinence.

- Minor degrees of stress incontinence may be helped by pelvic floor exercises.

- Urge incontinence that persists after treatment of the cause may be helped by bladder training — the interval between voiding being slowly increased over a defined period until a pattern is established that is tailored to suit the individual patient.

- Habit training may be useful where monitoring has shown that the patient is more likely to urinate at certain times of day or night.

- Privacy, and whenever possible independence, are essential to the preservation of dignity for the incontinent patient. Acceptance, understanding and empathy will help the nurse to avoid offering the indignity of unscreened commodes, loud discussions of the problem that can be overheard by others, and clothing that allows exposure.

- Only when the incontinence of urine has been *proven* to be unavoidable should it be accepted as such. The aims of treatment then become to improve the quality of life, to preserve dignity, to find an acceptable method of management, and to avoid the development of secondary problems.

- The patient and his or her relatives need help to understand the cause of the problem and the ways in which they may best be able to deal with it. Essentially they need to be involved in the planning of care and be enabled to participate in it if they are to learn to cope effectively for themselves. They also need to have information about where and when to seek advice — a list of names and telephone numbers of such people as the incontinence advisor can be provided.

- When an appliance is to be used it must be selected because it is the one most suited to the particular patient and his or her needs: the patient should be able to manage it unaided with careful instruction, supervision, and follow up; it should be acceptable to the patient; it should keep him or her clean, dry, odour free and comfortable. Appliances available work in one of three ways; by collecting urine externally in containers; by absorbing urine into pads or by collecting urine via a catheter or urinary diversion.

- Secondary problems of infection, odour, soreness, skin maceration and tissue damage will only occur if urine remains in contact with the skin. Perineal hygiene should be planned to remove all traces of urine whilst avoiding excessive use of soap, contamination of toilet articles, and the use of creams and powders.

Applicances available

Condom drains Soft latex rubber that can adapt to the altering size of the penis. Best results are achieved with a special skin adhesive attaching the condom at the base of the penis after the area has been shaved. This is the best appliance for persistent incontinence in males. It can only be used on the adequately sized non-retractable penis. If it fits poorly, allowing leakage around the scrotum, it may cause soreness of penile skin. The appliance is readily pulled off by confused patients.

External device for women These fit over the whole genital area and collect urine in a disposable plastic collecting bag. They restrict movement.

Urinals These are available for men and women but are only useful for patients with urge and frequency who can manage them without spillage. They cannot be left in situ for bedfast patients because of the risk of spillage and tissue damage.

Absorbent pads worn under pants Various types are available so that a choice can be made. Pads chosen must be ones that will absorb the amount of urine passed at one time. The greater the absorption the bulkier the pad. They must be changed before saturation point is reached. They are most effective for dribbling incontinence — it is important that the patient does if possible still try to micturate at intervals.

Marsupial pants These are made of fabric which allows only outward flow of urine. Urine flows through the material to be absorbed by the pad held in a plastic pouch stitched on the outside of the crutch of the pants. These were designed for day use.

Plastic pants These are inappropriate because they become wet in use, and PVC is affected by urine with resulting skin problems.

Inco pads These are suitable only for occasional incontinence when small amounts of urine are passed. They tend to move about the bed, to crease and to tear. They may add to the risk of pressure damage.

Indwelling catheters These should only be chosen when all other methods have been tried and found to be ineffective. There are many contraindications to their long term use.

Intermittent self catheterisation This is increasingly taking the place of use of the various appliances. It can only be suitable for certain patients and must be taught by a suitable instructor.

References
Josephs, C. (1983) Urinary incontinence, *Geriatric Medicine 13*, 9, 650–51.
Mundy, A.r. (1983) Urinary incontinence. *Surgery* **1**, 1, 1–6.

Bibliography
Irvine, R. (1983) Continence in the elderly, *Nursing Times* **79**, 17, 45–8.
Described the importance of attitude towards incontinence.
Mandelstam, D. (1980) Incontinence and its management. *Nursing* (1st Series, 18).
Discusses the problem of incontinence from many different perspectives.
Sines, D. (1983) Incontinence. Helping people with mental handicap. *Nursing Times* **79**, 33, 52–5.
Studies self help skills with handicapped people.

23

Management of male incontinence using a sheath

Virginia Playford, SEN
Nurse at the John Radcliffe Hospital, Oxford

The condom

The condom or sheath has been used for many years as a contraceptive device. Early condoms, which date back to the sixteenth century, were generally made from animal gut hemmed at one end. Fish membrane was also used, but was found to be inefficient. Vulcanised rubber sheaths were first made in the 1840s then, in the 1930s modern latex rubber began to be used.

A condom which is light and unobtrusive in wear may easily be adapted for use as a male urinary incontinence device by modifying the closed

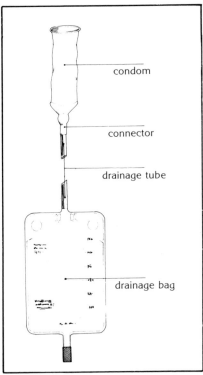

Figure 1. The condom and drainage bag.

end of the sheath to allow the connection of a tube and drainage bag (Figure 1). Most condoms used for incontinence are specifically designed for the purpose, though some attachments to convert normal contraceptive sheaths are still available. If correctly applied there is no need for the patient to wear absorbent pants or pads.

Problem of urinary incontinence   In males this can be eased when the correct appliance is fitted and well managed so that life is disturbed as little as possible. Sheaths or condoms are made from latex rubber and consist of a soft flexible sleeve which fits over the shaft of the penis and has a more rigid distal end for connection to a drainage bag via a plastic tube. They are suitable for patients with moderate to severe incontinence. Some may only need to wear the appliance during the day if it is difficult or impossible to get to a toilet or use a urinal.

Fixation of the sheath   This must be discussed with the patient to decide on a system which he can manage, taking his manual dexterity and mobility into account. Possible allergic reactions, the danger of over tightening fixation strips and the prevention of sores caused by incorrect application must be discussed and the patient must be encouraged to check his condom regularly.

Managing incontinence means treating the patient first, finding out the reason for his incontinence and, by attentive listening, encouraging him to express his fears and worries, to give him confidence and to make him feel that he is not alone. Careful explanation of the different appliances available to allow him to remain dry and enable him to return to as near his normal lifestyle as possible should be given (Table 1).

● Degree of incontinence.
● Patient's day — night requirements (different systems may be required).
● Attitude of patient.
● Sexual activities.
● Washing and disposal facilities.
● Availability of the incontinence aids.
● Patient's financial status.
● Availability of help with changing.
● Penis size.

Table 1. Factors to consider in choosing a sheath.

Sheath securing systems
The posey   A foam strip applied externally to the sheath, held in place with elastic and a Velcro fastening. The strip may be washed and reused.

Latex strip   A latex strip with an adjustable button fastening is used for external fixation.

The cuff An inflatable cuff incorporated in the shaft of the sheath, with a side arm to enable its inflation with a syringe.

Stomahesive strip A strip of stomahesive material which has an adhesive on both sides and sticks to the shaft of the penis, allowing the sheath to be rolled on and secured at its base.

Foam strip A double sided adhesive strip similar to the stomahesive strip, but made from a foam material.

Medical sprays Medical grade glue sprays or wipes may be used to apply a sticky substance directly to the penis allowing the sheath to be rolled on and secured.

Coated sheath A sheath with an internal coating of adhesive offering a very simple and secure fitting method.

To apply the sheath
When the sheath and different fixation methods have been explained, and a system has been selected, supervision may still be required until the patient gains confidence and is able to manage by himself. However, supervision must allow the patient sufficient privacy to enable him to feel at ease. He should be asked to wash his genital area and any long pubic hair around the base of the penis should be trimmed. Creams and powders should be avoided as they can spoil adhesion.

The rolled sheath should be placed on the end of the penis leaving a space of about 3cm between the end of the penis and the cone of the sheath. It should then be slowly unrolled along the shaft of the penis, avoiding creasing which might cause sores. The space between the end of the sheath and the penis acts as a small reservoir to accommodate any sudden gush of urine and reduces the risk of pressure problems resulting from the outlet of urine. The space, however, must not be too large as the sheath may become twisted and blocked. A well fitted sheath should be both comfortable and secure. Once fitted, the drainage bag may be connected and is normally secured to the patient's leg.

Possible complications
- Allergy to latex or medical adhesives.
- Constriction of the penis resulting in oedema, ischaemia and necrosis.
- Detachment of the sheath or drainage tube.
- Pressure sores caused by the sheath.
- Twisting of the outlet tube causing an obstruction to urinary discharge.
- Pooling of urine causing ammoniacal dermatitis.

● Blow outs. These may occur when there is a sudden voiding of a large amount of urine which cannot escape via a narrow or kinked outlet tube. This causes the sheath to become distended like a balloon and then pushed off the penis by the pressure.

Management

The patient should be encouraged to check the drainage tube and bag every two hours and empty it when necessary. Once the system and its management has proved satisfactory, and the patient feels confident, the sheath may be left in place for up to 48 hours before changing.

The sheath is removed by rolling it off the penis and any adhesive used will usually roll off with it. Some glues may require their own solvents but soap and water will normally remove any remaining glue satisfactorily. The patient should then check the foreskin and penis carefully for any signs of sores, sensitivity or constriction before applying a new sheath.

Many types of sheath, fixation and drainage bag are available. The factors mentioned earlier (Table 1) should be considered by the nurse and the patient together. The best choice for the patient is the system with which he feels most comfortable and which is easiest for him to manage. He can be greatly assisted in making his choice by good advice from a nurse with some expert knowledge of the problem.

Bibliography
Mandelstam, D. (1980) Incontinence and its Management. Croom Helm, Beckenham.
    A very informative book which is well worth reading.

24

Care of the catheter at home: a patient education handout

Janet Gooch, SRN, DipN(Lond), RCNT
Ward Sister, Brighton General Hospital

There is a wide choice of appliance available from which each patient can select the one most suited to his needs and life style. Several methods may be tried in the hospital ward before the final selection is made. If this choice later proves to be less successful than imagined then it is possible to ask for a known alternative.

Explanation

To know how to manage the catheter and drainage system correctly, and to minimize the risk of infection, it is necessary to understand how the system works and how problems could arise.

1. Urine is made by the kidneys and is normally stored in the bladder until you are ready to go to the toilet to pass the water. The catheter is a tube that is put into the bladder and kept there by a small balloon on its end. In this way the urine passes directly into the drainage bag attached to the catheter instead of remaining in the bladder. Ask your nurse if you are unsure of the reason for your catheter.

2. As long as the catheter and tubing are free of kinks or loops, and the bag is kept below the end of the catheter, there will be a free passage of urine. Interruption of this free flow can cause a "damming up" of urine which could increase the risk of infection.

3. Pulling on the catheter makes the balloon rub on the inside of the bladder and causes soreness.

4. Infection in the drainage system could come from dirty hands and from the area around the catheter where bacteria multiply if they are not removed by washing. It is therefore essential to wash the hands with soap and water before and after handling any part of the catheter, tubing, or bag. The area around the catheter needs washing at least once a day and after each bowel action — this washing should be from front to back so that bacteria from the back passage are not brought forward around the catheter.

5. A flow of urine washing down the inside of the tubing helps to keep the tube clean. To maintain a steady flow it is necessary to drink plenty of fluids to make the urine. It is better to drink small amounts regularly throughout the day rather than large amounts just once or twice.

6. Constipation can cause pressure on the catheter and block the flow of urine.

Other points

- People at home generally have divan type beds that are unsuitable for the bedside hanger used in hospital. A floor-standing hanger supplied

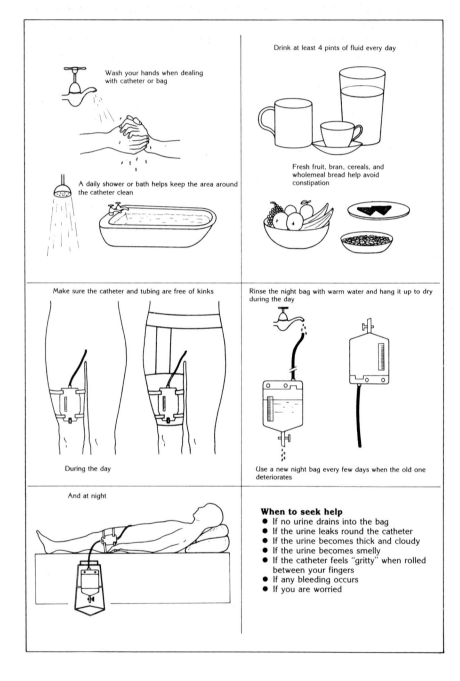

Wash your hands when dealing with catheter or bag

A daily shower or bath helps keep the area around the catheter clean

Drink at least 4 pints of fluid every day

Fresh fruit, bran, cereals, and wholemeal bread help avoid constipation

Make sure the catheter and tubing are free of kinks

During the day

Rinse the night bag with warm water and hang it up to dry during the day

Use a new night bag every few days when the old one deteriorates

And at night

When to seek help

- If no urine drains into the bag
- If the urine leaks round the catheter
- If the urine becomes thick and cloudy
- If the urine becomes smelly
- If the catheter feels "gritty" when rolled between your fingers
- If any bleeding occurs
- If you are worried

for use at night avoids lying the drainage bag on the floor.

- Painful spasms of the bladder sometimes occur when the catheter is first inserted. These are explained by the reaction of the body to the strange tube and stop once this is overcome. If they should recur it may be because the tube is blocked and help is needed to deal with this. In this case, your community nurse should be contacted.
- Very occasionally some bleeding occurs through or around a catheter. Unless you have been told to expect this, such bleeding should always be reported to your doctor.
- Remember that catheter bags (for both day and night use) are available on prescription.

25

A new kind of loving? The effect of continence problems on sexuality

Veronica Wheeler, RGN, RCNT
Clinical General Manager, Physical Rehabilitation Service, Aylesbury Vale Health Authority

Sexuality is not just concerned with sexual activity. Although this is a natural and important form of sexual expression, sexuality is also connected with the projection of sexual image and formation and maintenance of warm, loving relationships.

Recently, more recognition has been given to individual sexuality, indeed, the World Health Organisation (1983) proposed that "sexual health is the integration of the somatic, emotional, intellectual and social aspects of a sexual being, in ways that are positively enriching and that enhance personality, communication and love". While sexuality and sexual needs were identified, the report concluded that little relevant teaching on sexuality was offered in schools of medicine or nursing.

In 1974, Jacobson said nursing was behind in dealing with sexuality in patient and client care, and this is often still the case. She found few nurses or doctors gave patients information on how illness, drugs or procedures may affect their sexuality. Lack of education in this area, or the fact that young nurses and doctors may not yet have come to terms with their own sexuality were suggested as reasons for this. It is important, therefore, that nurses understand the development of their own self-image, as well as those of their patients.

According to Henderson (1969), an individual's health status cannot be fully understood without an awareness of their sexual identity. Without this, individuals' total needs cannot be met, so good healthcare should encourage healthy sexual expression. This is important for people who have to change or relearn their sexual behaviour following illness.

For many, continence problems will mean some modification of their original behaviour. While the principal nursing aim is continence promotion, there are times when this is not possible, and instead, nurses have to rely on bladder training to obtain controlled continence, teach intermittent self-catheterisation or rely on pants and pads for protection.

Since many people experiencing continence problems are over 40, some professionals may not discuss sexual implications of their condition because they think it is not relevant or may not be welcome. In fact many people - women as well as men - continue to engage in sexual activity well into their old age, so the subject should at least be raised with all clients, to give them a chance to ask for advice.

Many couples enjoy a warm, loving and active sexual relationship until late in life. For many, the period between 50 years and retirement is a time in which they face many changes in lifestyle and different demands, many of which are associated with relationships and sexuality (Duval, 1971). Even those with terminal illness, facing a permanent end to a relationship, may need sexual activity to show support and love. Illness, disability and incontinence can interfere with this.

The effects of continence problems

Interviewing women attending an incontinence clinic, Suthurst and Brown (1980) found 73 out of 208 said intercourse took place less frequently since they had developed continence problems, while 17 said it had stopped altogether. Reasons given for reduced frequency were dyspareunia (difficult or painful intercourse in women), wetness at night, embarrassment, depression, leakage during coitus, marital discord and the need for separate beds. Dyspareunia was the most commonly cited reason, because the women were constantly wet and sore.

Knowledge   Nurses need to develop an understanding of the development of sexuality; human sexual response; the relationship between age, illness, disability, treatments and sexual activity; and awareness of the variety of sexual behaviour.
Own values   Nurses need to be able to accept their own sexuality and be comfortable with their own behaviour to enable their clients to feel the same way. This will help nurses assess and identify clients' problems with sexuality.
Communication skills   Many people are reluctant to discuss sexuality, and it is important to be able to pick up non-verbal cues, interpret hidden questions and encourage further communication. It should be said, however, that without proper support and training, nurses are likely to find it just as difficult as others to discuss sexuality. However, it is important to be alert to the problem, so they can refer their clients on to someone who can help.

Table 1. Requirements for successful counselling of sexual problems.

Norton (1981), studied the emotional effects of urinary incontinence, using a sample of 55 women aged 22-78, with a mean age of 50. Nine women had no partner, and of the remaining 46, 26 said their incontinence had affected their relationship. If nurses are to deliver sexual healthcare as part of their holistic approach to patient care, there are three main areas of preparation to consider (Table 1).

The possibility of problems with sexuality can best be ascertained at the initial nursing assessment. The amount of information that can be collected depends very much on the client's feelings about sexuality and on the nurse's communication skills, but assessment should be a continuing process, so further information can be gathered later, when a closer relationship has been established. The initial assessment should identify how the client projects him- or herself as a sexual being (in appearance and dress), whether there is a regular partner (not necessarily opposite sex) and, for females, menstrual history.

Further assessments should identify whether clients' present condition affects their sexual life, concerns about future relationships and specific problem areas. For many people, the fact that someone mentions sexuality to them is enough to encourage them to talk about their concerns. Clients are also being asked to talk about their continence problems – another taboo subject, so the step from continence to sexuality should not be too difficult for most people.

The nurse's role

Nurses should not try to play the role of psychosexual counsellor, but they do need to be able to identify whether clients need this type of help. The real nursing role is to help clients and their partners overcome the problems brought about by their condition. This should include advice on other agencies who may be able to help, including psychosexual counsellors, family planning clinics and the Association to Aid the Sexual and Personal Relationships of People with Disabilities (SPOD). There are a number of areas about which patients may feel concerned when they suffer from incontinence.

Odour Careful hygiene will eliminate the problem of odour, which only occurs when urine is exposed to the air for a time. If there is any leakage of urine, the genital area should be washed frequently. The most convenient way for women is to sit on the toilet and squeeze water from a sponge over the genital area, although this will not be adequate if there has been heavy incontinence or a heavy void, when a proper wash is necessary. If the void happened while the client was sitting down, urine will have travelled up the back, so this area will also need washing. Careful drying, with talcum powder kept to a minimum, should prevent soreness. Pads should be changed every three to four hours to avoid odour, which can also be minimised by the use of neutralising deodorant.

For men, drip pouches or external collecting devices need to be changed regularly, and the skin washed and dried well, while leaving the penis free of appliances for some time each day will help keep the skin intact and healthy. Reusable appliances should be dismantled and rinsed under cold running water to remove all traces of urine before being washed in hot soapy water, rinsed and dried well. Proper care of appliances reduces odour and prolongs their life.

Pants and pads If it is decided a woman needs to wear pads or pants, their effect on sexuality should be considered when they are being selected. Obviously pants must be functional, but nurses should try to avoid the large asexual ones in favour of closer-fitting, more feminine designs, which look similar to normal pants when worn.

Pads should be carefully considered. They must be suitable for the amount of leakage, and comfortable and unobstrusive. For women who like to wear trousers, the bulk of the pad needs to be positioned at the back.

Male devices Couples in a sexual relationship can find appliances quite off-putting. Men may not feel they have a strong, masculine image if they wear a collecting device, while women may find them a 'turn-off'. Although the type of appliance to be used should be assessed carefully, the couple should also have the chance to examine it before it is applied, as this may help them come to terms with its use. Removal at night will help the penile skin to remain healthy and intact, and should also prevent the appliance interfering with the couple's sexual activity.

During the day, urinary devices can be unobtrusive, with the leg bag attached securely to the inner leg. For men who use wheelchairs, longer trousers will ensure the bag and tap are covered.

Sexual activity

While there are hygiene considerations associated with sexual activity and incontinence, the main problems tend to be aesthetic – it is not 'nice' to be incontinent. Other problems include fear of leakage, soreness and embarrassment. Communication is most important in relationships, and clients should be encouraged to discuss their problem with their partner. It is far better to discuss the possibility that leakage may occur than letting it happen without warning. Discussion also means preparations can be made, such as protecting the bed or emptying the bladder. Both partners must be made aware that leakage of urine during intercourse is not harmful unless the urine is heavily infected.

Women with unstable bladders may find intercourse causes bladder spasm leading to leakage. This can be minimised by keeping fluid intake to a minimum and emptying the bladder before intercourse. If the couple normally make love in the missionary position, a change of position may also help reduce leakage, putting less pressure on the woman's abdomen.

Men must also be encouraged to discuss appliances with their partners. If penile vaginal intercourse is not being attempted, there is no reason why the appliance should not be left in place, provided both partners are happy about this. If vaginal intercourse is going to occur and one partner uses an appliance, hygiene is vitally important, but this preparation can become part of the lovemaking.

While leakage is less likely when the penis is erect, the bladder should be emptied prior to intercourse (although men who find it difficult to get and maintain erections may find a partially distended bladder a good stimulation – in these cases clients must be made aware of the problems of going into retention). Dyspareunia is a common problem in women with continence problems, and may be avoided by strict hygiene and frequent pad changes. In these cases, lubrication may also be required, and this should be water soluble, like KY-Jelly; Vaseline should not be used, as it can harbour bacteria in the vagina.

Communication between partners is essential to overcome potential and existing sexual problems. Nurses should ensure both partners are present when they give advice of a sexual nature, and must impress upon them that a satisfactory sexual relationship is still possible.

Long-term catheterisation

For some people, the only satisfactory way to deal with urinary elimination is long-term catheterisation. This will improve the quality of life for many people, such as women who have mobility problems and must rely on others for toileting. The pros and cons of catheterisation should be explained to both partners, encouraging them to play a part in the decision-making process. All aspects of catheterisation should be discussed, and samples of leg bags and catheters shown. The care and hygiene associated with long-term catheters must be explained carefully and the area of sexuality broached early, assuring the partners this does not mean an end to sexual activity.

Any kind of appliance can make clients feel unattractive and unappealing, and careful consideration must be given to positioning of the leg bag to make it unobtrusive but still fully functional. It may be worth giving some clients a bag they can empty themselves.

It is vital that nurses appreciate the problems clients can experience with their sexuality if they are not fully continent, and that they also appreciate that sexual activity is not confined to the under 40s. Unless they come to terms with their own sexuality and become comfortable discussing issues of sexuality with others, nurses cannot give total care to their clients with continence problems.

References
Duvall, E.M. (1971) Family Development (4th Edn). Lippincott and Co., Philadelphia, USA.
Henderson, V. (1969) Basic Principles of Nursing Care. Karger, Basle.
Jacobson, L., (1974) Illness and human sexuality. *Nursing Outlook*, **22**, 1.
Norton, C. (1982) The effects of urinary incontinence in women. *International Rehabilitation Medicine*, **4**, 1.
Suthurst, J.R. and Brown, M. (1980) Sexual dysfunction associated with urinary incontinence. *Nursing Clinician North America*, **10**, 3.
WHO (1975) Education and Treatment in Sexuality. The Training of Health Professionals.

Report of WHO Meeting. Technical Report Series No. 572. World Health Organisation, Geneva.

Useful address
SPOD (Association to Promote the Sexual and Personal Relationships of People with Disabilities), 286 Camden Road, London N7 0BJ. Tel: 071-607 8851.

26

Early assessment of pressure sore risk

Moya J. Morison, MSc, BSc, BA, RGN
Clinical Audit Co-ordinator, Stirling Royal Infirmary

While surgeons generally take considerable interest in the management of wounds they have created, the day-to-day management of **chronic open wounds** is generally left to the nurse, who may not be or feel competent or confident to tackle this daunting task. While it is important to create the optimum local conditions at the wound site to promote healing through use of appropriate cleansing techniques (Morison, 1989) and dressings (Morison, 1987), delayed healing is inevitable unless the causes of the wound are identified and rectified at the same time. In the case of pressure sores, this involves identifying:

● the primary cause of tissue breakdown;

● any secondary factors of the patient's general health that may delay healing.

It is therefore a prerequisite to planning the nursing care for a patient with a pressure sore that nurses understand **how** it arose and which patient factors may be **exacerbating** the problem.

Pressure sores have been defined as: "a localised area of cellular damage resulting either from direct pressure on the skin, causing pressure ischaemia, or from shearing forces . . . causing mechanical stress to the tissues" (Chapman and Chapman, 1986). Research has shown that, of the general adult hospitalised population, between 6.5 per cent and 9.4 per cent of patients have at least one pressure sore at any one time (Jordan and Nicol, 1977; Lowthian, 1979; David et al, 1983) while their incidence in the elderly hospitalised population is much higher (Exton-Smith, 1987).

A number of classification systems have been developed (eg Barton and Barton, 1981; Forrest, 1980; Torrance, 1983) based on the cause, macroscopic appearance and clinical manifestations of the sore. Table 1 summarises Torrance's developmental classification, describing the clinical presentation of the sore at each stage.

Stage 1 Blanching hyperaemia
Momentary light finger pressure onto the site of erythema, following a prolonged period of pressure on the skin, causes the skin to blanch, indicating that the skin is intact.

Stage 2 Non-blanching hyperaemia
The erythema remains when light finger pressure is applied, indicating some microcirculatory disruption. Superficial damage, including epidermal ulceration, may be present.

Stage 3 Ulceration progresses through the dermis to the interface with the subcutaneous tissue.

Stage 4 The ulcer extends into the subcutaneous fat
Underlying muscle is swollen and inflamed. The ulcer tends to spread laterally, temporarily impeded from downward progress by deep fascia.

Stage 5 Infective necrosis penetrates down to the deep fascia
Destruction of muscle now occurs rapidly.

Table 1. Developmental classification of pressure sores (based on Torrance, 1983).

Factors affecting pressure sore development

The factors significant in the development and delayed healing of pressure sores are now well documented (eg Agate, 1976; Barton and Barton, 1981; David et al, 1983; and Torrance, 1983) and are summarised in Figure 1. Nearly all pressure sores are primarily due to **unrelieved pressure**, usually in relatively or totally immobile patients. Skin tissue is directly compressed between bone and another hard surface such as a bed, chair, operating table or trolley (Versluysen, 1986). The most common site for pressure sores is the sacrum, followed by the trochanter of the femur, ischial tuberosities and heels (Jordan and Nicol, 1977). The effect of body build is controversial (Bell et al, 1974), but studies have shown that underweight patients experience higher peak pressures than those who are obese.

Prolonged low pressure can be at least as hazardous as short-term high pressure (Kosiak, 1959). An external pressure which exceeds the mean capillary pressure (28–38mm Hg) is sufficient to cause tissue damage if it is maintained for long enough (Reswick and Rogerson, 1976), particularly in debilitated patients (Lee, 1985), but there is no scientific agreement about the **time** a given amount of pressure can be exerted before injury begins. However, it is generally assumed that any period of pressure exceeding two hours is likely to cause trauma (Versluysen, 1986).

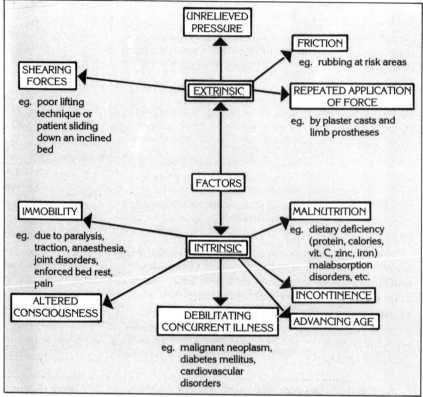

Figure 1. Factors significant in development and delayed healing of pressure sores.

Pressure interrupts the local microcirculation, and the ensuing hypoxia and build up of metabolic wastes can cause tissue necrosis.

Normally the patient experiences shearing forces and friction as well as pressure (Bennet and Lee, 1985), which can be particularly important in paraplegic, elderly and debilitated patients when in a semirecumbent position. As with excessive pressure, the effect of shearing is to disrupt the local tissue microcirculation (Chow et al, 1976), but by displacing, distorting or severing the blood vessels as skin strata move relative to one another. Paraplegic patients are particularly at risk (Grundy and Russell, 1986) because they cannot feel damage occurring. In general, chairbound patients are more likely to develop pressure sores than those who are bedbound (Jordan and Nicol, 1977).

There is a high correlation between incontinence and pressure sores (Exton-Smith, 1987). Urine can cause maceration and excoriation of skin, and superficial abrasion by friction becomes more likely in a constantly incontinent patient who is not catheterised.

Malnutrition does not directly cause pressure sores, but is an exacerbating factor. Once a sore has developed, a deficiency of protein, calorific intake, vitamin C, zinc and iron can all delay healing. Malnutrition is more common in the elderly than in the general adult population for many reasons including poverty, difficulties with buying and preparing food, difficulties with mastication due to ill-fitting dentures, difficulty with swallowing and problems of malabsorption.

Risk assessment

Abruzzese (1985) suggests that one of the major reasons why pressure sores form and are often so slow to heal is that insufficient care is taken with assessing a patient's *risk* of developing them, while according to Agate (1976) "There is hardly one pressure sore which could not be prevented." Prevention, however, can be costly, both in nursing time and in equipment. It is therefore vital that nurses' efforts at pressure sore prevention are *targeted* at those patients most at risk. A *valid* and *reliable* method of assessing pressure sore risk is needed which can discriminate between patients who have no risk, low risk, medium risk and high risk.

Various authors have attempted to group variables related to factors known to predispose patients to pressure sores (Figure 1) into assessment scales for use to determine patients' risk. The best known and simplest scale (Table 2) was devised by Norton et al (1962), who found an almost linear relationship between the patient's score and the incidence of pressure sores, a fact confirmed by Exton-Smith (1987) in a much more recent study in a geriatric unit. Patients with a score of 14 or less were found to be at risk, and those scoring less than 12 were particularly at risk.

Physical condition		Mental state		Activity		Mobility		Incontinence	
Good	4	Alert	4	Ambulant	4	Full	4	None	4
Fair	3	Apathetic	3	Walks with		Slightly		Occasional	3
Poor	2	Confused	2	help	3	limited	3	Usually	
Very bad	1	Stuporous	1	Chairbound	2	Very limited	2	urinary	2
				Bedfast	1	Immobile	1	Double	1

Table 2. The Norton Scale for risk assessment.

There have been a number of criticisms of the Norton scale. Goldstone and Goldstone (1982) found it tended to *over-predict* pressure sore risk in some patients. They showed that the sum of just the 'physical condition' and 'incontinence' scores was as successful in predicting patients' risk as the full Norton score. As Chapman and Chapman (1986) point out, Norton's scale was devised from a study of patients aged 65 years and over and so is only valid for this age group. It has been found to be ineffective in at least two groups of patients: children under six years old, and people of all ages who are only at risk for part of the day (Horsley, 1981). Pritchard (1986) found the scale *under-estimated* risk in patients recovering from a myocardial infarction who had been given strong analgesia. It may be a less appropriate tool in acute areas (Jones, 1986).

The Norton scale has also been criticised for not including any reference to nutrition or pain (Barratt, 1988). In Norton's defence, patients' nutritional status will be partly reflected by their 'physical condition'. A cachectic or otherwise anorexic patient is likely to score poorly in this category. A separate, detailed nutritional assessment by the dietitian is, however, a useful adjunct to the Norton assessment in patients deemed to be at high risk. The presence or absence of pain will certainly be reflected in the 'mobility' score, and the effects of powerful analgesia in 'mental state'. So long as its limitations are borne in mind, especially when assessing patients in an acute setting who may be at risk for only part of the time, the Norton scale, which has stood the test of time through its simplicity, remains a valuable *adjunct* to the nurse's direct observation and clinical judgement.

There have been several attempts to refine Norton's scale by including more parameters. Gosnell (1973) included skin appearance, tone and sensation, but did not give these parameters a numerical rating. More recent assessment tools, devised by Abruzzese (1985) and Waterlow (1985) have included nutritional factors, assessment of skin type and a 'weighting' for predisposing diseases – especially those involving sensory deprivation, and cardiovascular disorders, which could contribute to tissue ischaemia. Waterlow's risk assessment card has been updated and refined in the light of the findings of two local major pressure sore surveys (Waterlow, 1988). It has a wide applicability and is a useful aid for developing student nurses' awareness of pressure sore risk, observational skills and clinical judgement.

As Waterlow points out, no risk assessment scale is *any substitute* for sound clinical judgement, and it is of little use if the risk is not recalculated regularly as the patient's condition changes. Which risk assessment tool to use is largely a matter for personal preference, so long as the user is aware of its limitations. The problem (Torrance, 1983; Spenceley, 1988) seems to be to get nurses to use any assessment system at all!

References

Abruzzese, R.S. (1985) Early assessment and prevention of pressure sores. In: Lee, B.K. (Ed) Chronic Ulcers of the Skin. McGraw-Hill, New York.

Agate, J. (1976) Skin care: Medical factors in the causes of pressure sores. *Modern Geriatrics*, May, 33–37.

Barratt, E. (1988) A review of risk assessment methods. *Care – Science and Practice*, **6**, 2, 49–52.

Barton, A. and Barton, M. (1981) The Management and Prevention of Pressure Sores. Faber and Faber, London.

Bell, P.W., Fernie, G.R., Barbenel, J.C. (1974) Pressure sores; their cause and prevention. *Nursing Times*, **70**, 20, 740–45.

Bennet, L. and Lee, B.K. (1985) Pressure versus shear in pressure sore causation. In: Lee, B.K. (Ed) Ibid.

Chapman, E.J. and Chapman, R. (1986) Treatment of pressure sores: the state of the art. In: Tienery, A.J. (Ed) Clinical Nursing Practice. Churchill Livingtone, Edinburgh.

Chow, W.W. *et al* (1976) Effects and characteristics of cushion covering membranes. In: Kenedi, R.M. *et al* (Eds) Bedsore Biomechanics. McMillan, London.

David, J.A. *et al* (1983) An investigation of the current methods used in nursing for the care of patients with established pressure sores. Nursing Practice Research Unit, Harrow.

Exton-Smith, N. (1987) The patient's not for turning. *Nursing Times,* **83,** 42, 42–44.

Forrest, R.D. (1980) The treatment of pressure sores. *Journal of International Medical Research,* **8,** 6, 430–35.

Goldstone, L.A. and Goldstone, J. (1982) The Norton score: an early warning of pressure sores? *Journal of Advanced Nursing,* **7,** 5, 419–26.

Gosnell, D.J. (1973) An assessment tool to identify pressure sores. *Nursing Research,* **22,** 55–59.

Grundy, D. and Russell, J. (1986) ABC of spinal chord injury. *British Medical Journal,* **292,** 183–87.

Horsley, J.A. *et al* (1981) Preventing Decubitus Ulcers. Grune and Stratton, New York.

Jones, J. (1986) An investigation of the diagnostic skills of nurses on an acute medical unit relating to the identification of risk of pressure sore development in patients. *Nursing Practice,* **1,** 4, 257–67.

Jordan, M.M. and Nicol, S.M. (1977) Incidence of pressure sores in the patient community of the Borders Health Board Area on 13 October 1976. University of Strathclyde Bioengineering Unit and Borders Health Board, Glasgow.

Kosiak, M. (1959) Etiology and pathology of ischaemic ulcers. *Archives of Physical Medicine and Rehabilitation,* **40,** 62–69.

Lee, B.K. (1985) Chronic Ulcers of the Skin. McGraw-Hill, New York.

Lowthian, P. (1979) Pressure sore prevalence. *Nursing Times,* **75,** 9, 358–60.

Morison, M.J. (1987) Priorities in wound management: part 1. *The Professional Nurse,* **2,** 11, 352–55.

Morison, M.J. (1989) Wound cleansing – which solution? *The Professional Nurse,* **4,** 5, 220–25.

Norton, D. *et al* (1962) An Investigation of Geriatric Nursing Problems in Hospital. National Corporation for the Care of Old People, London.

Pritchard, V. (1986) Calculating the risk. *Nursing Times,* **82,** 7, 59–61.

Reswick, J.A. and Rogerson, J.E. (1976) Experience at Rancho Los Amigo's Hospital with devices and techniques to prevent pressure sores. In: Kenedi, R.M. *et al* (Eds) Ibid.

Spenceley, P. (1988) Norton v. Waterlow. *Nursing Times,* **84,** 32, 52–53.

Torrance, C. (1983) Pressure Sores: Aetiology, Treatment and Prevention. Croom Helm, Beckenham.

Versluysen, M. (1986) Pressure sores: causes and prevention. *Nursing,* **3,** 6, 216–18.

Waterlow, J. (1985) A risk assessment card. *Nursing Times,* **81,** 48, 49–55.

Waterlow, J. (1988) The Waterlow card for the prevention and management of pressure sores: towards a pocket policy. *Care – Science and Practice,* **6,** 1, 8–12.

27

Pressure sores: assessing the wound

Moya J. Morison, MSc, BSc, BA, RGN
Clinical Audit Co-ordinator, Stirling Royal Infirmary

Assessing the patient

The previous chapter on aetiology and risk assessment of pressure sores (Morison, 1989) evaluted a number of risk assessment tools. Risk assessment involves **assessing the patient as a whole** and includes assessing the patient's:

- general physical condition;
- skin appearance;
- mobility;
- nutritional status;
- continence;
- sensory functioning;
- cardiovascular status;
- conscious state and mental alertness;
- any debilitating concurrent illness;
- physical and social environment.

These factors identify any intrinsic or extrinsic factors that could lead to the development of a pressure sore. The importance of on-going risk assessment was emphasised.

Pressure sore risk assessment is just as important for a patient who has already developed a pressure sore. The very factors that **caused** the sore can **delay its healing** unless they are identified and alleviated.

Assessing the wound

After assessing the patient as a whole it is important to assess the wound itself, to identify any **local** factors that may delay healing, such as necrotic tissue, excess slough, infection or excess exudate. Accurate and on-going wound assessment is a prerequisite to planning appropriate care and to evaluating its effectiveness. It is facilitated where a reliable and systematic tool is available which:

- is easy and quick to use;
- includes all the parameters which may indicate whether a wound is healing or regressing;
- highlights the possibility of infection at an early stage;
- is applicable to a wide range of wounds and where information and trends are obvious at a glance.

A new assessment chart

There are few published wound assessment charts for nurses (eg, Jaber, 1986; Morison, 1987), and in an attempt to meet the criteria listed above, a new and comprehensive wound assessment chart (Table 1) has been

	DATE						
A. **TYPE OF WOUND**							
B. **LOCATION**							
C. **METHOD OF CLOSURE**							
D. **DRAINS (and TYPE)**							

TRACE THE WOUND WEEKLY (FOR OPEN WOUNDS): BE SURE TO MARK IN ANY SINUSES AND TRACKING. ALL OTHER PARAMETERS SHOULD BE ASSESSED AT EVERY DRESSING CHANGE.

DATE							
1. **WOUND DIMENSIONS** (mm) a. max length b. max breadth c. max depth							
2. **% OF TOTAL WOUND FLOOR WITH** (score 0–4) a. healthy granulation b. thick slough c. necrotic tissue							
3. **EXUDATE** a. colour b. consistency c. nature/type d. approx. vol/24 hrs							
4. **ODOUR** a. none b. some c. offensive							
5. **PAIN (SITE)** a. at wound itself b. elsewhere (specify)							
6. **PAIN (FREQUENCY)** a. none b. only at dressing changes c. intermittent d. continuous							
7. **PAIN (SEVERITY)** score patient's estimate (0–5)							
8. **WOUND MARGIN** a. colour b. oedematous?							
9. **ERYTHEMA OF SURROUNDING SKIN** a. present b. max. dist. from wound margin (mm)							
10. **ECZEMA OF SURROUNDING SKIN** a. wet b. dry							
11. **INFECTION** a. suspected b. wound swab sent c. organism(s) isolated							
WOUND ASSESSED BY							

Table 1. Wound assessment chart (for guidance in completing this, see Table 2).

devised for use with many types of wound, including **open wounds** and **surgically closed wounds**. The same form could be employed in medical, surgical and orthopaedic wards, as well as in the community.

Instructions for use

Guidance in completing the assessment summary is given in Table 2. Additional parameters can be added to the proforma to meet local needs. If the wound is being assessed more than once a day or there is no

---

Q.1. should be completed *weekly for open wounds   Qs. 2–11 at every dressing change for all wounds*

1. WOUND DIMENSIONS For open wounds:

Trace the wound margin carefully on to a piece of sterile double thickness transparent material (eg, a clear plastic glove) using a fine permanent marker pen. Be sure to mark in any tracking or sinuses and indicate their extent. Discard the portion next to the wound, date the tracing and keep it for future reference. Measure the maximum length and breadth of the wound and enter on the chart. Change in the surface area of an open wound is a useful measure of healing, but it should be noted that in the initial phases of healing, as devitalised tissue is removed, the wound may enlarge. To measure the maximum depth you require 2 sterile probes or quills.

Profile of wound:

Probe 1 is placed across the wound.

Probe 2 can then be used to obtain the max. depth accurately.

This measurement gives some indication of the extent of granulation from the wound floor, over time.

2. % OF TOTAL WOUND FLOOR WITH HEALTHY GRANULATION ETC

Estimate the % of the wound which is: a. healthy granulation; b. thick slough; c. necrotic tissue, using the following categories:

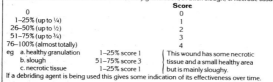

	Score
0	0
1–25% (up to ¼)	1
26–50% (up to ½)	2
51–75% (up to ¾)	3
76–100% (almost totally)	4

eg   a. healthy granulation   1–25% score 1   ⎫ This wound has some necrotic
        b. slough   51–75% score 3   ⎬ tissue and a small healthy area
        c. necrotic tissue   1–25% score 1   ⎭ but is mainly sloughy.

If a debriding agent is being used this gives some indication of its effectiveness over time.

3. EXUDATE

Note the characteristics of exudate under the headings given. A thick grey, cream or green exudate almost certainly indicates infection.

4. ODOUR

This is a subjective assessment, giving some indication only of the possibility of infection. However, from a social point of view odour can be extremely important to the patient.

5. PAIN (SITE)

Is the pain confined to the wound itself or are any other sites involved? Sometimes patients say that they feel no pain at the wound site but do experience pain at some other site due, for instance, to the bandage applied.

6. PAIN (FREQUENCY)

It is very difficult to assess a patient's pain. The patient is asked about his/her perception of its frequency.

7. PAIN (SEVERITY)

Different patients have very different pain thresholds and different abilities to cope with pain. The idea behind this question is to find out the patient's perception of his pain and whether for him the pain is getting better or worse with treatment. The patient could be asked to rate the pain on a five point scale:

None	Slight, but not distressing	Moderate, analgesia required	Bad enough to disturb sleep	Severe – "unable to cope"
0	1	2	3	4

8. WOUND MARGIN

The nature of the wound margin can indicate much about the 'health' of the wound itself. Local oedema and redness is to be expected during the early acute inflammatory response stage of healing, but prolonged problems at the margin can indicate infection and hypoxia.

9. ERYTHEMA OF SURROUNDING SKIN

This is a useful indicator of infection. Any spreading erythema should be reported to the doctor at once.

10. ECZEMA OF SURROUNDING SKIN

Wet or dry eczema is a common problem associated with chronic open wounds such as leg ulcers where there is venous stasis and local microcirculatory problems. Local topical agents may need to be prescribed by the doctor to alleviate itchiness and discomfort.

11. INFECTION

If the wound shows signs of infection, malodorous exudate, erythema, pain or oedema, send a wound swab to the Bacteriology Department for culture and sensitivity testing and note the result.

Table 2. Guidance for completing the wound assessment chart.

observable change, the next assessor can simply sign and date the bottom of the column completed at the previous assessment. In this way when any change occurs, it becomes more apparent, since it appears in a new column and information is condensed into more manageable form.

Parameters measured

The rationale behind the inclusion of the parameters listed in Table 1 is given in the explanatory notes (Table 2). It is worth, however, commenting in more detail on charting the surface area of an open wound. It is very important to trace open wounds weekly and to note the position and extent of any sinuses, skin flaps and tracking (Figure 1).

Change in the surface area of an open wound is a useful measure of healing or regression. It should be noted that an open wound may actually enlarge, as devitalised tissue is removed, before eventually getting smaller. For reasons which are not fully understood, a wound can also markedly change in shape without decreasing in total area. The breadth and depth of an open wound have been shown to be important parameters for predicting healing time in certain types (Marks, 1983).

Several methods for accurately assessing the surface area of a wound have been described (Bohannon and Pfaller, 1983; Anthony and Barnes, 1984; Anthony, 1985). Any two-dimensional representation of a three-dimensional wound inevitably leads to distortions. This may be important in clinical trials of dressing products where accurate measures of outcome are looked for, but for patients and most staff the absolute size of the wound is less important than the change in size with treatment. Where a reduction in size can be shown, this can be very encouraging and can act as a stimulus to further efforts towards wound healing.

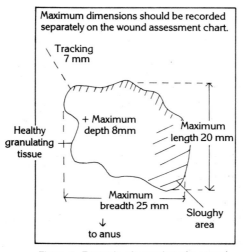

Figure 1. Example of a tracing of a sacral pressure sore.

Treatment aims

Having assessed the patient as a whole and the local wound environment and identified actual and potential problems, the nurse is now in a position to plan appropriate care.

References

Anthony, D. (1985) Measuring pressure sores. *Nursing Times*, **81**, 22, 57–61.

Anthony, D. and Barnes, S. (1984) Measuring pressure sores accurately. *Nursing Times*, **80**, 36, 33–35.

Bohannon, R.W. and Pfaller, B.A. (1983) Documentation of wound surface area from tracings of wound perimeters: clinical report on three techniques. *Physical Therapy*, **63**, 10, 1622–24.

Jaber, F. (1986) Charting wound healing. *Nursing Times*, **82**, 37, 24–27.

Marks, J. et al (1983) Prediction of healing time as an aid to the management of granulating wounds. *World J. Surg.*, **7**, 641–45.

Morison, M.J. (1987) Wound assessment. *The Professional Nurse*, **2**, 10, 315–17.

Morison, M.J. (1989) Pressure sore aetiology and risk assessment. *The Professional Nurse*, **4**, 9, 428–31.

28

Managing pressure sores: local treatment

Moya J. Morison, MSc, BSc, BA, RGN
Clinical Audit Co-ordinator, Stirling Royal Infirmary

It is important to assess a pressure sore and identify local problems that might be delaying healing at the wound site (Morison, 1989b). These problems can include the presence of necrotic tissue, excess slough and wound infection, and this article discusses priorities in the local management of these chronic open wounds. Wider aspects of care, such as providing appropriate patient support, improving mobility and nutritional status and providing psychological support will be discussed in the next chapter.

A local wound management policy
The aim of local wound management is to provide the optimum micro-environment for healing. Where the skin's integrity is breached, a dressing is usually required which will take over the functions of the missing tissue, protecting the underlying cells from the harmful effects of dehydration, fall in temperature, further mechanical damage and infection. No single dressing is suitable for all wounds (Turner, 1983; 1985), indeed each wound may require several different dressings as priorities change during the healing process.

Over the last 10 years a bewildering variety of new wound care products have come on the market. Table 1 includes just 30 of the most readily available primary wound dressing products, grouped into 10 categories according to physical and chemical properties, but does not include cleansing solutions, described in detail elsewhere (Morison, 1989a).

It is very difficult for nurses to know how to choose *one* product from within a particular category. Many of the products have not been subjected to extensive, properly controlled clinical trials, and there is often insufficient information available for even an 'informed' choice. Although products within one category may *look* alike, their physical and chemical properties may be significantly different. To overcome this problem many health authorities are now developing a wound management policy, enabling them to rationalise their use of products. In general, it is only necessary, usually, to select *one* dressing from *each category* (Table 1), in the full range of sizes. For hydrocolloids it is useful to

Category	Examples	Pharmaceutical company	FP10?	General indication of uses
Simple low-adherence dressings	Melolin Tricotex N.A.	Smith + Nephew Smith + Nephew Johnson & Johnson	√ √ √	Dry or very lightly exudating wounds.
Paraffin tulle dressings	Jelonet Paratulle Unitulle	Smith + Nephew Seton Healthcare Roussel	√ √ √	Clean, superficial low exudate wounds (with a secondary dressing).
Semipermeable films	OpSite Bioclusive Pharmaclusive Tegaderm	Smith + Nephew Johnson & Johnson Pharmacia 3M Health Care	√ √ √	Clean, shallow low exudate wounds – especially where it is useful to see the wound bed.
Hydrocolloids	Granuflex Comfeel Biofilm Dermiflex	ConvaTec Coloplast CliniMed Johnson & Johnson	√ √	Light to medium exudate wounds and for desloughing (contra-indicated where anaerobic infection is suspected).
Hydrogels	Scherisorb Geliperm Vigilon	Smith + Nephew Geistlich Seton Healthcare		
Alginate dressings	Sorbsan Kaltostat	Steriseal BritCair	√ √	Moderately exudating wounds (with a secondary dressing).
Foam dressings	Allevyn Lyofoam Silastic	Smith + Nephew Ultra Laboratories Calmic	 √	Medium to high exudate wounds.
Medicated dressings	Bactigras Sofra-tulle Inadine	Smith + Nephew Roussel Johnson & Johnson	√ √ √	Infected superficial wounds.
Bead dressings	Debrisan Iodosorb	Pharmacia Perstop Pharma	√ √	Sloughy, exudating or infected wounds, without tracking.
Deodorising dressings	Actisorb Plus Carbonet Kaltocarb Lyofoam C	Johnson & Johnson Smith + Nephew BritCair Ultra Laboratories		For infected, malodorous wounds.

Table 1. The major categories of primary wound dressings and their general uses.

include the dressing in a granule or paste form, to be used with the wafers, in deeper cavities. For alginate dressings, stock the ribbon or rope form for packing large, clean cavities, as well as sheet dressings.

The selection of products to be included in a local policy document is normally undertaken by the local Drugs and Therapeutics Committee, and it is valuable to have representation from all members of the healthcare team who have a special interest in, and responsibility for, wound management – including representatives from the community. As well as deciding which dressings to make *readily available*, it is helpful if the committee indicates those wound care products which should be *avoided*, or used with extreme caution, with the restriction that they can only be used when *formally prescribed* by the doctor on the drug prescription sheet. The action that should be taken by a nurse who feels that a *harmful* substance is being prescribed has been spelled out in the latest UKCC advisory document 'Exercising Accountability'.

Particularly where a local wound care policy does not exist, readers may find it helpful to refer to:
- Morgan, D.A. (1988). Formulary of Wound Management Products, Bridgend Hospital, Mid Glamorgan.
- Welsh Centre for the Quality Control of Surgical Dressings, Clwyd Health Authority: Dressing Information Sheets.

- Turner, A. (1985) Which dressing and why?
- Morison, M.J. (1987a,b, 1988). Priorities in Wound Management articles, and wallchart.

These will provide further information on the advantages and disadvantages of a number of wound care products and how to choose between them. The section which follows should also be of assistance. As a general principle:

> Before using *any* wound care product for the first time ALWAYS consult the manufacturer's recommendations, contraindications, precautions and warnings. If there is still any doubt about the suitability of a dressing, the pharmacist or the doctor should be consulted, so that the material selected is a team decision.

Priorities
What are the priorities in the *local* management of pressure sores? Essentially, the priorities are the same as for any chronic open wound.

Debridement   The first priority is to remove all debris such as any foreign material, devitalised soft tissue, excess slough and necrotic tissue which all delay healing and encourage infection. Methods for removing necrotic tissue and excess slough include:
- **Surgical excision** – the quickest method of achieving a 'clean' wound bed, but contraindicated for some patients, especially the severely debilitated.
- **Enzymatic treatment, eg, by Varidase** – a gentle, effective alternative at a physiological pH.
- **Hydrocolloid dressings, eg, Granuflex or hydrogels, eg, Scherisorb** which rehydrate necrotic tissue and create conditions that encourage the body's natural debriding processes.
- **Acid creams or solutions, eg, Malatex or Aserbine** – effective debriding agents, but care is needed to protect surrounding skin from possible irritation or maceration.
- **Hypochlorite and other chlorinated solutions, eg, eusol, Milton, Dakin's solution** – effective debriding agents but their toxicity to living tissues with prolonged use strongly militates against their use (Brennan et al, 1985, 1986; Leaper and Simpson, 1986).

Wound infection   There is a risk of a wound becoming clinically infected at *any* stage during the healing process. Until the epidermis is completely restored, there is no effective mechanical barrier to the entry of micro-organisms when the wound is exposed. Whether or not an infection develops depends upon:
- the dose of the contaminating organism;
- its virulence;
- the resistance of the host to infection.

Many micro-organisms are, however, commensal – living on the surface of a wound without causing an acute inflammatory tissue response. This is especially true for chronic open wounds such as pressure sores and leg ulcers. It is therefore only necessary to take a wound swab for culture and antibiotic sensitivity testing if a **clinical infection** is suspected, for instance if there is inflammation, localised heat, oedema of the wound margins, pain, copious cream, grey or green exudate, offensive odour or if the wound is refractory to treatment.

A systemic antibiotic may be prescribed where cellulitis is present, or where a very virulent micro-organism such as B-haemolytic *Streptococcus* is isolated. Without treatment this organism can spread systemically to other parts of the body, causing multiple tissue damage. However, the routine topical use of antibiotics, such as fucidin or cicatrin is frowned on as their injudicious use can encourage the emergence of multiple antibiotic-resistant strains of bacteria. In a heavily infected pressure sore extending into the dermis or deeper, Iodosorb or Debrisan can be effective treatments, but they should not be used where extensive tracking is present, as it may be impossible to retrieve them! Consult the manufacturer's recommendations for methods of application which aid subsequent removal. For shallow, open infected wounds, alternatives include Actisorb Plus, a charcoal dressing which also reduces odour, or non-adherent dressings impregnated with antiseptics such as Inadine or Bactigras.

There is increasing evidence that the wound exudate produced as part of the body's own defence against infection contains many bactericidal components (Hohn et al, 1977). Antiseptics should therefore only be required for severely debilitated patients or where wounds are extensive and there is a high risk of contamination.

Odour   Malodorous wounds can be very distressing for patients, and can lead to self-imposed social isolation, loss of appetite and depression. Treating the infection that leads to the malodorous exudate is important. The odour itself can be controlled by the use of an activated charcoal dressing such as Actisorb Plus. If there is a moderate amount of exudate present, an absorbent foam dressing which has a charcoal dressing backing, such as Lyofoam C, is helpful. Flagyl, when prescribed and given systemically or topically can also have a deodorising effect. While the problem of infection is being tackled, other simple remedies should not be forgotten, such as changing bed linen and clothing as soon as it becomes contaminated, changing the dressing if 'strike through' occurs, offering the patient a single room if possible, providing fresh air, using perfume and encouraging relatives to bring in scented plants. There is more to providing 'the ideal environment' for healing than simply choosing the most appropriate wound dressing, as the following chapter will demonstrate.

Excess exudate   Even when necrotic tissue and excess slough have been removed and a pressure sore is no longer clinically infected, it may still produce a moderate amount of exudate which can strike through non-occlusive dressings. This increases the risk of wound infection, or of macerating the wound margins if the surrounding tissues become waterlogged. The volume of exudate should lessen in time, but until this stage is reached an absorbent, non-adherent dressing is needed. There is a number of options including:

- Silastic foam – useful for clean, deep saucer-shaped cavities, without tracking, which can often be managed at home by a patient's relatives, or by staff in a nursing home, with new stents being made, as required, by the nurse, who can evaluate the wound's progress.
- Alginate dressings, eg, Sorbsan – a biodegradable dressing useful for packing clean, deep pressure sores where tracking is present. The wound should be lightly packed to prevent skin flaps from growing over cavities and encouraging the wound to granulate from beneath.
- Polyurethane foam sheets, eg, Lyofoam, Allevyn – for relatively shallow, medium-to-heavily exuding pressure sores. Cushioning effect helpful, but look out for possible maceration of surrounding skin with prolonged use in heavily exuding wounds.
- Extra absorbency hydrocolloids, eg, Granuflex E – this has all the characteristics of the ideal dressing and is designed to absorb more exudate than the original Granuflex wafers. Granuflex paste or beads are especially helpful in deep wounds with no tracking. However, the wafer dressing may 'bunch up' when applied to patients with a sacral sore, especially if the semirecumbent position is used. The problem can be alleviated by using a large enough dressing applied in a 'diamond' shape (corner towards the anus), by nursing patients from side to side, turning them carefully, and only allowing them to sit upright for short periods at mealtimes.

Your choice of dressing will be affected by such practical considerations as the site and size of the wound, the volume of exudate, comfort and cosmetic acceptability to the patient and, of course, the cost of the dressing (preferably calculated on a weekly basis, as this overcomes the bias against a product with a high unit cost if it requires less frequent dressing changes than a lower cost product).

Clean superficial pressure sores The aim here is to continue to provide a moist environment for healing and to protect the surface of the wound from further mechanical damage and from contamination. A semipermeable polymeric film such as OpSite is recommended.

Other therapeutic methods

The catalogue of substances used to treat pressure sores in the distant past (Forrest, 1982) and the present (David et al, 1983) makes depressing reading, and the more 'way out' solutions require no further comment here. Hyperbaric oxygen therapy remains of questionable benefit, but the use of ultrasound or ultraviolet light by the physiotherapist should be considered (Fisher, 1976; High and High, 1983). A well-illustrated account of methods for surgically closing pressure sores using skin grafts and skin flaps is given by Agris and Spira (1979).

Removing the cause of the wound

No matter how appropriate the wound dressing regime selected, if the underlying causes of the pressure sore are not alleviated, delayed healing is inevitable. Wider issues such as providing the most appropriate patient support system, improving mobility and nutritional status, and providing psychological support are important also.

References

Agris, J. and Spira, M. (1979) Pressure ulcers: prevention and treatment. *Clinical Symposia,* **31**, 5, 2-32.

Brennan, S.S. and Leaper, D.J. (1985) The effect of antiseptics on the healing wound: a study using rabbit ear chamber. *British Journal of Surgery,* **72**, 10, 780–82.

Brennan, S.S., Foster, M.E., Leaper, D.J. (1986) Antiseptics toxicity in wounds healing by secondary intention. *Journal of Hospital Infection,* **8**, 3, 263–67.

David, J.A. et al (1983) An investigation of the current methods used in nursing for the care of patients with established pressure sores. Nursing Practice Research Unit, Harrow.

Fisher, M.V. (1976) Pressure sores: treatment by ultrasound. *Nursing Times,* **72**, 8, 302.

Forrest, R.D. (1982) Early history of wound treatment. *Journal of the Royal Society of Medicine,* **75**, 198–205.

High, A.S. and High, J.P. (1983) Treatment of infected skin wounds using ultraviolet radiation. *Physiotherapy,* **69**, 10, 359–60.

Hohn, D.C. et al (1977) Antimicrobial systems of the surgical wound. *American Journal of Surgery,* **133**, 5, 597–600.

Leaper, D.J. and Simpson, R.A. (1986) The effect of antiseptics and topical antimicrobials on wound healing. *Journal of Antimicrobial Chemotherapy,* **17**, 2, 135–37.

Morgan, D.A. (1988) Formulary of Wound Management Products. Clwyd Health Authority.

Morison, M.J. (1987a) Priorities in wound management: Part I. *The Professional Nurse,* **2**, 11, 352–55.

Morison, M.J. (1987b) Priorities in wound management: Part II. *The Professional Nurse,* **2**, 12, 402–11.

Morison, M.J. (1988) Deciding priorities for wound management. *The Professional Nurse,* **4**, 2, (wallchart).

Morison, M.J. (1989a) Wound cleansing: which solution? *The Professional Nurse,* **4**, 5, 220–25.

Morison, M.J. (1989b) Pressure sores: assessing the wound. *The Professional Nurse,* **4**, 11, 532–35.

Turner, T.D. (1983) Absorbents and wound dressings. *Nursing,* **2**, 12, Supplement.

Turner, T.D. (1985) Which dressing and why? In: Westaby, S. (ed). Wound Care. London, Heinemann.

29

Pressure sores: removing the causes of the wound

Moya J. Morison, MSc, BSc, BA, RGN
Clinical Audit Co-ordinator, Stirling Royal Infirmary

Articles in the nursing press on the prevention and management of pressure sores probably outnumber any other single topic. This is perhaps not only a reflection of the size of the problem, but also of many nurses' feelings that more could be done to prevent pressure sores from developing and to improve their management. This chapter explores more general issues and outlines a very simple 10 point action plan aimed at *preventing* pressure sores in high-risk patients and *managing them appropriately* when tissue breakdown occurs. The general principles are the same.

General treatment aims

In the past, considerable research attention has been focused on the prevention of pressure sores, but relatively little on the effectiveness of the most commonly used treatment methods (Chapman and Chapman, 1986). Certainly, no definitive treatment for pressure sores has yet emerged but the general principles are clear:

- to remove the *extrinsic* factors significant in the development and delayed healing of pressure sores such as: unrelieved pressure, shearing and frictional forces;

- to alleviate the effects of the *intrinsic* factors that can contribute to tissue breakdown and delayed healing such as malnutrition, incontinence and debilitating concurrent illness (Morison, 1989b);

- to provide the optimum *local* environment for healing at the wound site (Morison, 1987; 1989d).

The 10 point plan (Table 1, overleaf) reflects these principles.

Since almost any patient problem can lead directly or indirectly to delayed wound healing it would be far too simplistic to suppose that all aspects of the care of a patient with a pressure sore could be adequately covered in one article. Ways of providing the optimum local environment for healing were described in the previous chapter (Morison, 1989d). There is only space here to refer to ways of alleviating the *intrinsic* problems such as malnutrition, incontinence, and debilitating concurrent illness. Key references to these problems are given in Table 1, so that nurses can follow up particular topics that interest them in the depth each deserves. Ways of removing the *extrinsic* factors that can cause pressure sores and delay their healing, are explored in this chapter.

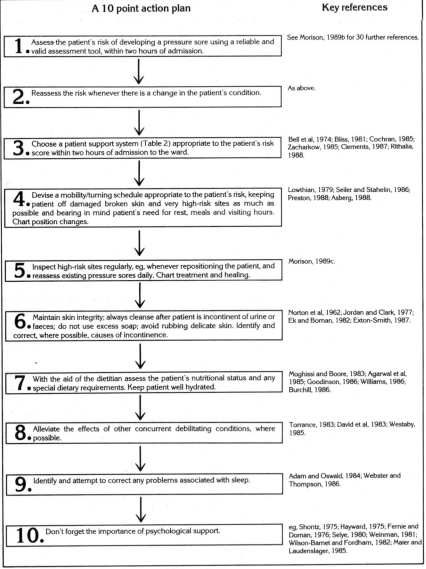

A 10 point action plan	Key references
1. Assess the patient's risk of developing a pressure sore using a reliable and valid assessment tool, within two hours of admission.	See Morison, 1989b for 30 further references.
2. Reassess the risk whenever there is a change in the patient's condition.	As above.
3. Choose a patient support system (Table 2) appropriate to the patient's risk score within two hours of admission to the ward.	Bell et al, 1974; Bliss, 1981; Cochran, 1985; Zacharkow, 1985; Clements, 1987; Rithalia, 1988.
4. Devise a mobility/turning schedule appropriate to the patient's risk, keeping patient off damaged broken skin and very high-risk sites as much as possible and bearing in mind patient's need for rest, meals and visiting hours. Chart position changes.	Lowthian, 1979; Seiler and Stahelin, 1986; Preston, 1988; Asberg, 1988.
5. Inspect high-risk sites regularly, eg, whenever repositioning the patient, and reassess existing pressure sores daily. Chart treatment and healing.	Morison, 1989c.
6. Maintain skin integrity; always cleanse after patient is incontinent of urine or faeces; do not use excess soap; avoid rubbing delicate skin. Identify and correct, where possible, causes of incontinence.	Norton et al, 1962; Jordan and Clark, 1977; Ek and Boman, 1982; Exton-Smith, 1987.
7. With the aid of the dietitian assess the patient's nutritional status and any special dietary requirements. Keep patient well hydrated.	Moghissi and Boore, 1983; Agarwal et al, 1985; Goodinson, 1986; Williams, 1986; Burchill, 1986.
8. Alleviate the effects of other concurrent debilitating conditions, where possible.	Torrance, 1983; David et al, 1983; Westaby, 1985.
9. Identify and attempt to correct any problems associated with sleep.	Adam and Oswald, 1984; Webster and Thompson, 1986.
10. Don't forget the importance of psychological support.	eg, Shontz, 1975; Hayward, 1975; Fernie and Dornan, 1976; Selye, 1980; Weinman, 1981; Wilson-Barnet and Fordham, 1982; Maier and Laudenslager, 1985.

Table 1. The prevention and management of presure sores.

Ongoing assessment

The plan in Table 1 emphasises the importance of early and ongoing risk assessment – even for a patient who already has a pressure sore. Which risk assessment tool to use is largely a matter of personal preference, so long as the user is aware of its limitations (Morison, 1989b), but it is of paramount importance that the patient is assessed as soon as possible after admission, and that the risk is reassessed whenever there is a material change in his or her condition. The underlying tissue damage that can lead to a pressure sore can occur very rapidly, for example when a patient is waiting to be seen in the A&E Department, or to be transferred from there to a ward; in the X-ray department during a special procedure which requires the patient to be placed on a hard surface; or on operating theatre tables and trolleys (Nightingale, 1978; Stewart and Magnano, 1988). Some patients are at risk for only part of the day, during the acute phase of an illness or for a few hours immediately post-surgery. Whether through pain or sedation, they move less than they normally would (Exton-Smith, 1987). Nursing interventions need to keep pace with the changing nature of the patient's problems. Patients of *all* ages can develop pressure sores given the right (or rather the wrong) circumstances, although the elderly and chronically debilitated are obviously most at risk (David et al, 1983).

Relief of pressure, shearing and friction

It is a commonly quoted adage that the nurse can put anything on a pressure sore – except the patient. To encourage healing, all pressure should ideally be removed from the site. In practice, however, this is usually not possible, especially in severely deformed patients where repositioning can put undue pressure on other vulnerable sites. The ideal

Table 2. Some pressure relieving beds and mattresses.

1. Devices to alternate the area of the body under pressure				
TYPE & EXAMPLES	DESCRIPTION AND PRINCIPLES BEHIND USE	ADVANTAGES	DISADVANTAGES	REFERENCES TO TRIALS
Alternating pressure (ripple-type) mattresses Large-cell ripple mattress	Alternates the area of the body under pressure. The mattress consists of two sets of tubular air cells which are alternately inflated and deflated by means of an electric air pump controlled on a time switch.	1. Can be very effective in preventing the lesions even where positional change is restricted, eg, traction. Large-cell mattress much more effective than medium or small-cell types. 2. Relatively cheap and easy to use, even at home. 3. Lightweight and fits on top of an ordinary mattress.	Their effectiveness is easily reduced by incorrect assembly, kinking or disconnection of the tubing, incorrect setting and lack of maintenance.	Bliss & Murray (1979); Bliss (1981); Exton-Smith et al (1982).
Pegasus Air wave System	Two layers of air cells; produces a deep rhythmic wave effect from feet to head by deflating every third cell in a 7½ minute cycle. A continuous air flow ventilates the mattress and reduces problems caused by sweat and urine.	As above and: 4. Regular zero skin pressure, for about 2 minutes every 7½ minute cycle, allows blood recirculation and prevents local ischaemia over high-risk sites. For 75% of time the interface pressure is less than that causing capillary occlusion. 5. Very low interface pressures minimise forward slide and hammocking. 6. Feet to head airwave effect aids venous return and lymph flow. 7. Rapidly deflatable in case of cardiac arrest. 8. Reliable, hard-wearing and easy to clean. 9. Microprocessor controlled.		

Table 2. Continued.

2. Devices to reduce and distribute pressure more evenly				
TYPE & EXAMPLES	DESCRIPTION AND PRINCIPLES BEHIND USE	ADVANTAGES	DISADVANTAGES	REFERENCES TO TRIALS
1. *Water beds* Beaufort-Winchester	Patient's weight is evenly distributed in a controlled volume of water (based on Pascal's law) so that there are no pressure gradients and tissue distortion does not occur. Only in deep tank models, however, is there a sufficient volume to displace the patient's mass without developing tension on the enveloping membrane.	**1.** Good systems are capable of providing the total hydrostatic support needed for severe risk patients. **2.** Most patients find them comfortable. **3.** Pain relief often reported.	**1.** Hammocking can occur when the load is taken up by the membrane, leading to shearing at the interface, and efficiency of pressure distribution is reduced. **2.** Bottoming out, in shallow water beds, can lead to pressure points. **3.** Can cause nausea and disorientation. **4.** Heavy. **5.** Quite expensive. **6.** Some nursing procedures not easy. **7.** Unsuitable for confused, immobile, psychiatric or incontinent patients.	Bell et al (1974).
2. *Air fluidised beds* Clinitron	Uses dry flotation to provide hydrostatic support. A flow of warm air is pumped through fine particles, eg, sand or glass microspheres to provide fluid-like support characteristics.	**1.** Provides true hydrostatic support suitable for intensive care. **2.** Patient does not sink into the bed to the same extent as in some water beds and is less likely to become disorientated. **3.** Air temperature can be controlled. **4.** System can absorb exudate. **5.** Air fluidisation can be continuous or intermittent; patient handling is easier when fluidisation is switched off. **6.** Can be used with traction. **7.** Fluidisation can be stopped instantly in case of cardiac arrest.	**1.** Expensive to hire (but may still be worth it for *very* high-risk patients). **2.** Takes up a lot of space.	Turnock (1983); Viner, (1986).
3. *Low air loss bed systems (LALBS)* Mediscus	The LALBS consists of 21 waterproof but vapour permeable sacs arranged in groups of 5 with pressure valves controlling each group to suit body contours. The bed is hinged and bellows at the head and foot control posture. There is automatic deformation of the bed to accommodate body form.	**1.** Uniform pressure on maximum body surface area. **2.** Low shear stresses. **3.** Water can evaporate from support surface. **4.** Temperature and humidity are controllable. **5.** Air sacs are easily removable for washing/disinfection. **6.** Minimum lifting of patient, variable positions possible. **7.** Mobile.	**1.** Expensive. **2.** Requires more space than a conventional bed to accommodate control unit.	Jeneid, (1976); Love, (1980).
4. *Low pressure Air bed* Simpson-Edinburgh	Consists of two standard air beds placed one on top of the other on a wooden base and with padded sides. An air pump inflates the mattresses to a pre-set pressure and when the patient is placed on the bed air is discharged to keep the pressure constant.	**1.** Prevents the patients from grounding. **2.** Adjustable pressure control ensures bed is not over-inflated. **3.** Relatively economical.	**1.** Difficulty in rolling the patient on to his side and when using bedpans. **2.** Difficulty in changing the bottom sheet.	Laing and Walton, (1979).
5. *Cut foam mattresses* Polyfloat Clinifloat	Consists of two layers of foam bonded together with the upper layer cut into almost independent blocks to reduce the hammock effect from the tension in the otherwise solid foam mattresses.	**1.** Inexpensive. **2.** Considerable improvement on solid foam mattresses, reducing shearing. **3.** Effective for patients at moderate risk of developing pressure sores. **4.** Light and easy to use.	Effectiveness of both mattresses is greatly reduced if sheets are tucked in.	
6. *Silicone padding mattresses* Spenco	Made up of horizontal fibre-filled tubes.	**1.** Easy to use and maintain, machine washable. **2.** Patients like them. **3.** Easily placed on top of bed.	Only suitable for low-risk patients.	

Table 2. Continued

	3. Devices to aid turning			
TYPE & EXAMPLES	DESCRIPTION AND PRINCIPLES BEHIND USE	ADVANTAGES	DISADVANTAGES	REFERENCES TO TRIALS
Net suspension beds Mecabed Egerton	Patient is supported on a slightly elastic open-mesh net suspended from a frame which either fits over the bed, or is free-standing. Operated by two winding handles.	1. Bed conforms to body contours. 2. Provides a ventilated skin environment. 3. One nurse can easily turn even heavy patients.	1. Patient is raised much higher than normal and may feel insecure and embarrassed. 2. Not suitable for confused patients.	Gibbs, (1977). Graham, (1981).

way to reduce pressure on high-risk areas is to encourage early mobility (Asberg, 1988), but for patients who are paralysed, sedated or unconscious, who are on a form of treatment which restricts mobility (such as traction) or who are on enforced bed-rest for medical reasons, regular repositioning by nurses will be required. The aim is to reduce the pressure per unit time over high-risk sites so that irreversible tissue breakdown is prevented.

A number of turning schedules have been devised (eg, Lowthian, 1979; Seiler and Stahelin, 1988). The *30° tilt technique* is particularly effective since the pressure is transferred to low-risk 'soft' sites such as the gluteal muscles, which can tolerate pressures up to three-and-a-half times higher than those tolerated over bony prominences (Preston, 1988). This makes four hourly turning feasible for many patients. Extended periods of eight hours or more without turning are possible for some, allowing a complete night's sleep. As sleep favours the anabolic healing processes (Adam and Oswald, 1984) wound healing should be greatly facilitated.

The ideal support system

The actual surface that a patient rests on is also very important (Bliss, 1981; Cochran, 1985; Zacharkow, 1985). An ideal support system should:
- distribute pressure evenly, or provide frequent relief of pressure by varying the areas under pressure;
- minimise friction and shearing forces;
- provide a comfortable, well ventilated patient support interface which does not restrict movement unduly;
- be acceptable to the patient;
- not impede nursing procedures;
- be easily maintained;
- be inexpensive.

None of the devices currently available can fulfil all these requirements. Those most effective at providing pressure relief are expensive and can be difficult to maintain, while the cheaper devices are less effective in pressure distribution. The advantages and disadvantages of a number of commonly available beds and mattresses and the principles behind their use are given in Table 2. For further information on this complex subject nurses are referred to:

- **Torrance (1983)** Pressure sores: aetiology, treatment and prevention – a useful summary of all aspects of pressure sore prevention and treatment with an informative review of patient support systems.

- **Kenedi et al (eds) (1976)** Bed sore biomechanics – an informative collection of seminar papers on current knowledge and research on support systems.

- **Bliss (1981)** Excellent article on clinical research in patient support systems.

- **Jay (1983)** Review of wheelchair cushions.
  (Full references are given at the end of this article.)

The beneficial effects of even the most sophisticated support systems can be counteracted if nurses handle patients carelessly, and it is nurses' responsibility to understand when a support system is not functioning properly so that it can be reported for repair. The value of inexpensive and well-tried alternatives should not be underestimated. Sheepskin fleeces under the buttocks and heels can reduce frictional forces, paraplegic patients can be taught to relieve pressure from the sacral area while in bed by using monkey poles and rope ladders. Bed cradles should be used to remove the pressure of bedclothes from the lower limbs of vulnerable patients, especially those with peripheral vascular problems who are particularly susceptible to trauma, and where the consequences of a pressure induced wound could be severe enough to precipitate amputation. It seems unlikely that there will ever be enough high-technology beds for all our high-risk patients, so it is important to make the best use of existing resources, matching those at highest need to the best pressure relieving aids. It is also important to prolong the useful life of even the humblest equipment, as Larcombe (1988) explains for the basic hospital mattress.

Developing a pressure sore policy
If relevant research into the prevention and management of pressure sores is to be put into practice, its results must be made available to nurses at ward level by nurse educators (Morison, 1989a). The role of management in ensuring theory is put into practice should not be underestimated – it is, after all, the budget-holders who ultimately determine how much is spent on pressure sore prevention and care, and senior nurse managers who have considerable influence on how the money is spent. If a hospital is given, say £10,000 from a local charity appeal, is it better to spend the money on one low air loss bed, four Airwave alternating pressure air mattresses, 60 large cell ripple mattresses, 500 full-length sheepskin fleeces or a combination of these?

There is no easy answer to this question. It will depend on the equipment the hospital already has and its special needs. It helps where a health authority has a pressure sore prevention and treatment policy, based on the latest research, which is known and carried out by all staff and which includes monitoring equipment in use, planning equipment acquisition and deciding on priorities for the future (Livesley, 1987; Hibbs, 1988).

References

Adam, K. and Oswald, I. (1984) Sleep helps healing. *British Medical Journal*, **289**, 24 Nov. 1400–01, (letters section).

Agarwal, N. et al (1985) The role of nutrition in the management of pressure sores. In: Lee, B.K. (Ed) Chronic Ulcers of the Skin, McGraw-Hill, New York.

Asberg, K.H. (1988) Early activation for elderly patients in acute medical wards. *Care: Science and Practice*, **6**, 3, 69–73.

Bell, P.W., Fernie, G.R., Barbanel, J.C. (1974) Pressure sores: their cause and prevention. *Nursing Times*, **70**, 20, 740–45.

Bliss, M.R. (1981) Clinical research in patient support systems. *Care: Science and Practice*, **1**, 17–36.

Bliss, M. and Murray, E. (1979) The use of ripple beds. *Nursing Times*, **75**, 7, 280–83.

Burchill, P. (1986 Body builders. *Community Outlook*, August, 19–22.

Chapman, E.J. and Chapman, R. (1986) Treatment of pressure sores: the state of the art. In: Tierney, A.J. Clinical Nursing Practice. Churchill Livingstone, Edinburgh.

Clements, S. (1987) And so to beds. *Community Outlook*, September, 16–17.

Cochran, G.V.B. (1985) Measurement of pressure and other environmental factors at the patient – cushion interface. In: Lee, B.K. (Ed) Chronic Ulcers of the Skin, McGraw-Hill, New York.

David, J.A. et al (1983) An investigation of the Current Methods Used in Nursing for the Care of Patients with Established Pressure Sores. Nursing Practice Research Unit, Harrow.

Ek, A.C. and Boman, G. (1982) A descriptive study of pressure sores: the prevalence of pressure sores and the characteristics of patients. *Journal of Advanced Nursing*, **7**, 51–57.

Exton-Smith, A.N. et al (1982) Use of the Airwave System to prevent pressure sores in hospital. *Lancet*, **1**, 1288–90.

Exton-Smith, N. (1987) The patient's not for turning. *Nursing Times*, **83**, 42, 42–44.

Fernie, G.R. and Dornan, J. (1976) The problems of clinical trials with new systems for preventing or healing decubiti. In: Kenedi et al (Eds) Bedsore Biomechanics, MacMillan, London.

Gibbs, J.R. (1977) Net suspension beds for managing threatened and established pressure sores. *Lancet*, **1**, 8004, 174–75.

Goodinson, S.M. (1986) Asssessment of nutritional status. *Nursing*, **3**, 7, 252–57.

Graham, E. (1981) A new nursing aid. *Nursing*, **25**, 1090–93.

Hayward, J. (1975) Information: a prescription against pain. Royal College of Nursing, London.

Hibbs, P. (1988) Action against pressure sores. *Nursing Times*, **84**, 13, 68–73.

Jay, P. (1983) Choosing the best wheelchair cushion for your needs, your chair and your lifestyle. Radar, London.

Jeneid, P. (1976) Static and dynamic support systems: pressure differences on the body. In: Kenedi Ibid.

Jordan, M.M. and Clark, M.O. (1977) Report on the incidence of pressure sores in the patient community of the Greater Glasgow Health Board Area on 21 January 1976. University of Strathcylde Bioengineering Unit and The Greater Glasgow Health Board, Glasgow.

Kenedi, R.M. et al (Eds) (1976) Bedsore Biomechanics, MacMillan, London.

Laing, E. and Walton, S.K. (1979) Report on the clinical evaluation of the Simpson – Edinburgh Low Pressure Air Bed 1978/79. Bioengineering Unit, Princess Margaret Rose

Hospital, Edinburgh.

Larcombe, J. (1988) One good turn deserves another. *Nursing Times*, B84, 11, 36–38.

Livesley, B. (1987) An expensive epidemic. *Nursing Times*, **83**, 79.

Love, C. (1980) A problem sore. *Nursing Times*, **76**, 13, 560–64.

Lowthian, P. (1979) Turning clocks system to prevent pressure sores. *Nursing Mirror*, **148**, 21, 30–31.

Maier, S.F. and Laudenslager, M. (1985) Stress and health: exploring the links. *Psychology Today*, **19**, 8, 44–49.

Moghissi, K. and Boore, J. (1983) Parenteral and Enteral Nutrition for Nurses. Heinemann Medical Books, London.

Morison, M.J. (1987) Priorities in wound management: Part I. *The Professional Nurse*, **2**, 1, 352–55.

Morison, M.J. (1989a) Delayed pressure sore healing can be prevented. *The Professional Nurse*, **4**, 7, 332–36.

Morison, M.J. (1989b) Early assessment of pressure sore risk. *The Professional Nurse*, **4**, 9, 428–31.

Morison, M.J. (1989c) Pressure sores: assessing the wound. *The Professional Nurse*, **4**, 11, 532–35.

Morison, M.J. (1989d) Pressure sore management: Part I – local treatment. *The Professional Nurse*, **5**, 1, 34–38.

Nightingale, K.M. (1978) Out of sight: out of mind: an enquiry into the incidence of pressure injuries in the operating department. *NAT News*, August, 22–26.

Norton, D. et al (1962) An Investigation of Geriatric Nursing Problems in Hospital. National Corporation for the Card of Old People, London.

Preston, K.W. (1988) Positioning for comfort and pressure relief: the 30 degree alternative. *Care: Sci. and Pract*, **6**, 4, 116–19.

Rithalia, S.V.S. (1988) What inflation pressure and which air mattress? *Care: Science and Practice*, **6**, 2, 45–47.

Seiler, W.O. and Stahelin, H.B. (1985) Decubitus ulcers: preventive techniques for the elderly patient. *Geriatrics*, **40**, 7, 53–60.

Selye, H. (Ed) (1980) Selye's Guide to Stress Research, 1. Van Nostrand Reinhold, London.

Shontz, F.C. (1975) The Psychological Aspects of Physical Illness and Disability. MacMillan, New York.

Stewart, T. P. and Magnano, S.J. (1988) Burns or pressure ulcers in the surgical patients? *Decubitus*, **1**, 1, 36–40.

Torrance, C. (1983) Pressure Sores: Aetiology, Treatment and Prevention. Croom Helm, Beckenham.

Turnock. H. (1983) Benefits of a bead bed. *Nursing Mirror*, 16 Nov. (reprint).

Viner, C. (1986) Floating on a bed of beads. *Nursing Times*, **82**, 8, 62–66.

Webster, R.A. and Thompson, D.R. (1986) Sleep in hospital. *Journal of Advanced Nursing*, **11**, 4, 447–57.

Weinman, J. (1981) An Outline of Psychology as Applied to Medicine. John Wright, Bristol.

Westaby, S. (Ed) (1985) *Wound Care*. Heinemann Medical Books Ltd, London.

Williams, C.M. (1986) Wound healing: a nutritional perspective. *Nursing*, **3**, 7, 249–51.

Wilson-Barnett, J. and Fordham, M. (1982) Recovery from Illness. John Wiley, Chichester.

Zacharkow, D. (1985) Wheelchair Posture and Pressure Sores. Charles C. Thomas, Springfield.

30

Mental health problems in old age

Lesley Donovan, BSc, RMN, RGN, Cert Ed.
Senior Lecturer in Nursing, Bristol Polytechnic

Throughout our lives we continually face and attempt to adjust to the various life stages we pass through. Old age is seen as the final stage, a very vulnerable time in life which involves distinct life changes. For many it is seen as a 'wearing out', a 'running down' of both physical and mental ability. The ageist society that we live in compounds these negative attitudes through its lack of resources and opportunities for the elderly. Puner (1979) goes as far as to state that as we get older we are so indoctrinated into believing that our mental competence and capacity must break down, that it sometimes becomes self-fulfilling, and mind and memory fail in old age simply because they are expected to. Yet research has shown that we continue to learn as long as we live and memory should not have any age limits at all.

What must be recognised is that the stresses in life can increase dramatically in old age and an individuals coping mechanisms are pushed to their limits. Mental health problems developing in these mature years are often the result of an overload of anxiety and life traumas not a reduce capacity to cope. (Little 1986).

Obviously, an elderly person is susceptible to any form of mental health problem. The following three mental disorders were chosen as they are recognised as being the most prevalent for this age group. (Isaacs & Post, 1978; Brooking, 1986; Little, 1986).

- confusional states
- depression
- dementia.

Before going on to consider each of the above in detail it is important to note that although some symptoms, eg, confusion may be present in each disorder it is possible, through a thorough and extensive assessment to differentiate between them. The nurse is often the key person in this process and must therefore be competent and knowledgeable when carrying out the assessment in order to prevent misdiagnosis. If the wrong diagnosis is arrived at then inappropriate treatment will be implemented. This is not an uncommon phenomenon (Jorm, 1987) and may result in the elderly person never recovering from a curable disorder.

Confusional states

This is often seen as a perplexing term leading to confusion itself! These confusional states are also called acute organic states or more recently the term acute brain failure has been used. Many mental health workers are now adopting the latter terminology as they believe it reinforces the pathophysiology involved in this state as in the failure of any human organ. Acute organic states are generally reversible. This syndrome is not to be confused with illnesses identified under the heading chronic organic states or chronic brain failure. These states are irreversible and the onset tends to be insidious, often developing over several years. A classic example of this form of mental disorder is dementia which will be discussed in detail later.

Signs and symptoms   These include:
- clouding of consciousness
- confusion
- disorientation
- restlessness
- apprehension
- sudden onset (Little, 1986; Wattis, 1986)

and are the physical signs and symptoms associated with the following possible causes of confusional states (Table 1).

Table 1. Possible causes of confusional states

CAUSE	EXAMPLE
Infection	Septicemia, pneumonia, meningitis, any acute systemic infection
Intoxication	Alcohol, hypnotics, industrial chemicals
Metabolic disorder	Hepatic and renal failure, hypo/hyperglycaemia, malnutrition, electrolyte disturbance
Cerebral catastrophe	Head injury, cerebrovascular accident, neoplasm, demyelinating disorders, subdural heamatoma
Cardiovascular disorders	Cardiac failure, severe anaemia, anoxia, hypercapnia
Postoperative and postanaesthetic complications	
Epilepsy	
Profound physical exhaustion	

(from Little, 1986, p.385).

It is apparent from the above table that there are multifarious factors which may lead to a person presenting with a confusional state. It is also evident that an elderly person is more likely to suffer from one of the above due to physical deterioration and/or social factors. Why an elderly person is more prone to suffer acute confusion as a result of the identified causes is as yet unclear (Brooking 1986). Thorough assessment is therefore vital with the focus on the patient's physical state. If an underlying physical cause is missed in a patient presenting with the psychological symptoms previously described then they are likely to be labelled as suffering from dementia and their physical problems will go untreated (Wattis, 1986).

The physical cause must be ascertained and the patient treated accordingly. Most confusional states are reversible although some may progress to a chronic organic state due to residual damage.

Depression

As has been identified earlier the ageing process is often viewed as a time of great change for the individual. A sense of loss can be associated with this process. Physical deterioration may result in an inability to carry out usual hobbies and activities and therefore an increase in dependence on others. Debilitating illness such as arthritis or chronic obstructive airways disease once again may result in loss of ability, as well as having to cope with chronic pain. The loss of a social network due to retirement, decreased financial resources and limited access to activities leads to loneliness; as does the tragic loss of partners and close friends. To top all this, society's lack of respect and often uncaring attitude leaves the elderly person in a world to which they feel they no longer belong.

These circumstances often result in an intolerable increase in life stressors, and a breakdown in the individual's coping mechanisms. This breakdown will often result in the person developing a depressive illness. Depression is common among the elderly and the suicide rate, especially in men, increases with age (Brooking 1986). Murphy in his work on depression and old age pinpointed the following risk factors:

- death of a spouse or loved one.
- separation from spouse or loved one.
- a debilitating physical illness.
- poor health of someone close.
- difficulty in family or marital relationships (Murphy, 1982).

He also states that the elderly most vulnerable to the effects of such circumstances were the elderly who lacked a confiding intimate relationship.

Signs and symptoms An in depth analysis of the clinical manifestations of depression is not within the remit of this book and the reader is advised to consult an up to date text on mental health. However, low mood, tearfulness, anxiety, apathy and poor communication are signs and symptoms . Cognitive abilities are slow, thought processes muddled with obvious memory impairment. The elderly person experiencing this syndrome will often present as confused and disorientated. Rational thought may be lost and the person may be experiencing delusions or hallucinations. These disorders usually involve unpleasant beliefs or perceptual disturbances, eg, that the individual's body is rotting inside, or voices are telling the person that they are worthless. The person may be irrationally suspicious and untrusting of other persons.

Physical picture   There is loss of interest in physical appearance and hygiene. In addition, neglect of diet and fluid intake often result in dehydration and constipation. Slow laconic movement can be seen.

Social picture   Reduced social contact and even shunning of friends and loved ones may result in social isolation and a breakdown in relationships. Inappropriate and socially unacceptable behaviour may be exhibited if they are experiencing hallucinations, delusions. Loss of control of finances mean that debts may rise.

Some or all of the above may occur when an elderly person is experiencing a depressive illness. Also it is important to note that the severity of the symptoms will also vary. If an elderly person is well dressed and communicative it does not mean that they cannot be depressed!

Another factor which must be considered is the detection of such an illness. With the elderly person living alone and having reduced contact with others, the depression is often not discerned until the illness is well established, making treatment more difficult.

Depression vs dementia

It is important to recognise that this is an area where misdiagnosis is common (Jorm, 1987). The implications for an incorrect diagnosis can be dire. Although an elderly person with a depressive illness can present with almost identical symptoms to those of the early onset of dementia, depression is curable. Dementia, as can be seen in the next section, is not. Therefore if a person is wrongly labelled as having dementia when they have depression they will be treated inappropriately and recovery will not occur (Jorm, 1987; Brooking, 1986; Little, 1986). Once again thorough assessment is imperative, particularly of the patient's cognitive functioning. Robins *et al* (1984) offer some criteria for diagnosing 'reversible dementia' caused by depression.

1. The onset of the illness is most likely to have been recent; a matter of months rather than years.
2. Person was more likely to have experienced a depression before.
3. Current depressed mood.
4. Irrational beliefs expressing feelings of hopelessness, that they were to blame for their predicament and that they were physically ill.
5. Likely to have a disturbed eating pattern.

Dementia

"Dementia is the global impairment of higher cortical functions including memory, the capacity to solve problems of day to day living, the performance of learned perceptio-motor skills, the correct use of social skills and control of emotional reactions in the absence of gross clouding of consciousness. The condition is often irreversible and progressive." (Royal College of Physicians, 1981).

Dementia is a syndrome, and disorders which can produce this syndrome are Alzehimer's disease, multi infarct dementia, Huntingtons Chorea, Parkinson's disease, Pick's disease, depression and AIDS.

For the elderly person there are three main disorders which can result in dementia

- Alzheimer's
- multi-infarct (due to the narrowing of the arteries) cerebral disorder
- mixed causation (Brooking, 1986; Jorm, 1987).

Why a person develops Alzheimer's disease is as yet unproven but there is increasing evidence to link it with the aluminium levels in the brain, plus the suggestion of hereditary risk. Dementia does have a distinct cerebral pathology depending on the type. Alzheimer's produces senile plaques and neurofibralliry tangles while multi infarct dementia reveals narrowing of the lumen of the arteries and necrotic tissue (Marsden, 1978). Therefore a finite diagnosis of the type of dementia cannot be made until after the death of the sufferer. There is now a tendency to use Alzheimer's disease to describe the condition of any elderly person suffering from this chronic organic state.

Signs and symptoms The American Psychiatric Association (1980) propose that the following features must be present for dementia to be diagnosed.
1. Loss of intellectual abilities which is severe enough to interfere with social or occupational functioning.
2. Memory impairment.
3. At least one of the following:
    - impairment of abstract thinking
    - impared judgement
    - other disturbances of higher brain functions, involving language, complex sequences of action, perception or construction.
    - personality change
4. Not delirious or intoxicated.
5. Either one of the following:
    - evidence from the history, physical examination, or laboratory tests of some organic factor which could plausibly produce the disorder.
    - in the absence of such evidence an organic factor can be presumed if other psychiatric disorders have been ruled out. (Cited in Jorm, 1987, p.2).

This criteria recognises the importance of ruling out any other illnesses which may produce similar symptoms, but it does not differentiate or clarify the symptoms. Therefore it is important to remember that dementia   is an insidious chronic disease, it is progressive and irreversible. If an elderly person is suffering from dementia then the symptoms will gradually become more severe.

A useful analogy to try to help understand the destructive nature of the illness is to liken a person's life to a book. The first page contains the most recent memories, experiences and learning. When dementia strikes it is as if page after page is being torn from the book. Gradually the person loses their memories and learning, resulting in a regression back through earlier periods of their lives, and a loss of social skills. Progressively the individual's personality changes until they often become unrecognisable to loved ones.

As can be seen dementia is a devastating and frightening illness. Fortunately public awareness of the disease is increasing and with that the illness is no longer being swept under the carpet but has a higher profile. Relatives of the sufferers are being encouraged to talk about their problems in caring for their loved ones and support groups such as the Alzheimer's Disease Society have been formed. The person suffering from dementia ultimately finds themself in a world of their own and it is the carer who needs support and guidance to cope with the illness.

References

Brooking, J.I. (1986) In Redfern, S. *Nursing Elderly People*. Churchill Livingstone, Edinburgh.

Isaacs, A.D. and Prost, F. (Ed) (1978) *Studies in Geriatric Psychiatry*. John Wiley & Son, London.

Jorm , A.F. (1987) *Understanding Senile Dementia*. Croom Helm, London.

Lyttle, J. (1986) *Mental Disorder: Its Care and Treatment*. Bailliere Tindall, London.

Murphy, E. (1982) Social origins of depression in old age. *British Journey of Psychiatry* **141** 35–42.

Robins, P.V. *et al* (1984) Criteria for diagnosing reversible dementia caused by depression. *British Journal of Psychiatry* **144** 488–92.

Wattis, J. (1986) Seven stages towards a less confused patient. *Geriatric Medicine*, February, 45–50.

31

Management of mental health problems

Lesley Donovan, BSc, RMN, RGN, CertEd
Senior Lecturer in Nursing, British Polytechnic

The foundation underpinning the approach to the management of any patient problem is a detailed assessment. Once again it cannot be reiterated enough that in the realms of mental health the elderly are at risk of being misdiagnosed and, as a result, problems may be mismanaged.

There are many nursing models which offer a framework for the assessment of the individual. Roper (1989) in particular is often associated with and applied in care of the elderly settings. None of the nursing models to date offer the nurse the structure and focus needed to assist in the assessment of the mental functions of the elderly. Fortunately there are tools available to support the assessment procedure which specifically focus on the cognitive abilities of the individual. For example, the Clifton Assessment Procedures for the Elderly (CAPE) was developed by psychologists as a succinct and uncomplicated method of assessing the cognitive and behavioural abilities of elderly people (Pattie and Gilleard, 1979). It is important for nurses to be aware of and familiarise themselves with such tools. A variety of tools which as part of the assessment focus on different aspects of the elderly person's abilities will lead to a comprehensive and meaningful assessment. No single assessment tool exists which tells the nurse everything they need to know about a patient (Barker, 1985).

Once an exhaustive assessment has been completed the nurse will then become aware of the patient's problems and implement an effective plan of care to manage these.

The following are some of the therapies which can be executed to help manage certain mental health problems as experienced by an elderly person. The most commonly used interventions will be examined, but it is important to note that this is not inclusive of all therapies available.

Reality Orientation (RO)
Aim of therapy   The title of this therapy actually describes the aim of this approach to care. It is to orientate the individual to reality; that is to encourage an awareness of what is happening in the here and now and what the here and now is. The main objective is to improve the patient's

cognitive functioning by focussing on their deteriorating memory.

Reality orientation is used in the rehabilitation of an individual experiencing memory loss, confusion and time – place disorientation. (Lyttle, 1986; Drummond, 1978). This therapy has certainly been subject to the most scrutiny by the caring professions and several studies conclude that RO is a viable method of treating the confused elderly person (Hanley *et al*, 1981; Holoden and Woods, 1982).

Implementing the therapy   There are two main types of RO
1. 24-Hour or informal RO.
2. Classroom or structured RO.

With 24-Hour RO the role of the nurse is to provide the stimulus for the patient through the interaction and control of the environment. The first approach involve the nurse through her interactions with the patient reminding them of the time, place and person, eg, "It is 12.30 now Mrs Jones. I am taking you to the dining room for lunch." "Hello Mrs Jones, I am Sally. Did you enjoy your breakfast? What did you have?"

It is important that this dialogue is seen to be as natural as possible and should not consist of a bombardment of questions as the patient may feel they are undergoing a 24-hour memory test! The nurse should approach the patient with kindness and respect as there is a risk of sounding patronising when carrying out reality orientation.

The nurse can also use memory prompt to reinforce and help the patient to focus on the subject of the orientation, for example when out walking identifying the daffodils as flowers associated with spring. Memory prompts can be created in the ward as well as at a personal or environmental level. Examples of personal memory prompts:
- patient's favourite pictures.
- photographs/photo album.
- own clothes.
- favourite ornaments.

Examples of environmental memory prompts:
- large signs to identify rooms.
- colour coded doors.
- large clocks.
- date display.
- weather board.
- current affairs board.

Classroom RO should be considered as a supplement to 24-Hour RO. In classroom RO the nurse would facilitate a group of elderly patients through a specific aspect of the orientation, eg, the nurse may want the patients to focus on the month of the year and encourage discussion of events, weather related to that month, or she may want the patients to learn each others' names. The emphasis is on group interaction and the experience should be an enjoyable one for the patient. Therefore the nurse utilising this form of RO must not only have a good knowledge base but be competent in facilitating groups.

Benefits to patients

If employed correctly the benefits of this therapy are the enhancement and maintenance of the memory resulting in an improvement in the patient's quality of life, and promoting a feeling of security.

There has been a growing dissatisfaction by nurses with RO over the years. This stems from what is seen as the indiscriminate use of RO and the narrowness of the therapy (Morton and Bleatham, 1988; Akerlund and Norberg, 1986; Jones, 1985).

RO can, if used unwisely, be damaging to the patient's emotional stability. As Morton and Bleatham so aptly state,"RO can do little except drag the unwilling subject back to an intolerable reality – provoking anger, misery and pain." This view may be a little extreme but it is an inherent danger if RO is mismanaged.

For the above reasons a different group of therapies have emerged which concentrate not on improving the patient's memory but on the feelings and emotions the patient is experiencing. These should not be seen as an alternative to RO but as its companions in trying to improve the quality of life of the confused elderly patient. These therapies will now be examined in more detail.

Therapies

These three therapies, validation therapy, group psychotherapy and resolution therapy, all attempt to focus on the patient's feelings and emotions. They ignore any memory and intellectual impairment, resolving not to correct misconceptions, but encouraging the patient to explore how they feel. Again these therapies are for implementation with an elderly person who is experiencing confusion and memory loss.

Group psychotherapy   In group psychotherapy, the nurse directs a group of patients to discuss topics of their choice. The facilitator will explore the feelings and emotions behind what the patients are saying in an effort to identify problems and perhaps examine solutions. The emphasis is on the group members exploring feelings and thereby stimulating discussion at a higher cognitive level. A small study conducted by Akerland and Nerberg (1983) concluded that patients involved in the group psychotherapy did function at a higher cognitive level than a control group only experiencing RO. This psychodynamic approach appeared to support the patient's mental processes.

These findings must be interpreted within the limitations of the study size and the country where the research was conducted, which was Sweden. Nevertheless these findings are promising and more research should be encouraged in order to develop this area further.

Validation therapy   Validation therapy also focuses on the analyses of feelings by encouraging the re-experiencing of past enjoyments or emotions, or attempting to resolve past conflicts and problems (Jones, 1985). Validation can be used individually or facilitated through group work. Here factual errors are overlooked and meaningful dialogue encouraged. For example if the patient states that they are worried about their sister, the nurse does not remind the patient that her sister is dead but encourages the patient to express exactly what her worries are. The focus is on the "subjective experience not the objective fact." (Morton and Bleatham, 1988).

Resolution therapy   Lastly resolution therapy is a concept proposed by Goudie and Stokes (1989). For this therapy the authors recommend a break away from a psychodynamic approach and the adoption of a more open and accepting stance, rather than the analytical emphasis of the other therapies discussed. The rationale behind this is as follows. Firstly staff may misinterpret the feelings and content of the patient's dialogue because of the emphasis on the analytical and problem-solving approach adopted. Secondly, and a very important issue, not all elderly people suffering from confusion have the intellectual ability and the cognitive processes necessary for abstract reasoning and problem solving (Goudie and Stokes, 1989); these therapies are often implemented with patients suffering from dementia. Therefore the emphasis of this therapy is not on the interpretative but the supportive, allowing the expression of feelings and emotions but not looking for the reason why. It finally explores ways in which the individual can cope with these feelings.

Implementing the therapies

The nurse must decide which therapeutic approach is applicable to her patient. Once again a good understanding of the patient's needs and their cognitive abilities is paramount.

In order to carry out any of the above therapies the nurse must be skilled in the art of counselling and group facilitation. She must have a thorough understanding of the processes involved in each therapy and to this end should have received appropriate education. The aims and objectives for the instigation of the therapy must be clearly identified.

Benefits to patients   It is important to give an elderly confused person the recognition they deserve. They are valuable, feeling human beings. These therapies offer a route to achieving this end. By encouraging the expression of feelings and giving value to them the nurse can try to engender a sense of worth within the individual; then, if appropriate she can try to help the patient resolve or manage his feelings. One can only hope that the person's experience of their illness will be less distressing.

Reminiscence therapy

This therapeutic intervention is usually implemented for an individual who is experiencing a depressive illness without confusion. The title of this therapy also indicates the aim of the therapy, that is to encourage the elderly person to reflect upon past experiences. It is hoped that unresolved issues may be concluded through dealing with conflicts and ambiguities they raise (Lyttle, 1986).

Implementing the therapy Once more the role of the nurse as a facilitator comes to the fore. Interactive skills especially counselling are also at the root of this therapy. The nurse must encourage the patient to reflect on their past experiences and examine the meaning of significant events. The feelings and emotions associated with these past events will also be discussed and brought to the fore. The nurse will then focus on strategies available to help the patient cope with these.

Reminiscence therapy using more general stimuli, records, film, magazines, may also be used with confused elderly people. It aims to stimulate interaction between patients around particular themes, thereby making them less isolated and affirming them as useful, communicating beings. Its use can certainly enrich the patient's environment and provide meaningful activity. In recent years however there has been much indiscriminate use of reminiscence by inexperienced staff and there is a definite need for further research into the effective use of the therapy in this manner with the elderly mentally infirm.

Benefit to patients By facilitating the examination of 'unfinished business', hopefully the patient will be able to resolve many of their feelings and become more positive about the present and the future.

New coping strategies can be developed by the identification of the factors which cause the patient to feel stressed. Specific problem areas may be identified which would have otherwise gone undetected. For example, it may become apparent through the patient's reminiscence that they have not grieved properly for the death of a spouse; if this is the case then the appropriate intervention can be brought about. In this case bereavement counselling could be started.

Finally it is important to highlight the danger of distressing the patient unduly. Never force a patient to talk about a situation which makes him or her feel uncomfortable.

Music and art therapy

Music and art therapy are two approaches to care worth mentioning when caring for a patient who has problems associated with depression. These therapies can be utilised in two ways. Firstly they may be used as vehicles for the release of feelings and thoughts. For example, a sad piece of music will allow sad feelings and thoughts to flow, while a jaunty, jolly piece of music may facilitate happy positive feelings (Lyttle, 1986). Secondly music or art therapy can help in the analysis of feelings and emotions, through encouraging the patient to explain and interpret the picture he has painted or the piece of music chosen. Again care is needed not to read too much into the patient's art or choice of music; these activities are very subjective and should be seen simply as tools to facilitate discussion of feelings between the nurse and the patient.

The main aim of these therapies therefore is to enable the patients to project their feelings and thoughts through the art or music. Often patients feel more comfortable with this form of expressing themselves rather than just having to talk about how they feel.

Implementing the therapy   The nurse does not have to be a budding Picasso or Chopin. But she must be confident in her ability to start a therapy that may cause distress to the patient in a similar way as discussed when considering reminiscence therapy. These therapies can be executed in groups, or on an individual basis. If in groups the nurse must have control of the situation and must be able to guide and support all the group members. It is also important to provide the correct environment especially for the music therapy ie. comfortable chairs, dim lighting, no background noise, good quality recordings.

Benefits to patients   The obvious benefit is that the patient is allowed to, and actively encouraged to express their feelings in an indirect way. As has already been identified this method is often seen as less threatening than a direct one to one dialogue. Nurse/patient interaction is centred around an event and discussion is encouraged. Hopefully, the patient's awareness of their feelings, emotions and how these are affecting him will be enhanced.

The patients can learn to use these therapies themselves allowing them to control the expression and release of their own emotion through increasing their self awareness.

Drug therapy

This is the last therapy to be discussed in this chapter and it has been purposefully left to last as drugs are so often reached for before other therapies are considered. It is important to remember that any drug therapy for the elderly person can potentially lead to the creation of further problems. Elderly people are most at risk of drug toxicity often due to a higher sensitivity to the drug prescribed (Redfern, 1986). Another factor to bear in mind is the interaction between different drugs. Again the elderly person is more likely to already be taking a variety of drugs to improve their physical health.

If the patient is suffering from dementia there is no drug yet discovered which can in any way interfere with the chronic deterioration of mental functions (Wattis, 1986). Where drug therapy may be applicable is in the treatment of behavioural problems associated with dementia such as physical and verbal aggression. Here a tranquilizer may be used to help calm the patient and render their behaviour more socially acceptable. The patient therefore is less likely to be rejected and become socially isolated because of threatening behaviour. The drug would probably belong to the phenothiazine group, eg, thioridazine.

A patient experiencing a depressive type of illness is more likely to be prescribed drugs. It is important to see this drug regime, if it must be implemented, as a small part of the overall approach to care. Tricyclic anti-depressants are an ever expanding group of drugs and have been shown to be effective in improving a patient's mood. Initially the patient may require anti-depressants to lift his mood and make him more susceptive to other forms of therapy such as counselling or reminiscence therapy.

If the patient is experiencing debilitating anxiety the anxiolytics such as Ativan and Valium can be used. Again this should be seen as a short term measure as these drugs are notoriously addictive.

Drug therapy must be considered as a part of any treatment regime. Often however, it is all too easy to control a person's behaviour through drugs rather than to offer more stimulating and meaningful therapies. Against this the nurse must be perpetually vigilant.

References
Ackerlund, B. and Norberg, A. (1986) Group psychotherapy with demented patients. *Geriatric Nursing*, March/April, 83.
Bleathman, C. and Merden, I. (1988) Does it matter whether it's Tuesday or Friday. *Nursing Times*, 10 Feb, **84** (6).
Drummond, L. (1978) A practice guide to RO: A treatment approach to confusion and disorientation. *The Gerontologist*, **18** (6).
Gaudie, F. and Stokes, G. (1989) Understanding confusion. *Nursing Times*, Sept 27 **857** (39).
Hanley, L.G. *et al* (1981) Reality orientation and dementia: a controlled trial of two approaches. *British Journey Phychiatry*, **138**, 10–14.
Holden, V.P. and Woods, R.T. (1982) *Reality Orientation: Psychological Approaches to the 'Confused' Elderly*. Churchill Livingstone, Edinburgh.
Jones, G. (1985) Validation therapy: a companion to reality orientation. *The Canadian Nurse* **81** (3) 20–3.
Lyttle, J. (1986) *Mental Disorders: Carers and Treatment*. Bailliere Tindall, London.
Paltie, A.H. and Gilleard, C.J. (1979) *Clifton Assessment Procedures for the Elderly* (CAPE), Hodder & Stoughton, London.
Redfern, S. (Ed) (1986) *Nursing Elderly People*, Churchill Livingstone, Edinburgh.
Wattis, J. (1986) Seven stages towards a less confused patient. *Geriatric Medicine*, Feb.

32

Tablets to take away: why some elderly people fail to comply with their medication

Sally Quilligan, RGN, DipN
Currently studying BEd (Hons) at South Bank Polytechnic

In 1981, Bliss revealed that drug related problems accounted for 10 per cent of all hospital admissions in elderly people. While some of these could be explained by the age-related changes in physiological and metabolic processes and by polypharmacy, some were also a consequence of patients failing to take their medications correctly (Bliss, 1981). My own experiences as a medical ward sister appeared to support this finding and stimulated me to investigate the problem at a local level. In doing so I was surprised to see that, although nursing studies about discharge planning and self-medication briefly mention the problem of non-compliance with medication, there have to date been few detailed nursing papers (Entwistle, 1989).

Increased life expectancy

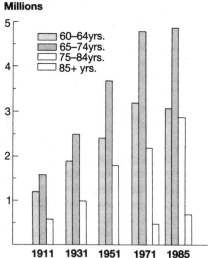

Figure 1. Population trends above 60 years, adapted from Social Trends (1987).

In 1980, Williamson reported that one quarter of all elderly patients admitted to hospital suffer from four or more chronic conditions, and that 80 per cent of all elderly patients take some prescribed medication. Statistics (Figure 1) clearly demonstrate that elderly people have an increase in life expectancy, and although this demographic trend may be attributed to many causes, a major factor is medication.

There is, however, strong evidence to suggest that elderly people frequently fail to comply with their medication regime – the Royal College of Physicians (1984) emphasised this in their report demonstrating that 75 per cent make errors in their compliance to prescriptions, of which 25 per cent are potentially serious. An extensive literature search seems to demonstrate that compliance with long-term medication is about 50 per cent. Non-compliance with a drug regime may disrupt or reverse the possible benefit of the preventive, curative or palliative effect the drug provides. It may involve the patient in further investigative procedures, cause discomfort and physical suffering. Illness

1. The medication to take home is checked by a trained nurse, but invariably given to the patient by a student nurse.

2. The medication is handed to the patient at their bedside less than an hour before discharge.

3. Little attempt is made to check the patient's knowledge about the medication.

4. With the occasional exception of patients on Warfarin and steroids, no explanation of likely side-effects is given.

5. Patients' ability to open containers, dispense their medication, or read the labels is not checked.

6. No mention is made about the danger of hoarding previously prescribed medication.

7. Occasionally, family members are told when to administer the drug, but there are no planned teaching sessions.

8. No explanation is given of how to obtain a new prescription unless the patient asks.

9. No reference is made in the care plan to this aspect of discharge preparation.

Table 1. Outcome of observations.

and possible readmission to hospital may upset daily routines, disrupt social relationships with family and friends and possibly induce deep anxiety for the elderly person. With dwindling resources and the current NHS crisis, the additional cost generated must also be considered.

This appears to suggest that failure of elderly people to take their medicines correctly after discharge from hospital does have far-reaching consequences. It is surely in the healthcare professional's and society's interest to ensure elderly people are able to administer their drugs safely and correctly.

Fully aware of the importance of correct medication administration among elderly people after discharge from hospital, I decided to review current practice within my own clinical area, a four ward medical unit. This proved a salutary experience as shown by the outcome (Table 1), and I would suggest that the results might be mirrored on hundreds of other wards up and down the country.

Factors affecting non-compliance

"Reasons for error and non-compliance are varied and . . . external factors such as poor record keeping by healthcare professionals . . . inadequate labelling, packaging and presentation may all contribute to the problem, as may the patients' knowledge of their medication and the availability or lack of adequate instructions in their safe and appropriate use" (Parish, 1983).

Size, shape and colour of pills   "The white one is my water pill." Past experience has shown me that some patients relate the action of their drug to its colour. The World Health Organisation (1981) recognises this and suggests that where several drugs are prescribed they should be of different shapes and colours. This may however be failing to treat the patient as an individual, assessment might reveal many elderly people who would know exactly which tablets and what dose to take. The shape of the tablet also needs to be easy to handle. Limited movement and painful joints are a feature of the lives of many old people and they may find it difficult to pick up small, round tablets. Even if a suitable form of medication is prescribed, a repeat prescription may, as Warren (1985) notes, be a different brand or generic product, and this variation in the tablets' appearance may be a contributing factor to drug non-compliance.

Containers   "We have established beyond reasonable doubt that it is difficult, if not impossible, for some elderly patients to open childproof containers and remove tablets from bubble packs without shooting them across the floor" (MacGuire, 1987). In 1983 Parish clearly stated that healthcare professionals should be alert to the fact that child resistant containers are a potential source of medication error. This is reinforced by Halworth's (1984) outpatient study of 92 elderly people, in which he found that a quarter of them admitted to having transferred their tablets to an alternative container. Clearly, blister packaging, foil packaging and childproof containers present difficulties, indeed childproof would appear to generally be synonymous with elderly proof.

Davidson (1973) demonstrated that a glass container with a screw top lid was the most convenient for elderly people to use. However, this requires a firm handgrip, and handgrip becomes progressively weaker with age, which may explain Bellamy's (1981) more recent finding that many elderly people could not completely close screw-capped containers. The ability to open a container depends on eyesight as well as manual dexterity, and Coote (1984) proposes that people with poor eyesight should place each prescription in a different shaped bottle. In my experience I have found patients prefer a clear glass palm-sized bottle with screw cap or push-on lid. There are, however, those with particular needs who will find even these difficult. Coote (1984) suggests that for people with severe hand tremors, the use of Dines high impact polystyrene tubs with pull-off lids may be beneficial.

Labelling   "Pharmacists should provide typewritten labels with clear and complete instructions and ensure that the patient can read and understand the label" (*Drug and Therapeutics Bulletin*, 1980).

It is common knowledge that part of the ageing process results in a loss of visual acuity and may result in a loss of ability to read effectively. Although labels are now computer printed, they are often too small and difficult for elderly people with poor eyesight to read. It is, then, somewhat alarming to consider that in Halworth's (1984) outpatient study, 34 per cent stated that if the instructions were not on the label they would not remember how to take their drugs correctly. It is also disturbing to note that Bliss (1981) revealed that 50 per cent of GPs' repeat prescriptions have no instructions other than take as directed.

Instructions themselves can cause problems if ambiguous. 'One tablet three times daily', or 'one tablet at breakfast, lunch or dinner' may, as MacGuire (1987) notes, cause problems – when is dinner, what is lunch? It may then be better to state take one tablet at 08.00 hrs, 12 noon, 18.00 hrs. What is certain is that research has demonstrated associating specific times of day with medication may improve compliance (*Drug and Therapeutics Bulletin*, 1980).

Written instructions   "Written information about the medication each patient is taking, which they could take home, may help to increase their knowledge level and indirectly compliance" (Waters, 1987). In 1970, Skeet argued that written instructions for patients to take home would increase understanding and memory. Although not all elderly patients need additional instructions, those with memory or hearing impairment may find some useful.

The progressive hearing loss associated with ageing results in a progressive loss of ability to hear high frequencies and may significantly affect ability to understand speech. In a community survey of over-70 year-olds, Gilhome (1981) found 60 per cent had some hearing impairment and, of more concern, 25 per cent of these refused to accept any suggestion that they might have a hearing impairment. This must alert nurses to the fact that elderly people may try to hide their hearing loss and that verbal instructions may often need to be written down.

Memory aids   "Intellectual decline is not a universal and inevitable part of growing old" (Redfern, 1985), but 25 per cent of the population over 80 are moderately severely demented (Cormack, 1985) and many others who are not demented experience short-term memory loss. People with memory or orientation problems may experience difficulty and fail to take their medication as directed, and will require to be given extra time when preparing for their discharge. Even after this, some may have such severe problems that they are unable to manage, but others may benefit from learning to use a memory aid.

Memory aids range from the simple device made by the family, such as setting out doses for a day or week in egg cartons, to the more complex commercial product such as the Dosett Box. I could find no recent research to support the type of simple device already discussed, but it may act to encourage the family and or friends to become involved in reminding the patient about adhering to the drug regimen. The use of commercial aids to improve compliance is somewhat debatable. A ward using the Dosett Box system within my clinical area found it complicated, and the *Drug and Therapeutics Bulletin* (1980) notes that they may be difficult to use and awkward to refill.

Patient teaching   "We believe that teaching patients to take their medication correctly should form part of the rehabilitation programme for patients leaving hospital" (Crome *et al*, 1980). The review of current practice indicated that the information given to patients about their medication was hopelessly inadequate, and Wilson Barnett (1985) suggests that the implication of discharging patients home unprepared and without adequate knowledge is that they will fail to cope.

The benefits of using teaching plans as a means of improving knowledge and compliance have been clearly demonstrated (MacDonald, 1987). However, the author found little evidence that nurses recognise their role in relation to teaching about medication, and no reference to formal teaching on medication on any of the care plans.

The literature does appear to identify that there is no framework for patient education. Instruction is sometimes given in the form of informal chats in response to questioning, or as Price (1984) notes, as a menu or list of facts to be taught after a specific operation or procedure. This type of patient education is self-limiting and a framework is required which all nurses, including students, can use with ease. The familiar format of the nursing process as utilised by Wilson Barnett (1985) provides a basis for such patient teaching.

The way forward

This review of the literature has shown that many of the factors that influence medication compliance have been recognised for as long as a decade. It is suggested that in many clinical areas the importance of this information is being ignored and that nurses need now to consider the significance of their role in this important aspect of care.

References

Bellamy, K. *et al* (1981) Letter: Granny-proof bottles. *Journal of the Royal College of General Practitioners*, **31**, 2, 124.

Bliss, M.R. (1981) Prescribing for the elderly. *British Medical Journal*, **283**, 203–06.

Coote, J. (1984) Helping the elderly with their medicines. *The Pharmaceutical Journal*, November 17, 608–09.

Cormack, D. (Ed) (1985) Geriatric Nursing – A Conceptual Approach. Blackwell Scientific Publications, Oxford.

Crome, P. *et al* (1980) Drug compliance in elderly hospital in-patients. *The Practitioner*, **224**, 782.

Davidson, J. (1973) Presentation and packaging of drugs for the elderly. *Journal of Hospital Pharmacy*, 31, 180–84.

Drug and Therapeutics Bulletin (1980) Helping elderly patients to manage their medicines. *DTB*, **18**, 23, 89–91.

Entwistle, B. (1989) A problem of compliance. *Nursing Standard*, **20**, 3, 33–35.

Gilhome-Herbst, K.R. and Humprey, C.M. (1981) Prevalence of hearing impairment in the elderly living at home. *Journal of the Royal College of Practitioners*, **31**, 155–60.

Halworth, B.R. and Goldberg, L.A. (1984) Geriatric patients' understanding of labelling of medicines. *British Journal of Pharmaceutical Practice*, **6**, 6–14.

MacDonald, E.T. *et al* (1977) Improving drug compliance after hospital discharge. *British Medical Journal*, **2**, 618–21.

MacGuire, J. *et al* (1987) Two pink and one blue. *Nursing Times*, **83**, 2, 32-33.

Parish, P. *et al* (1983) The elderly and their use of medicine. Kings Fund Project Paper, No. 40, Kings Fund, London.

Price, B. (1984) From hospital to home. A framework for patient education. *Nursing Times*, **80**, 8 Aug, 28–30.

The Royal College of Physicians (1984) Medications for the Elderly. Report of the Royal College of Physicians. *Journal of the Royal College of Physicians*, **18**, 7–17.

Skeet, M. (1970) Home from Hospital. Macmillan, London.

Waters, K. (1987) Discharge planning: an exploratory study of the process of discharge planning on geriatric wards. *Journal of Advanced Nursing*, **12**, 71–83.

Wilson-Barnett, J. (1985) Principles of patient teaching. *Nursing Times*, **81**, 13, 28–29.

Williamson, J. (1978) Principles of drug action and usage. In: Isaacs, B. (Ed) Recent Advances in Geriatric Medicine. Churchill Livingstone, Edinburgh.

World Health Organisation (1981) Health Care in the Elderly. Report of the Technical Group on use of medicaments by the Elderly. *Drugs*, **22**, 279–94.

33

When should you take your tablets? Teaching elderly people about their medication

Sally Quilligan, RGN, DipN
Currently studying BEd (Hons) at South Bank Polytechnic

If 10 per cent of hospital admissions of elderly people can be linked to drug-related problems (Bliss, 1981), this must in part reflect that the present level of patient teaching about medication is inadequate. As Wilson Barnett (1985) has suggested, the implication of discharging a patient home without adequate knowledge is that they will fail to cope.

In 1977 MacDonald found that a predischarge counselling session of 15 minutes improved compliance by as much as 50 per cent, and there is much recent evidence to demonstrate that teaching is beneficial and may improve knowledge and compliance (Johnston, 1986). There is, however, little documented data to show that nurses recognise their role, in relation to teaching about medication. Within my own clinical area, while patient teaching was viewed as important, it was often omitted when the ward was busy. In addition, there was no reference to formal teaching about medication on any of the care plans. This accords with Water's (1987) experience in the North of England.

Lack of framework

What the literature does appear to identify is that there is no framework for patient education. Instruction is sometimes given in the form of informal chats in response to questioning, or as Price (1984) notes, as a menu or list of facts to be taught after a specific operation or procedure. This type of patient education is self-limiting – we need a framework which all nurses, including students, can use easily. The familiar format of the nursing process (Wilson Barnett, 1985) provides such a basis.

Who should perform the teaching? This appears to be another point for debate. Many writers suggest pharmacists should counsel patients (Sweeney, 1989; Johnston, 1986), whereas others suggest that because nurses spend most time with patients, it should be primarily their role (Royal College of Physicians, 1984). I would argue that it is the teaching *per se*, rather than who does the teaching, that matters.

·Teaching patients to take their medication correctly should, as Crome (1980) suggests, form part of the rehabilitation programme, and should begin with the first nursing assessment following admission. The nurse must assess what precipitated this admission and ask the next of kin to bring in all the tablets patients have at home. It may also be necessary to ascertain how willing the family are to become involved in a teaching plan. As patients' conditions improve, the drug round can be used to assess their knowledge about both their disease and why they have to take their medication. Drug rounds thus become part of the learning process, and where appropriate, this could eventually be in the form of carefully supervised self-medication. Patients would then have a chance to familiarise themselves with their medication and discuss any needs or worries, while the nurses would have the opportunity to assess patients' knowledge, evaluate previous teaching and also identify those patients who may fail to take their medication due to physical or mental impairment and thus alert the community services. Following the drug rounds, nurses and patients could establish new goals – further individualised teaching sessions, involving patients' families wherever possible, can then be planned around patients' needs.

The drug round could thus provide continuous assessment and evaluation, and nurses would, as Redfern (1985) suggests, prepare patients for discharge throughout their hospital stay. Progress and teaching sessions given could then be formally documented within patients' care plans.

Suggested framework
The following framework is one way of ensuring elderly patients are given enough support in learning about their medication. It takes the steps of the nursing process as its structure.

Patient assessment
1. Does the patient understand his or her disease, and why their tablets must be taken?
2. Does the patient want to learn? Is he or she able to learn?
3. Can family be involved in the process?

Planning teaching Use realistic, clear, *joint* goals on agreed topics and if possible arrange discussions when family can be present. Set dates and times for the sessions to ensure they are not missed.

Implement Limit teaching to three topics in each session. Discuss the patient's worries and check previous knowledge. Remind the patient of the topic and goal, and limit the session to 15 minutes maximum.

Evaluate On-going assessment of medication and the teaching programme is required (see Table 1).

By using this simple framework the patient's individual needs may be accounted for. Below is a checklist of areas that, ideally, most patients

1. Patient must be able to explain to the nurse at the end of session what has been discussed.
2. The patient's knowledge, needs and worries should be reassessed when he or she receives drugs on drug round, thus demonstrating change in knowledge.
3. A follow-up questionnaire should be conducted on discharge, to gain feedback on whether the teaching helped.
4. The nurse should assess the experience and recognise any lack of knowledge.

Table 1. Evaluation.

should be aware of.

Many intrapersonal factors such as motivation may influence compliance with medication following discharge and over this the nurse has no control. With a little planning the nurse can provide the elderly person with a real choice. With a sound knowledge base and user friendly medication they can now decide whether or not to comply rather than being in many cases simply unable to comply.

References

American Society of Hospital Pharmacists (1984) Guidelines on pharmacist conducted patient counselling. *American Journal of Hospital Pharmacy*, **41**, 331.

Bliss, M.R. (1981) Prescribing for the elderly. *British Medical Journal*, **283**, 203–06.

Crome, P. *et al* (1980) Drug compliance in elderly hospital in-patients. *The Practitioner*, **224**, 782.

Gooch, J. (1985) Medication to take home. *Professional Nurse*, **1**, 1, 15–16.

Johnston, M. *et al* (1986) Facilitating comprehension of discharge medication in elderly patients. *Age and Ageing*, **15**, 304–06.

MacDonald, E.T. *et al* (1977) Improving drug compliance after hospital discharge. *British Medical Journal*, **2**, 618–21.

Price, B. (1984) From hospital to home: a framework for patient education. *Nursing Times*, **80**, 32, 28–30.

Redfern, S. (1985) Nursing Elderly People. Churchill Livingstone, Edinburgh.

The Royal College of Physicians (1984) Medications for the Elderly. Report of the Royal College of Physicians. *Journal of the Royal College of Physicians*, **18**, 1, 7–17.

Sweeney, S. *et al* (1989) The impact of the clinical pharmacist on compliance in a geriatric population. *The Pharmaceutical Journal*, Feb 18, R4–R6.

Warren, J. *et al* (1985) Drug compliance in the elderly after discharge from hospital. *The Pharmaceutical Journal*, April 13, 472–73.

Waters, K. (1987) Discharge planning: an exploratory study of the process of discahrge planning on geriatric wards. *Journal of Advanced Nursing*, **12**, 1, 71–83.

Wilson-Barnett, J. (1985) Principles of patient teaching. *Nursing Times*, **81**, 8, 28–29.

34

Surgery in old age

Gill Garrett, BA, RGN, RCNT, DN (London), Cert Ed (FE), RNT, FP Cert
Freelance Lecturer, Bristol

In recent years new surgical techniques have transformed the lives of many elderly people; classically the replacement of arthritic hip joints has meant a new lease of life for older people previously seriously immobilised and in pain and new ophthalmic procedures have restored useful vision to many. Improved anaesthesia has ensured that surgery is now safer for those in later life whose respiratory or cardio-vascular status would have rendered them inoperable in the past. Judicious timing of elective surgery in early old age, for example, repair of inguinal hernia, which pre-empts the need for emergency surgery (further to the hernia's strangulation) at a later, less robust stage, is now routine surgical practice. Consequently at any one time a high proportion of surgical beds will be occupied by older people and the surgical nurse will require knowledge and skills to meet their specific needs.

For, despite the great forward strides indicated above, surgery does present greater problems later in life, demanding of the nurse perceptive assessment, careful identification of actual and potential problems and meticulous care planning and implementation. An understanding of the processes of ageing and their effects on daily living activities, post-operative progress, the likely speed of rehabilitation and discharge needs is essential. The ability to communicate effectively, especially in anxiety-provoking, emergency surgery situations, and the skill to motivate and remain realistically optimistic are similarly pre-requisites.

Although an option in the treatment of many conditions, surgery may not however always be the one of choice, either by the surgeon or the elderly patient. In addition to assessing the patient's chance of surviving operation, the surgeon must also consider the natural course of the disease as against the patient's life expectation and the quality of life without surgery; if operation is decided upon, should it be radical and heroic or modified and palliative (Vowles, 1979)? Much is now spoken of 'informed consent'; only when the patient and her family are in receipt of all the necessary information concerning their condition, the expected outcome and alternative methods of treatment available can this be a reality. The information will be viewed in the light of their own personal circumstances, beliefs and perceived needs and decisions made should be respected and honoured. Difficulties may arise where mental incapacity clouds the issue or individual and family views appear to be at odds and the responsibilities of the health care team are weighty indeed in these circumstances.

Pre-operative assessment and preparation

On admission to hospital old people have on average nine separate diagnoses (Redfern, 1989). Medical and nursing assessment may thus be much more complicated than with younger patients. To obtain a clear picture of the patient's medical, functional, social and psychological situation requires a multidisciplinary approach and collation of community and hospital acquired information. Consequently it cannot be 'done overnight' and for elective surgery it can be built up over a period of time, perhaps beginning with outpatient consultation, continuing through any investigation admission and completed when the patient actually comes in for surgery.

Allowing sufficient time for thorough pre-operative assessment also permits the older patient time to acclimatise to the hospital ward, personnel and procedures. Post-operative confusion, not infrequently seen in the elderly, is much lessened when the patient is familiar with her environment. Anxieties are much more easily discussed when one has become more confident with the staff and the nurses should use the opportunity to find out about home circumstances, the suitability of housing and any carer's state of health so that post-operative planning can take account of these realities.

A surgical ward can prove a very stressful environment with its rapid turnover of patients, emergency intakes and flurries of activity on theatre days. To the staff this becomes just the way of life and they sometimes become unappreciative of the meaning of 'routine', 'minor' surgery to the actual patients, for whom of course it is neither routine nor minor. Careful, and often repeated, explanation of all procedures is vital and apprehension must be recognised and allayed by discussion and appropriate intervention.

When surgery is planned there is time to ensure that the elderly patient is in the best possible condition pre-operatively. There is time, for example, to reduce obesity which greatly contributes to the development of post-operative complications; to correct dehydration or to improve nutrition (and thereby promote more ready wound healing). Surgery which will leave the patient with an altered body image (such as mastectomy, amputation of a limb, creation of a stoma) requires additional specific preparation; the psychological trauma precipitated at any stage of life may well be compounded by the age factor. The introduction of the appropriate specialist (appliance officer, stoma therapist) at an early stage allows for formation of a supportive relationship in which fears can be discussed and post-operative management explained.

Attention is paid to all general pre-operative nursing measures such as identification of the patient, recording of baseline observations of vital signs, urine analysis, skin preparation and encouragement of exercises as taught by the physiotherapist. 'Routine' removal of prostheses should not compromise the patient's dignity or independence however and should be timed appropriately; the hearing impaired patient for example will need her hearing aid left in situ until the induction of anaesthesia and resited as soon as she regains consciousness post-operatively.

Elderly patients tolerate periods of fluid deprivation less well than younger ones and long periods of having 'nil by mouth' should be avoided. Intravenous fluids may be commenced pre-operatively and oral hygiene or frequent mouthwashes should be available to keep the patient comfortable.

Drowsiness may exacerbate frailty or unsteadiness and once the patient has been given her premedication she should be asked to remain at rest in bed. Depending on the type and extent of the surgery to be performed, in some units prophylactic antibiotics and subcutaneous heparin are given to minimise the likelihood of the post-operative complications of chest and wound infections and deep vein thrombosis.

Emergency surgery

The mortality rate for emergency surgery in the older age group is double that for elective; the elderly patient is often in a very poor state pre-operatively and post-operative complications (both physiological and psychological) are more likely to ensue. When the hazardous early stages are survived, rehabilitation is often prolonged.

Much of the above mentioned preparation is precluded by emergency surgery. The elderly patient may be bewildered and confused by her sudden illness or injury, rapid admission to hospital, subjection to urgent investigation and preparation for theatre. It is most important that staff, all too easily pre-occupied with her physical needs, should be aware of the anxieties and fears of the patient and her family in this situation and that they should do their best to allay them.

Post-operative care

Care in the post-operative phase is directed, as in any age group, towards the prevention of complications or their early detection and management should they occur. Certain age related difficulties may be experienced with older patients however requiring of the nursing staff informed awareness and particular vigilance. Often different reactions are seen in older patients with a less florid and dramatic picture than in younger individuals. 'Silent' infarcts may occur with little or no pain; fever may not result in a pyrexia but in an acute confusional state. Prompt and accurate diagnosis is essential; inappropriate drug therapy (such as sedation rather than antibiotic) will infinitely worsen the condition.

The specific post-operative care elderly patients will receive will obviously vary with the type of surgery carried out, the sort of anaesthesia employed and personal idiosyncrasies or conditions suffered (for example, diabetes). Here however the general points important in management will be discussed.

On return from theatre pain relief is essential both to ensure patient comfort and to obtain cooperation with mobility and deep breathing, both vital factors in preventing complications. Analgesics generally need to be given with anti-emetics; they may be given by intermittent intramuscular injection or (increasingly) by slow intravenous infusion. This last method gives a more consistent analgesic effect with smaller doses; the older patient requires careful observation however to ensure that respiratory depression does not occur. It must be remembered that analgesics are not the only method of pain relief: suitable positioning and regular change of position are important and anxiety, a potent inducer of pain, needs to be dealt with appropriately.

Vital signs must be closely monitored and significant deviation from the patient's norm promptly acted upon; even moderate hypotension is poorly tolerated by older people and untreated may herald cardiac or renal complications. Intravenous fluids require meticulous regulation as circulatory overload readily occurs and central venous pressure readings may be necessary to monitor the situation. Fluid balance should be accurately recorded.

Elderly patients with defective thermoregulatory mechanisms can easily become hypothermic during surgery with exposure on the operating table and the infusion of cold fluids. They should not be put back into cold beds on return to the ward but left in their theatre blankets until their temperature has been checked and found satisfactory. A low peripheral temperature demands the observation of a core temperature, recorded rectally; if this is below 35 degrees Centigrade the patient must be rewarmed in a room temperature of at least 25 degrees with a 'space blanket' and intravenous fluids infused through a warming mechanism.

Chest complications are particularly prevalent in older patients with decreased chest expansion and a weaker cough reflex; there may also be underlying pathologies such as chronic bronchitis adding to the likelihood. As soon as the general condition allows the patient should be supported in the upright position and encouraged with deep breathing exercises and expectoration; manual support is given to chest or abdominal wounds to make this less painful.

Wound healing is affected by many factors. In later life it may be delayed by underlying disease (such as malignancy), medication the patient is receiving (such as steroids or anticoagulants) or by poor physical status generally. In malnourished patients this may be a real problem. One study found that 30% of surgical patients examined had clinical evidence of malnutrition and, a very worrying finding, this number rose to 60% after a week or more in hospital (Hill, 1977). Where ensuring adequate nutrition pre-operatively is difficult, perhaps because of persistent vomiting or oesophageal obstruction, parenteral feeding should be considered to improve the patient's condition before surgery. Post-operatively a high protein diet assists with wound healing and additional carbohydrate is required to meet .extra metabolic needs. Imaginative presentation and encouragement with diet may be necessary with older patients with poor appetites, however.

Many elderly patients experience difficulty with elimination post-operatively – incontinence may be an early problem or retention of urine may require the temporary insertion of a urethral catheter. Whenever possible the patient will be more comfortable and able to pass urine more easily if assisted out of bed to do so. Once any fluid restriction is removed, the provision of a daily intake of at least two litres will assist in preventing urinary infection, as will mobilisation to prevent the stasis of urine.

Early ambulation post-operatively assists in the prevention of many complications, such as deep vein thrombosis and pulmonary embolism, as well as in maintaining skin integrity. It may not be easy to achieve however with elderly arthritic or debilitated patients and needs to be gentle and slowly progressive. The patient's capabilities should not be overtaxed in the early post-operative period; fatigue may lead to frustration, loss of confidence and subsequent lowering of motivation. It is not encouraging dependency to assist as required with the activities of daily living at this time, support can be gradually withdrawn as the patient's ability to cope unaided returns (Garrett, 1987).

After care

Changes in the organisation of surgical care in recent years have led to earlier discharge from hospital with community carers, both informal and professional, assuming far greater responsibility for patient care. The surgical ward now deals with short term needs and problems immediately consequent upon surgery; in the home situation the longer term needs must be met and adaptation, perhaps to a changed body image or lifestyle, must take place. Whilst preparation for discharge from hospital generally has improved of late, especially from geriatric and medical wards, anxiety has been voiced (Garrett, 1987) that discharge from surgical wards may be precipitate (dictated more by the need for the bed than by the patient's condition) with inadequate preparation of patient and family and poor organisation of community services.

To overcome such criticisms it is important that in surgical nursing the need to prepare for discharge is viewed as part of pre-operative care planning. Obviously plans at that stage are tentative only, to be reviewed in the light of post-operative progress, but full assessment of the home situation, the patient's feelings about discharge and perception of her needs will indicate possible areas of concern and allow time and opportunity to plan for these. Relatives can be informed of projected time scales and reassured concerning support, for example from district nursing staff. Their involvement in teaching sessions, concerning medication perhaps or the management of prostheses, should be actively encouraged where appropriate.

Liaison between hospital and community staff is essential to ensure continuity of care for the elderly surgical patient. Some surgical units have designated liaison workers who see patients on the wards, join in the multidisciplinary team meetings and relay the necessary information to the district staff; others depend on a variety of structured forms which travel with the patient to convey a care plan to her own community nurse. The design of these forms depends on local needs and preferences but an essential feature should be the actual name and designation of the referring nurse so that ready contact can be made after discharge if necessary.

With increasing longevity and an ageing population in the UK the coming decades will see many more elderly people requiring surgical intervention and follow up. Undoubtedly resources will need to be increased to meet this demand but with good forward planning and skilled nursing and after care there is no reason why this should not prove cost beneficial in restoring function and fitness (thus reducing the cost of other supportive services) and improve elderly people's quality of life tremendously.

References

Garrett, G. (1987) *Health Needs of the Elderly*. MacMillan, London.
Hill, G.L., Blackett, R.L., Pickford, I. *et al.* (1977) Malnutrition in Surgical patients: An Unrecognised Problem. *Lancet* i, 689.
Redfern, S. (1986) *Nursing Elderly People*. Churchill Livingstone, London.
Vowles, K.D.J. (1979) Surgery in the Aged. In: Vowles K.D.J. (ed) *Surgical Problems in the Aged*. Wright, Bristol.

Working With Older People

The title of this section of the book reflects an increasingly appreciated concept in elderly care, that we do not 'care for' but 'work with' our elderly clients. The former terminology casts the client in a passive, subjugated position; the latter recognises their active role in a partnership approach to problem-solving. As Stephen Wright states in the introductory section to this book, health care workers are now empowering older people to get involved in and assume more control over their health needs and how they are met. For many conventionally trained professionals this is a totally new approach and it requires of them a radical rethink of basic philosophies.

When 'caring for' rather than 'working with' older people was the order of the day, it was assumed that 'basic nursing skills' were the only prerequisites. Such work was accorded low status and regarded as a clinical and professional backwater. It has only been with the adoption of the 'whole person' approach in recent years that there has been a realisation of the enormous professional and personal challenges that older people present. The demands they make upon us far exceed the need for a kind heart and a strong back; they include a wide knowledge of the process of ageing, age related disorders and their management and available sources of help; very varied practical and interpersonal skills and sensitive, respectful and non-judgemental attitudes.

The chapters in this section illustrate the complex, multifaceted nature of the nurses role with older clients and emphasise the need for appropriate preparation at basic, post-basic and continuing educational levels.

35

Teamwork: an equal partnership?

Gill Garrett, BA, SRN, RCNT, DN(Lond), Cert Ed(FE), RNT, FP Cert
Freelance Lecturer, Bristol

From being one of the fundamental tenets in the care of groups such as elderly people and those with mental handicaps, the vital nature of the team approach has become recognised and accepted in all areas of nursing. Many patients have a multiplicity of needs – medical, nursing, therapeutic, social – which no one discipline can hope to meet; only by close collaboration and cooperation can different practitioners bring their skills into concert to attempt to meet them.

Increasingly in recent years, the validity of this contention has been appreciated by both hospital and community workers, and the gospel has been preached. But how effective has the concept been in practice? While no doubt in many parts of the country teams are working efficiently and harmoniously together to the benefit of all concerned, it would seem that in others there are areas of concern which demand urgent consideration and action if the concept is not to prove a meaningless cliché. With this in mind, this chapter considers the prerequisites for effective teamwork, points out a few of the common problems which may arise and offers some suggestions as to how these problems may be ameliorated.

Who makes up the team?
One very basic question to ask before considering the work of the team is who makes up the team? On multiple choice papers, students will indicate the doctor, nurse, therapists, dietitians – all the professional partners in the venture. But integral to every team must be the people most meaningful to the individual patient: her family if she has any, her supportive neighbour, or whoever. If our aim is to rehabilitate the patient or to maintain her at her maximum level of functioning, these are people we neglect at our peril – and much more importantly, at the patient's peril. As professionals we must learn that we do not have a monopoly on care, nor do we have a dominant role in an unequal partnership. The contribution of relatives or friends, as agreeable to the patient, is vital – whether discussing assessments, setting goals or reviewing progress; their non-contribution, if excluded from active participation, may indeed frustrate all professional efforts. Although most of this

chapter concentrates on those professionals who are conventionally seen as team members (primarily because of the space available), this point cannot be overstressed.

Why are teams necessary?

Perhaps an even more basic question is, why does the team exist? It is easy to lose sight of the fact that its sole *raison d'être* is the patient and her need. An old adage runs, "The patient is the centre of the medical universe around which all our works revolve, towards which all our efforts trend". In economic terms we are quite used to this concept of 'consumer sovereignty', but in our health and social services management at present, all too often our consumer exists more to be 'done to' rather than canvassed for her opinion, offered options and helped to make choices. A thorny question often raised about the multidisciplinary team is, which professional should lead it? An equally important one not so often posed is, who should be the 'director' of team activity? If we recognise the patient as an autonomous, independent person (albeit with varying degrees of support), surely we must have the humility to acknowledge that this directing role falls inevitably to her. For patients with mental or other serious impairment, of course, the question of advocacy then arises – again an issue subject to much current debate.

Having allocated the role of director to the patient, the team leader then becomes the facilitator of action. It has been said that, "Fundamental to the concept of teamwork is . . . division of labour, coordination and task sharing, each member making a different contribution, but (one) of equal value, towards the common goal of patient care" (Ross, 1986). What do these elements demand? To make for efficient division of labour there has to be an accurate assessment of a situation and the input needed to deal with it, a recognition of who is the best person for which part of the job, and the carrying through of the appropriate allocation. Coordination demands the ability to see the overall, the sum of all the individual parts, and to recognise their relative weightings in various circumstances; it needs effective communication skills and the ability to use feedback to take adjustive action as required. Task-sharing demands that team members have an understanding of different roles and their effect upon one another, that they recognise areas of overlap and are prepared to shoulder one another's problems should the need arise. Such demands are not light; they require considerable training and practice to perfect.

Status and power within the team

Consideration of the second part of the Ross quotation brings us to one of the common problems experienced in multidisciplinary teamwork: ". . . of equal value towards the common goal of patient care". Is that how all team members view their own contribution or that of their partners? Status and power imbalances can make for great difficulties in team functioning; tradition accords high status and consequent power to the medical establishment, for example, with much affection but little standing to nurses. But if nurses have been seen as lacking in power and status, even lower on the rungs of the ladder comes the patient; in general, society grants a very low status to ill and disabled people, and institutional care strips all vestiges of power from inhabitants.

For workers who see themselves as being the juniors in teams, the presence and influence of more powerful members may prove intimidating, and consequently they may make only tentative and limited contributions to discussions and meetings. It is important that they realise that, however 'junior', they have a right to contribute, indeed a duty to do so, if they have what has been described as the "authority of relevance" (Webb and Hobdell, 1975) – if they have knowledge relevant to the patient's own feelings of need or wellbeing which must be brought to the team's attention. So often it is those members who spend more time in close proximity to the patient who possess such authority, rather than the senior medical personnel who may visit her only on a weekly basis.

'Follow my leader'   A second problem may arise out of the power and status imbalance, especially when team members have become used to suppressing their views or do not recognise their authority of relevance – regression into the 'follow my leader' phenomenon. There may be the tendency to leave all the thinking to another group member who is perceived as being more prestigious or simply more articulate, often the consultant. His thinking and directions are seen as definitive, with team members abdicating their own professional responsibility to think and speak for themselves and for their patient from their own vantage points. Except in the unlikely event of the team leader being qualified in a multidisciplinary capacity, this obviously acts to the detriment of patient care – we can none of us prescribe or wholly substitute for each other's contributions. A variation on this 'follow my leader' phenomenon is sometimes seen where two leaders emerge from subgroups in a team, each with his or her own following. In addition to the drawbacks already mentioned, the results in situations like this are invariably divisive too.

'Groupthink'   This is the name that has been given to another possible problem in teamwork; it is generally seen in well-established, long-lived teams whose members over time have grown very used to working with each other. Team meetings are always amicable and 'cosy', there is no bickering or dissension and everyone gets on terribly well with everyone else. The group gives the appearance of having its own internal strength, with a marked sense of loyalty and supportiveness. But this denies that disagreement and conflict are facts of life and often signs of constructive enquiry and growth; all too often such teams ". . . become rigid, committed to the status quo . . . less open to input and feedback. Hierarchies become established and bureaucratic qualities emerge which resist questioning and change" (Brill, 1976).

Patient confusion   In case this should all seem a little esoteric, consider for a moment one last very basic possible problem in multidisciplinary teamwork – potential confusion for the patient. Unless each member of the team extends to her the courtesy of an introduction to their personal role, with an explanation of how this fits in with the overall individual plan of care, especially in the acute phase of an illness, the patient (particularly if elderly) may well find so many professionals overwhelming and muddling. If she is to feel in any degree in control of the situation and if any confusion is to be lessened, time must be taken to ensure a personal approach, with all care being presented as part of a concerted whole, and with common goals identified towards which all the team are working.

This last problem, then, is usually amenable to a common courtesy and common sense solution. But what about the others? The problems associated with status and 'follow my leader' have a more deep-seated origin and, although rectifiable in the short term in individual teams, in the longer term they demand a close scrutiny of, and changes in, professional education. 'Groupthink' demands flexibility of individuals and a system which encourages and permits a regular turnover of personnel to maintain healthy group dynamics.

Common core training?

If in effective teams there is no room for professional superiorities or jealousies, what is needed is an open, trusting relationship based on knowledge of, and respect for, one another's professional expertise. But this demands in turn an insight into other trainings and backgrounds to understand one another's terms of reference – the differences in emphasis we have in relation to patient care. While individual effort and inservice training programmes can go some way towards this, the difficulties with late attitudinal change are only too well known. Most of our basic feelings about our own profession and those with which we work are formed during our initial training period. Nursing is currently implementing Project 2000, with a common core foundation programme for all nurse practitioners. Is it not time we were much more adventurous, and explored avenues of common core training for all health professionals? Certain knowledge, skills and attitudes are prerequisites whether we are to be doctors, nurses, therapists or social workers – if we learned them together how much easier it would be to practise them together. The intention of such common training would not be to reduce all teaching to the lowest common denominator, but rather to look at areas of mutual concern, highlighting the unique contribution of each professional, and the bearing this has on the work of the other team members.

Value of difference

Educational change may also help us to recognise the value of 'difference' and the constructive use to which conflict may be put, so that 'groupthink' becomes a less likely problem. Better training in interpersonal skills – including assertiveness – should help the creation of a climate in which there is freedom to differ, to look more dispassionately at dissent, while acknowledging the areas of basic trust and agreement that do exist and can be built upon. The need for turnover in team membership has to be balanced, of course, by the need for reasonable stability over a period of time. Change every five minutes for the sake of it helps no one, but there must be recognition that long-term team stagnation (however well camouflaged) is beneficial neither to the group nor to the professionals within it – and certainly not to the patient and her family.

Realism

A brief overview of a very important area has been provided. Readers' personal experiences may differ considerably from the scenarios which have been outlined. It would seem, however, that most experienced nurses have had experience of needing to temper idealism in striving for effective teamwork with realism, given the situations in which they work. But recognition of this is in itself a step forward; we must have in mind that "under the aegis of teamwork, strange bedfellows are discovering, in time, they they must *learn* to work together before they *can* work together . . . teamwork is not an easy process to understand or to practise" (Brill, 1976).

References
Brill, N.I. (1976) Teamwork: Working Together in the Human Services. Lippincott, New York.
Ross, F.M. (1986) Nursing old people in the community. In: Redfern, S. (ed) Nursing Elderly People. Churchill Livingstone, Edinburgh.
Webb, A.L. and Hobdell, M. (1975) Coordination between health and personal social services: a question of quality. In: Interaction of social welfare and health personnel in the delivery of services: Implications for training. Eurosound Report No. 4, Vienna.

36

The dynamics of ageing: their implications for care

Brendan McMahon, BA (Hons), SRN, RMN, Cert Dynamic Psychotherapy
Patricia Fitzgerald, RMN, Cert Ed
Both Clinical Nurse Specialists in Dynamic Psychotherapy, Derby

It is difficult for the young to imagine what it is like to be old. What ageing does to the body is fairly easy to see, but its effects on the mind and in particular on the sense of self, are more difficult to comprehend. The processes of ageing are complex, and no two people will age in the same way. The way in which an individual responds to the challenge of ageing will be heavily influenced by his or her attitudes and beliefs, his or her past experience and the kind of person he or she is. We are to a large extent the authors of our own lives and, as George Orwell remarked, at fifty everyone has the face that he or she deserves. The issue is complicated by social expectations, which are reflected in employment practice, and in the creation of stereotyped 'elderly' roles in popular culture: old people have been seen as dependent, economically useless and 'sick'. Economic shifts and growing self-consciousness (and self-confidence) on the part of the elderly, as evidenced, for instance, by the Third Age movement, are changing these stereotypes as we write, and fewer and fewer grandmothers are content to spend their declining years knitting by the fireside. This is no more than a rediscovery of the truth that healthy old people have always had the capacity to lead active and creative lives. Dostoevsky was sixty when he completed *The Brothers Karamazov*, and Freud and Becket produced some of their most challenging work in advanced old age.

Development tasks

Erikson proposed a model of psychosocial development according to which each stage of life presents its own conflict to be resolved (Erikson, 1959). In the first year of life, for instance, the central issue is basic trust versus mistrust, as the infant forms his or her first trusting relationship with his or her mother. The adolescent struggles with role confusion in a quest for identity, and the adult in middle-age must learn to be creative (or 'generative') if he is to avoid stagnation. From the age of fifty the individual strives for 'ego-integrity' the alternative to which is despair. In all of Erikson's formulated eight stages of development, from infancy to old age, each stage represents a choice or crisis for the developing self. The effects of maturation, experience and social institutions on the growing individual are encompassed in the theory, and the resolutions of each successive crisis are seen as determining the future developments of the personality. This may be viewed as a process of adjustment to the changing demands of the external world of family and society on the one hand, and of the internal world of emotional need on the other. A different psychological issue comes into focus at each stage of development, but the same issue is also present in later stages: that is to say, a 'solution' at any stage of development has its effects on all subsequent stages, and an individual cannot successfully resolve, say, the issue of ego integrity if he or she has not successfully resolved issues of intimacy and generativity. This is not an academic point: each individual responds to ageing in his or her own way, on the basis of his or her unique life-experience, and the nurse should beware of generalisation.

Integrity provides the individual with the wisdom to understand and accept his or her own life as he or she has lived it, including the fact that it is about to reach its conclusion. In order to achieve this he or she needs to establish a meaningful connection between past and present, and old age is characteristically a time for reminiscence. The therapeutic applications of this concept are beginning to be explored through reminiscence therapy (Hanley and Gilhooly, 1986). But this kind of remembering has an important interpersonal, social aspect too. Grandparents tell their grandchildren what they did in the war and in non-literate cultures, past and present, the history, law and myth of the race is passed from the old to the young by word of mouth. In our own culture the segregation of the elderly, though by no means the norm, mitigates against the process. This communication across the generations is important for the young, because it provides them with a sense of continuity and a respect for the past, and for the old, because it gives them a role and a sense of value, at a time when other sources of self-esteem may be denied them. This is particularly important in our own time, in which the individual's sense of continuity is under attack from the twin forces of rapid social and technological change and a growing cultural rootlessness.

Psychodynamic approaches

The development theory outlined above has great therapeutic potential, though this has not always been recognised in psychoanalytic thought. Freud, perhaps because of his own anxiety about ageing (Gay, 1988), paid little attention to the subject and its therapeutic possibilities. In 1905 he wrote "The age of patients has this much importance in determining their fitness for psychoanalytic treatment, that, on the one hand, near or above the age of fifty the elasticity of the mental processes, on which the treatment depends, is as a rule lacking – old people are no longer educable – and, on the other hand, the mass of material to be dealt with would prolong the duration of the treatment indefinitely".

In retrospect this seems both pessimistic and patronising. A number of analysts have in fact carried out successful analyses of elderly patients, and Leszcz and others have published an interesting account of a psychotherapy group of cognitively intact men aged 70–95 years (Leszcz *et al*, 1985).

Setting up a psychotherapy group

One of us has been involved in setting up a psychotherapy group on a psychogeriatric ward, the aims of which were to:

- facilitate the delivery of psychotherapy to the client group.
- provide a setting in which patients can use the time to examine their problems and relationships with others who have also experienced the traumas of old age.
- offer ward staff the opportunity to learn and develop the basic principles of the psychodynamic model.

The group met in the same room at the same time every week, for one hour, and was facilitated by two nurses, one of whom was an experienced group therapist. It was agreed that no patients or nurse should be called out of the group, except in case of emergency, and that feedback to all staff on the process of the group would be given on a weekly basis. The group provides the possibility for relationships to be formed between individuals who have experienced similar difficulties, and for the provision of feedback from other group members in order to generate, within the safe environment of the group, a matrix for change.

King (1986) has identified five areas of conflict which may emerge in the psychoanalysis of older clients. These are:

- fear of the dimunition or loss of sexual potency.
- the threat of redundancy or displacement at work by younger people, and the problems of coping with retirement.
- the changing dynamic of the marital relationship as children grow up and leave home.
- growing awareness of ageing, and anxieties about possible physical illness and dependency.
- coping with the prospect of death.

It will be seen that the common factor here is loss and the fear of loss, and that it is of dual nature. That is to say, the feared loss is partly external, to do with income, status and role as breadwinner or mother for instance, but that, these external factors relate to internal objects, the threat to which may be even more unbearable. Being a father, mother, teacher, nurse is not just something we do: it is an important part of what we are. The successful negotiation of each developmental stage involves a renunciation of previous certainties as well as the facing of new challenges. So, for the adolescent, the wonder of discovering the world for him or herself is tempered by the pain of detaching from his or her parents. Although most people remain capable of loving sexual relationships to the end of their lives (Greengross and Greengross, 1989), the feared loss of sexual capacity can threaten one of our most potent sources of self-esteem. Death, the prospect of actual physical non-existence, is the greatest challenge of all, and the way in which we meet it will depend on the extent to which we achieve a sense of integration in our later years. Life must have value and meaning for us if we are to renounce it with grace and dignity.

The general nurses involved in the physical and perhaps terminal care of elderly patients must keep these issues in the forefront of their minds if they are to be able to respond to their patients' needs. The psychiatric nurse, who is well used to working with issues of bereavement and loss of role is, one suspects, often reluctant to tackle such issues with elderly patients. The reasons for this may be conjectured. It may be that the medical model, with its emphasis on cure, and the wider cultural preoccupation with wonder drugs and pioneering surgery, lead to a tendency to regard failing health and death in particular as a shameful failure to be shunned, rather than as a developmental task to be achieved, in which the nurse can play a crucial facilitating role. It may be that we are reluctant to accept that we too must grow old and die.

The recognition of mortality

The individual has his or her first ideas about death quite early in childhood. Small children ask questions and express concern about dead animals and birds and about the death of relatives. It cannot be said that they understand the implications of death, yet they feel deeply about dead things and people. It may be that this feeling mirrors aspects of the child's own early experience, such as the withdrawal of the breast or the temporary absence of mother which the baby may experience at the time as an irretrievable loss. Children's conscious worries about death are often expressed in terms of fear of losing their parents or grandparents, and for them, the most important aspect of death is the loss of a loved and needed person. It may be that children are incapable of fully conceptualising their own death, which seems such a long way off that it can easily be disregarded or denied.

When a person enters the teenage years his or her capacity to deny his or her own mortality erodes somewhat. This is a gradual transition and is an intrinsic part of the growth of adult identity. By the twenties and thirties the idea of one's own death has usually taken firm root. The evidence for mortality mounts as relatives and friends die and as the individual is exposed to illness and accident. This growing consciousness is adaptive, since it spurs us on to clarify our goals in life and to set about achieving them.

By the beginning of the fifth decade our awareness of mortality develops into the sense that our lives are half over, and that we are running out of time; for some this can be a profoundly depressing realisation. By this time most of us have made irrevocable choices in terms of career and personal relationships, and it is no longer easy to believe that the world is our oyster. If we can accept both our limitations and our achievements, then the middle years can be a time of great creative energy and sense of purpose, and this is the best preparation for ageing and death.

Nurses are people too, and must learn to recognise their limitations along with their achievements. We too must die. In helping our clients to face the challenge of death, we also confront the challenge for ourselves, and through this can become richer, more vital human beings.

References

Erikson, E.H. (1959) *Identity and the Life Cycle*. International Universities Press, New York.

Freud, S. (1953) *On Psychotherapy. Standard Edition of the Complete Psychological Works of Sigmund Freud*, Vol. 7. Hogarth Press and the Institute of Psychoanalysis, London.

Gay, P. (1988) *Freud. A Life For Our Time*. J.M. Dent Ltd, London, P.134.

Greengross, W. and Greengross, S. (1989) *Living, Loving and Ageing. Sexual and Personal Relationships in Later Life*. Age Concern, Mitcham.

Hanley, I. and Gilhooly, M. (1986) *Psychological Therapies for the Elderly*. Croom Helm, London.

King, P.H.M. (1986) Notes on the psychoanalysis of older patients. *J. Anal. Psychol*, **19**, 22–37.

Leszcz, N. *et al* (1985) Group psychotherapy in the elderly. *Int. J. Group Psychotherapy*, **35** (2), April, 177–96.

37

Communicating with elderly people

Kevin Teasdale, MA, Cert Ed, RMN
Director of In-Service Training and Post Basic Nurse Education, Pilgrim Hospital, Boston, Lincs.

Personal relationships can be seen as a series of bargains, negotiated from differing positions of power. This Exchange Theory suggests that as people enter the later stages of their lives, they have less to bargain with – physically, materially and socially. They are then vulnerable to learned helplessness – the belief that whatever actions they take, they can no longer get what they want, no longer control their environment which may be applied to all aspects of the person's life, resulting in a state of apathy, passiveness and introversion. The following situations could form the basis for discussion between you and your colleagues.

Situation 1 – Learning to be helpless

A newly admitted elderly woman is taken to the ward bathroom by a nurse. The woman tells the nurse: "Please don't worry. I can manage to get myself bathed on my own." "That's all right," says the nurse. "Here, let's run the water and get you undressed."

The elderly woman can interpret what has happened in a number of different ways. Look at the following possible interpretations and discuss the psychological effects of each one on future behaviour.

a) "I should have spoken up louder and really insisted on bathing myself."

b) "The nurses here just see the patients as pets to be looked after."

c) "Look at the state of me. I can't even get myself undressed and into the bath any more."

d) "I disliked that nurse the moment I saw her. She thinks she's the matron telling everyone what to do."

a) The woman is interpreting what happened to her on this occasion as resulting from a lack of effort on her part. It will probably lead her to take a more assertive stance on the next similar occasion. She has limited the damage to the specific event, but blames herself for lack of effort.

b) This interpretation is damaging in the sense that the woman has generalised from the behaviour of one nurse to that of all the nurses in the ward. However she is also attributing the fact that she did not get what she wanted to a source outside herself. It may lead to passive behaviour while on the ward, but she may continue to see herself as fully capable when discharged home.

c) This is the most damaging interpretation, and most likely to lead to helplessness and dependence. The woman internalises the fact that she has not got what she wanted, she interprets it as evidence of a permanent state of helplessness. It will usually take a whole series of adverse events to cause such a pessimistic interpretation, but nurses may have no idea of what has happened to new patients prior to admission.

d) This interpretation strongly reinforces the woman's view of herself as capable of influencing events. She attributes what happened to the nurse's bossy nature, and limits the problem to interactions with this particular nurse.

Situation 2 – Controlling language

The way a nurse talks to an elderly person may suggest that the nurse is in complete control and is offering the patient no choice in the matter. Frequently the words and the non-verbal communication are those of a parent to a child, rather than one adult to another.

Analyse the following sentences to find out which phrases emphasise the control exercised by the nurses. How could they be rephrased to achieve an adult-to-adult interchange?

a) "Now then Martin, lie on your side so that I can wash your bottom, there's a good chap."
b) "We'll just sit you down here in the day room."
c) "You will eat up all your dinner for me now, won't you?"
d) "Now don't you worry about what's going on at home. You just concentrate on getting better."

a) Try saying this aloud to hear the tone of voice that naturally accompanies the words. It is fine if Martin is six years old, but what if he's sixty-six? The use of the first name may not be appropriate, it depends on the relationship between the nurse and the patient. It could be rephrased as, "Please can you lie on your side so that I can wash your bottom."

b) The implication is that the patient's body is an object which the nurses move around at will. The word 'just' is often used as a softener, when a nurse wants to do something to a patient without fully explaining it, or without giving any choice in the matter. An improved version might be, "We'll help you to sit down in the day room. Would you like to sit on this side of the room, or on the other side?" The phrasing shifts the nurses back into a helping role. Even if there is no choice about sitting in the day room, it is worth giving a limited choice on where to sit.

The other two examples can be analysed in the same way. It would help even the most experienced nurse to get an elderly patient's permission to tape record a conversation, and then listen to it for examples of the nurse using a patronising, 'parent' tone of voice. It can be an enlightening experience!

Situation 3 – Regaining control

A communicating/counselling process can systematically help an elderly person to move towards a realistic view of themselves, through realising that there are still major areas over which the person can reasonably expect to exercise control.

A 70 year old woman whose husband died last year after a long illness complains to her health visitor that she cannot seem to talk to anyone in the village any more, which is why she now stays in the house as much as possible. Consider the following alternatives to the "Pull-yourself-together" approach to problem solving. Discuss the good points of each approach.

a) "You seemed to have a large circle of friends before your husband became ill. Would you say that people enjoyed your company then?"

b) "Next week when you go to the post office for your pension, give a smile and comment on the weather. Then we'll talk about what sort of response you got."

c) "You and I have talked a lot about what your husband meant to you, but other people could be afraid of upsetting you by mentioning him."

d) "You told me that your neighbours on the right always kept themselves to themselves, even while your husband was alive, but the woman across the road was very supportive when he was ill. How could you make contact with her again?"

a) Trying to help her to recognise that if she once had the capacity to maintain successful social relationships, she can probably do so again. She is encouraged to see her loneliness as being temporary.

b) Giving her graded tasks in which she is likely to be successful. Then encourage her to generalise from one success to the possibility of others, thus reversing the learning process.

c) Instead of attributing her loneliness to something in herself, she is encouraged to consider the possibility that part of the problem is external, due to the lack of understanding on the part of other people. Generally speaking an external attribution of failure is less damaging than an internal attribution.

d) Trying to help her to establish limited, realistic expectations of success and failure. Certainly, some people will not want to make contact, but others will be only too pleased to do so. The principle is one of changing an unrealistic global attribution of failure to a limited and specific one.

Situation 4 – When the person is disorientated

You are working in an assessment ward for the elderly mentally ill. As you wake up one patient and prepare to help him get dressed he reaches across the bed and says, "Where's my Elsie? Why isn't she in bed with me?" You know that Elsie, his wife, died last year before he was admitted to hospital.

Consider the following ways of handling the situation. What principles are illustrated in each, and on what basis could you decide which is the more suitable course of action?

a) "I think Elsie's already got up before you. Come on Mr Jones, why don't you get up too?"

b) "Now then Mr Jones, it's time to get up and come down to the ward dining room. Which shirt would you like to wear today?"

c) "You're in a hospital ward at the moment, Mr Jones. I remember that yesterday you were telling me about Elsie. Where did you say the two of you used to live?"

d) "I'm very sorry Mr Jones, but your wife died last year. This is a hospital you're in at the moment, not your own home."

a) Reinforcing the false belief, then using distraction. As a general rule (to which there are always exceptions) avoid this approach. It is important that if an elderly person is disorientated, the whole environment should be supportive, and all contacts should reinforce reality.

b) Distraction. If a person raises a subject which is likely to evoke a strong emotional reaction, the nurse needs to consider whether she can give enough time to this individual to help and support him through that reaction. It may be much the best course to distract the patient now, but give him another opportunity to talk about his wife later.

c) Emphasising reality in time and place, and encouraging the patient to go back to his intact long term memories and then gently work forward to the time of his wife's death. An adult approach, encouraging the patient to keep in touch with reality. Needs the right time and place. The nurse must understand the grieving process, and the likelihood of renewal trauma at rediscovering the death.

d) Reinforcing reality. It may be effective, it may also be cruel. The situation reveals the importance of assessing each patient individually. One suggestion is to try confronting the patient with reality when he is confused about something which is *not* emotionally charged – what was on the lunchtime menu for example. How does the patient react when he realises he has made a mistake? Even patients in the later stages of senile dementia may become frighteningly aware of the tragedy which has happened to them, and become severely depressed as well as demented.

Conclusion

All aspects of working with the elderly, particularly communication, demand great skill. Nurses can draw on research to guide them, and they themselves have a duty to develop their own body of applied research through evaluating the effects of their interventions.

Bibliography

Holden, U.P. and Woods, R. (1982) Reality Orientation. Churchill Livingstone, London.
  Sound sense from authors who understand how to apply research to practice.
Hanley, I. and Hodge, J. (1984) Psychological Approaches to the Care of the Elderly. Croom Helm, London.
  Includes detailed explanation of learned helplessness and how it may be overcome.
Lanceley, A. (1985) Use of controlling language in the rehabilitation of the elderly. *Journal of Advanced Nursing*, **10**, 125–135.
  A nurse opening up this area for future research.

38

Coping with other people's emotions

Philip Burnard, MSc, RGN, RMN, DipN, Cert Ed, RNT
Lecturer in Nursing Studies, University of Wales College of Medicine, Cardiff

Nurses in all specialties regularly come into contact with people who are upset. In the psychiatric hospital, they are frequently asked to cope with those who are distressed as a result of depression, anxiety or fear. In the general hospital they also face the emotional release of others: in the intensive care unit, in medical, surgical and children's wards and also when relatives are distressed for any number of reasons. While there is an increasing focus on interpersonal and communication skills in all the nursing syllabi, the question of what to do when someone expresses strong emotion is still rarely addressed in a practical manner. Here I shall outline some of the options available to the nurse and suggest some guidelines for further training.

A healthy activity

The first consideration is that the release of emotion generally seems to be a *healthy* activity. We all have the capacity to express strong emotion (laughter, tears, anger and fear) and the release of such feeling tends to enable us to regain a certain equilibrium. Conversely, when we bottle up emotion we tend to function less effectively and often feel less healthy. Unfortunately, a cultural norm in this society seems to be that we should not outwardly show strong emotion: that we should maintain the 'stiff upper lip'. As a result, many people in our culture carry around with them a lot of unexpressed emotion. This can manifest itself in a variety of ways.

Physical tension A person carrying around a great deal of unexpressed anger, for example, will often experience considerable tension in the shoulders and upper trunk. One who cannot cope with their own unexpressed sorrow will ofter experience tension in their stomach. The mapping out of the physical effects of this emotional bottling up has been described by Reich (1976), who argues that release of such repressed emotion can lead to the person feeling more physically, as well as emotionally, stable and secure.

Emotional problems Emotional release often leads to the resolution of emotional problems. Thus the person who is grieving and allowed to express their grief will more readily come to terms with the loss they have experienced. It seems that the free expression of emotion is one of the means by which we come to terms with our problems. Again, the cultural norm runs counter to this principle and as a result many people think that it is not acceptable to express feeling openly. Such a sanction on the expression of feeling extends to nurses who often feel incompetent to deal with other people's emotional release.

Emotional release is a healthy process which can help people both physically and psychologically. The first way to help others in this area is to *allow* them to express feelings. If a relative or patient starts to cry, it is usually helpful to let them continue. For many nurses, the ingrained reflex when someone cries is to rush in and 'reassure' them in a rather desperate attempt to stop them crying. If we can resist that reflex and allow them to cry we will usually be helping them far more than if we offer them glib reassurance.

Such reassurance is often more for the nurse than for the patient. It is almost as if the patient's tears stir up our own unexpressed emotion and make us unhappy. As a result, we feel compelled to stop them. In the first place stopping them saves us the embarassment of not being able to deal with the emotion and in the second, it stops our own feelings from being churned up. If we, as nurses, are to deal with the emotional release of others frequently, we must take some time to consider our *own* emotional status. If we carry around a great deal of unexpressed emotion, we cannot expect to be much help to others when they are distressed. If our emotion is just beneath the surface, we will tend to avoid allowing others to freely release their feelings because we will find it too distressing.

Exploring our emotions

The first practical issue in helping others to express emotion, then, is to explore our own emotions. This can be done in a variety of ways. A support group can be set up to enable nurses to talk through their feelings about their job and, if necessary, their personal lives. Such groups can help relieve job-related stress and do much to ward off the development of burnout – the insidious process of exhaustion caused by job-related pressure. These groups can be set up by nurses who have had some experience and training in running groups, and training is regularly available in short workshops as part of extramural programmes of universities and colleges.

Support groups should meet once a week for an hour to be most effective. Any discussions which take place within them are confidential to group members. A useful book on running such groups is Ernst and Goodison's In Your Own Hands: a book of self-help therapy (1981), which gives details of how to set up, run and overcome teething troubles in support groups.

Individual nurses can make a contract with themselves to set aside time each day or week to talk through problems with a friend or trusted colleague. This may sound very formal, but unless we consciously set aside time to do this, the tendency is to allow ourselves to 'carry on as normal'. The net result is often that we do not communicate our feelings to others but continue to bottle them up. The process of setting aside time each week, in a fairly formal way, to talk things through can be very therapeutic. This can be shared equally between the two people involved and soon becomes a regular and very healthy part of the week.

Growth groups

A third approach to exploring personal feelings is to join a regular 'growth' group of some sort. Various types of women's and men's groups are now running up and down the country and they can be useful vehicles for the development of self-awareness and personal development. To some, the time taken up by such activities may seem self-indulgent, but if we are to truly help others, we must first help ourselves. Apart from the single sex groups mentioned here, there is a wide range of short courses and ongoing groups available through universities and colleges which aim to enhance self-awareness and develop communication skills. Co-counselling also offers a useful medium for exploring self development among trusted colleagues and friends. After initial training, co-counsellors meet regularly in pairs. One of the partners spends an hour in the role of 'client' and the other in that of 'counsellor', then the roles are reversed. The hour may be spent as the 'client' chooses: exploring problems, releasing pent-up emotion or planning for the future. Further details of co-counselling and co-counselling networks are described by Heron (1978).

Allowing the expression of emotion

This self-development is the first stage in preparing for helping others to express their emotions. The next stage is what to do when a person begins to express feelings, whether through tears, anger, fear or laughter. This expression is healthy, so the first 'rule' is to *allow* the expression of emotion. We have to learn to refrain from rushing to reassure the other person and from suggesting that they stop! If someone is 'allowed' to cry or express anger, the emotion usually runs its own course and they feel better as a result. If we rush in too quickly to stop the emotion, we encourage them to bottle things up and create potential problems for themselves later.

All we have to do, then, is to sit and allow the other person to release their feelings. This is easy to write about but often very difficult to do! We are nearly all readily programmed by our socialisation to jump in quickly to stop tears or anger. To sit back and 'allow' it is far more difficult. With conscious effort, backed up by exploration of our own emotional status, such acceptance can become our norm.

Nurses who regularly have to cope with profound emotional release are well advised to consider further training in cathartic methods. Issues such as when to intervene, when to encourage the release of emotion and *how* to encourage such release, need to be considered. Heron (1986) discusses many of these issues and his description of cathartic methods, their use and abuse makes useful reading. Cathartic work usually involves rather lengthy periods of time with the patient, and many nurses may feel that such an investment of time is an expensive one, but we are committed to caring for the *whole* person, then caring for their emotional needs is a high priority.

Therapeutic touch

One simple skill that all nurses have literally at their fingertips is the use of touch. Light touch can often promote and encourage emotional release, while an arm round the patient's shoulder is often comforting and assists their emotional release (Heron, 1986; Montague, 1978).

The third aspect of coping with other people's emotion is to allow a period after the tears or anger for them to 'make sense' of what has happened. This quiet period after the emotion has died down is an important aspect of the whole process. After expressing strong feeling, people are often flooded with new insights into their condition. It is as if the expression of feeling has allowed a veil to be lifted and that they now see things more clearly. Usually during this period, nothing need be said by the nurse at all. The patient (or relative) only needs to sit quietly and think things through. The insight that occurs during this period is often personal and it may not be expressed to the nurse. What is perhaps more important to the other person at this time is that they have *company* and are *allowed* the time they need to think things through in this way.

These, then, are three practical aspects of coping with other people's emotional release. First we explore our own emotions so that they do not 'get in the way' when the other person expresses feeling; second, we 'allow' full expression of the feeling, and third we allow time and space for the piecing together of the insights that usually follow such emotional release.

Emotional release is only part of a wide spectrum of interpersonal skills the nurse requires to satisfy patients' emotional needs. Heron (1986) offers a comprehensive and practical list of all possible types of therapeutic interventions which he calls Six Category Intervention Analysis (Heron, 1986). The therapeutic interventions that Heron identifies are as follows:

Prescriptive: the nurse offers suggestions or advice.

Informative: the nurse offers the patient factual information.

Confronting: the nurse challenges the patient.

Cathartic: the nurse helps the patient release pent-up emotion.

Catalytic: the nurse helps the patient to further consider their own thoughts and feelings by asking questions and generally 'drawing out' the patient.

Supportive: the nurse validates and encourages the patient.

Heron argues that the skilled practitioner can use all of these interventions appropriately. He also identifies non-therapeutic use of them and explains how each type of intervention can be misused. The nurse who develops skills in each of the six categories can become an effective helper in a range of interpersonal situations, with patients and their relatives and with her colleagues and friends. Once again, a variety of training courses in Six Category Intervention Analysis are available through various university departments and practical methods in the six categories are described elsewhere (Burnard, 1990).

It is interesting to note that recent research has suggested that trained nurses see themselves as skilled in using the prescriptive, informative and supportive categories but far less skilled in using the catalytic, confronting and cathartic categories (Burnard and Morrison, 1987).

The principles described in this article apply in almost all nursing settings: in clinical and community situations as well as in management and educational environments. All nurses can learn the basic skills involved in helping those who are emotionally distressed and so practise more therapeutically.

Increasingly, colleges of nursing are using a range of experiential learning methods to facilitate the development of a wide range of interpersonal skills, such as counselling and group leadership. Perhaps more time needs to be set aside for the development of the specific skills of helping people to release emotion. Given the stressful nature of nursing, such competence can only help both nurse and patient. Perhaps, too, gradually and slowly, the cultural norm of keeping a stiff upper lip will change and a more completely human person will emerge.

References

Burnard, P. (1990) Learning Human Skills: A Guide for Nurses, 2nd edition. Heinemann, London.

Burnard, P. and Morrison, P. (1987) Nurses' perceptions of their inter-personal skills. *Nursing Times*, **83**, 42, 59.

Ernst, S. and Goodison, L. (1981) In Our Own Hands: A Book of Self-help Therapy. The Woman's Press, London.

Heron, J. (1978) Co-Counsellor's Teachers Manual. Human Potential Research Project, University of Surrey, Guildford.

Heron, J. (1986) Six Category Intervention Analysis (2nd Ed). Human Potential Research Project, University of Surrey, Guildford.

Montague, A. (1978) Touching: The Human Significance of the Skin. Harper and Row, New York.

Reich, W. (1976) Character Analysis. Simon and Schuster, New York.

39

Helping clients to come to terms with loss

Teresa Lombardi, RGN, RSCN, RNT, Cert Ed, Dip Counselling
Director, Professional Development, West Sussex College of Nursing and Midwifery

Working with terminally ill people, although rewarding and challenging, is far from easy, for a variety of reasons. It is impossible to identify a 'right and wrong' way of communicating with them, as each client has individual needs and ways of expressing him or herself. Similarly, each situation is different, and as nurses we bring our own individual attitudes, values, beliefs, experiences and skills into them. We also bring our feelings of anxiety and helplessness and our need to 'make it better' for patients or clients, which it is not always possible to do.

Witnessing strong emotions in others and learning to cope with and accept them may remind us of our own areas of difficulty and losses, whether real or feared. This can make us vulnerable to feelings of anxiety, inadequacy and pain. If we are not sufficiently aware of our own values, beliefs and areas of 'unfinished business', it may affect the way we relate to our clients and hinder the development of the qualities of warmth, acceptance, genuineness, empathy and flexibility that are so essential when working with this client group. Finally difficulties arise because ultimately 'effective helping' requires a degree of self confidence and courage and it is often easier to 'opt out' and avoid the situation. This is a normal coping strategy that we all need to do when we are vulnerable. We must care for ourselves as nurses or we will not be free to effectively care for others.

Tasks of mourning

Although each client and situation is different, there are certain principles that can be followed to make our helping skills more effective. It may be useful to consider these within the framework of the four tasks of mourning (Worden, 1983).

When clients are informed of their situation they often feel a sense of disbelief, that 'it is not really happening'. During this first stage the nurse's prime aim is to help the client become aware and accept that the situation is real, it is happening and is not a figment of the imagination. This is essential, as only when reality is accepted can the client progress and experience the pain of grief, ultimately moving through to resolution. One of the best ways to help clients accept their loss is to encourage them to talk. Many clients mentally relive where they were when they first heard of their diagnosis, what happened and who said what. They may need to talk through this again and again, over weeks or even months. While family and friends may grow tired and even impatient the effective nurse is a patient listener who encourages the clients to talk.

Acknowledging grief

The second task of mourning is to acknowledge and experience the pain of grief. Feelings such as anger, guilt and sadness may not be acceptable to either family or friends or to clients themselves. They may therefore try to suppress or even deny their pain in order to avoid burdening, distressing or embarrassing their loved ones, while other clients may think they are 'going mad'. During this stage clients need to be helped to give themselves 'permission' to be angry or sad, or to cry, and must be given opportunity to talk through their guilt and unburden themselves. A nurse's quiet acceptance and acknowledgement of the pain of grief will facilitate this difficult task, which means that clients are not left to carry the burden of their pain with them into the next stage of their lives.

Adjustment

The third task of mourning is that of adjusting to the loss, real or impending. Essentially the nurse helps clients to identify problems and then to explore alternative ways of dealing with them. For example, this may mean identifying short term goals, of looking at today and next week rather than next month or next year. This is an active stage and may involve adopting and coming to terms with a new role or learning new skills such as coping with a prosthesis.

The final stage of mourning involves withdrawing emotional energy from the loss and reinvesting it in another relationship or diverting it to other channels. At this point the intense pain of grief diminishes and although clients will still experience a sense of sadness they will be able to channel their emotions into living and dealing with their lives today.

Skills for effective helping

Effective helping can be viewed as a problem solving activity. Most nurses use a variety of skills throughout the helping process and although there is no standard classification of such skills, for convenience they can be divided into two main stages.

Stage one — attending   Effective helpers are those who can establish a caring, non threatening relationship with their clients. Many nurses begin this relationship with an advantage in that the client's trust is already invested in them because of the nurturing nature of the nursing role. Trust will also develop if the nurse can be open and honest — relationships bound by any degree of mutual pretence will lead to feelings of insecurity and non-acceptance in clients (Glaser and Strauss, 1965), who will then be more likely to withdraw into their lonely worlds.

The first contact between nurse and client is crucial in developing and maintaining a warm trusting relationship. The client will have doubts and fears, and some problems will seem too large, too overwhelming or too unique to share. He may ask himself, "Can I really trust this person?", "Is she really interested in me?" "Does she have the time for me?" Answers to such questions will be provided not merely by words but by other more subtle and powerful means of communication. The physical setting, the way the nurse greets the client and her gestures and tone of voice can all convey sensitivity and consideration.

Observing and reacting

From the first meeting nurse and client will engage in the process of observing and reacting to the other. Success in helping depends upon the client's perception of the nurse's manner and behaviour. He will look for, and must experience, empathy, respect and sensitivity. Being with, attending to and listening are supportive and comforting behaviours which convey respect and concern for the client.

At this stage an opening statement such as, "I wonder what worries you have about your illness?" may provide the necessary invitation for the client to take the lead and talk freely while the nurse 'attends'. This involves 'being with' the client physically and psychologically. Body communication, posture, degree of relaxation and eye contact indicate interest in and attention to the client. Attending behaviour encourages the trust that is so necessary for promoting exploration and will also help the nurse listen more effectively.

Listening is an active, complex process and perhaps the most important of all helping skills. It involves first observing and interpreting the client's non-verbal behaviour and then listening to and interpreting his verbal messages. During the process of listening, the skill of reflection can be used by the nurse to sensitively communicate to the client her understanding of his concerns. It is an empathetic response that involves restating in fresh words the client's core feelings. For example:

Client: "I'm bewildered, there's so much to take in and consider, and so many different doctors each with their own ideas."

Nurse: "It all seems so confusing, even overwhelming and almost out of your control."

Client: "Yes, that's it, it feels like that."

An accurate reflection, while not halting the flow of talk can help clarify and bring less obvious feelings into the client's awareness so that they can be 'owned' and acknowledged. Reflection also increases the degree of trust which will ultimately facilitate further exploration.

Stage two — responding This stage of helping involves maintaining the good relationship developed in the first stage and taking the process further by helping the client explore, clarify and define his problem or area of concern. Responding skills help the client progress through the stages of mourning, the appropriate and effective ones at this stage are those which enable the client to extend and develop his understanding of himself and his difficulties.

Effective helping will be determined by the nurse's ability to respond accurately to the needs and cues provided by the client. This 'staying with the client' demonstrates empathy and acceptance. To achieve this the nurse needs to avoid directing and leading, eg "I don't think you should be spending so much time talking about your illness."; reassuring, eg "That's a common problem, but you'll be alright."; advising, eg "I wouldn't tell your family about this;" or not accepting the client's feelings and hiding behind the professional facade, eg "Your depression will pass, it's just part of the body's response to your treatment."

Staying with the client may also mean staying silent if he needs time to gather thoughts and feelings together. Although there are many different meanings for a silence, it is often a productive time and it is helpful if the nurse simply waits quietly until the client is ready to go on. This is perhaps a very difficult strategy to adopt as we are used to commenting on, advising or teaching.

Other skills

Other responding skills which will help exploration and clarification are probing, questioning and summarising. Prompts and probes are verbal tactics which help clients talk about themselves and define their problems more concretely. A prompt may be a head nod or a simple "Aha" or "I see" while a probe may take the form of a statement, eg "When you were told you had cancer you said you were both relieved and depressed. I'm wondering how you've been since then."

The careful use of questions can also help focus and clarify. These should be open questions, usually beginning with 'how', 'what' or 'who', which leave the respondent free to answer as he wishes, eg "Can you explain what you mean?", or "What was it about your treatment session today that was so upsetting?". Asking too many questions, however, may make the client feel interrogated, anxious and insecure, which will interfere with the rapport between nurse and client. Questions which begin with 'why', such as, "Why did you feel like that?" are also unhelpful, as they lead the client to search for intellectual explanations to justify his feelings.

Summarising

Summarising is the process of tying together all that has been communicated during part or all of a helping session. It can also be a natural means of finishing the session or beginning a new one. This then paves the way for the client to commit himself to further exploration and to developing awareness. Thus, with continuing emotional support the client, finding and utilising his own inner resources, moves on with hope to another day.

These strategies have been identified to help the nurse care for clients who are experiencing loss, but it should be remembered that the nurse has to deal with her own personal feelings of grief in response to the client's situation. In addition she may be constrained by fears that she will make the situation worse for the client through lack of skill. Only the client can judge what is helpful and is likely to seek a nurse who can support, comfort and care, and is herself — a real person with strengths and weaknesses like anyone else.

Bibliography

Brammer, L. M. (1979) The Helping Relationships Process and Skills, Prentice-Hall, New Jersey.
   Provides more in-depth discussion of the issues raised in this paper.
Egan, G. (1982) The Skilled Helper Model, Skills and Methods for Effective Helping. Brooks Cole Publishing Company, California.
   Describes in detail the skills and methods needed for effective helping.
Munro, E. A., Nanthei, R. J., Small, J. J. (1983) Counselling: A Skills Approach. Methuen, New Zealand.
   A clearly-written text with some very practical exercises and examples of helping skills.
Nelson-Jones, R. (1983) Practical Counselling Skills, Holt, Rinehart and Winston, London.
   Applies the theory of counselling in a very practical way using exercises to aid skill development and case studies as examples.

References

Glaser, B. and Strauss, A. (1965) Awareness of Dying. Aldine, Chicago.
Worden, W. J. (1983) Grief Counselling and Grief Therapy. Tavistock Publications, London.

40

Bereavement: patients with advanced cancer and their families

Jenny Penson, MA, SRN, HVCert, Cert Ed, RNT
Senior Lecturer in Nursing Studies, Dorset Institute of Higher Education

"Bereavement" means "to be robbed of something valued" – this definition seems particularly helpful as it indicates that this someone or something has been wrongly or forcibly taken from you. A key concept to understanding bereavement is that of loss. As Caplan (1964) and others have suggested, the grief experienced after losing someone close to you may be similar to the emotions felt after other types of loss, life transitions such as redundancy, divorce, failing an important exam or losing a much loved pet. As nurses we become aware of the emotions that patients experience after operations such as mastectomy, amputation of a limb or the loss of body image caused by suffering from a disfiguring disease.

When people are bereaved they suffer not only the loss of a person but also a substantial part of themselves, because everything they have shared with that person cannot be repeated with anyone else. The bereavement experience, therefore, is one of strong, violent and sometimes overwhelming reactions. These feelings actually begin from the moment the relative is told that the patient will not recover, referred to by Lindemann (1944) as "anticipatory grief".

The patient

Kubler Ross (1970), states: "We cannot help the terminally ill patient in a really meaningful way if we do not include his family." She determined that family members undergo stages of adjustment similar to the five phases she described for dying patients – denial, anger, bargaining, depression and acceptance as they come to terms with the reality of terminal illness in the family. She advocates that when there is time to do so, the family should be encouraged to express grief as much as possible prior to the death of a loved one which serves to alleviate, to some extent, the pain that is felt afterwards. If members of a family can

Through this article bereaved people are referred to as 'family' or 'relatives' for ease of comprehension. Terms such as 'key people' or 'significant others', while rather unwieldy, may more accurately describe the grieving person who is, for example, a life-long friend.

share these emotions they will gradually face the reality of the impending separation and come to an acceptance of it together.

Unresolved family stress can significantly affect the outcome of the patient's illness, so the care of the family is part of the total care of the patient. It is also about understanding him as a member of the family group, and being aware that he and his family are not separate entities. Each constantly influences the other, thus affecting the health and happiness of both. It is possible that nursing actions may affect the long-term adjustment of the bereaved relatives after the death of the patient.

Molter (1979) studied family needs as they identified them, and looked at whether these were being met, and if so, by whom. The results showed that relatives could identify their needs during an intensive phase of hospitalisation. Their universal and strongest need was for hope. Nurses can go some way towards meeting this need by helping to set short-term goals for the patient. A weekend at home, a visit from a favourite friend, planning something special to enjoy together all helps to relieve that sense of helplessness which is often felt. They also go some way towards providing good memories to look back on. Reassurance that the patient will not be allowed to suffer pain or great distress, that someone will be with them when they die, and that support is available after the death if they need it, are all significant to those for whom no hope of an ultimate recovery can be given.

Hampe (1975) also found that spouses believed that the nurse's primary responsibility was to the patient and therefore they would be too busy to help relatives. One of the principal needs she identified from her study was for the family to be able to visit the dying patient at any time and for as long as they wished. They also wanted prompt help with the physical care and a demonstration of friendliness and concern in their relationship with the nurse.

My own experience indicates that encouraging involvement of the family in the care of the patient may minimise feelings of guilt during bereavement. There is a sense of not having failed when one was needed and the satisfaction of having done something tangible to give comfort and show love.

Hospital or home care?

This must be borne in mind when discussing the pros and cons of hospital versus home care. Where dying at home is possible because both the patient and their relatives want it, and there are enough resources available when needed, the family are likely to feel a sense of achievement, of not having failed the patient. On the other hand, relatives do derive comfort from the security of constant professional expertise and the knowledge that any emergency will be dealt with by a 24-hour service. However, they still need to feel involved and should be encouraged to give to the patient in any way they can. This might range from helping with nursing care to arranging photos and flowers or bringing in special food or drink that the patient may ask for which the hospital cannot supply.

To tell or not to tell

Whether or not to tell the patient of his diagnosis and prognosis is a dilemma which causes much distress to family, patients and nurses. Sometimes relatives are advised by doctors and/or nurses not to be truthful with the patient and this can create a barrier between them, described by Solzhenitsyn (1971) as "a wall of silence" which separates them.

There is an obvious conflict in many relatives' minds between the idea of the patient's right to autonomy to knowing the truth if he wishes it, and the idea of paternalism, having the right to withhold it on the grounds of protecting the patient and giving him hope. Relatives will often say such things as "it will be too much for him", "he will give up", "I know he won't be able to stand it", "he will be frightened". These sort of statements may well be true but they may also reflect the relatives' own fears.

The cue to how much information is given should lie with the patient and the nurse's role with the relatives is often to explain to and sustain them during that gradual realisation that comes to most patients near the end. This may or may not be expressed and shared. However, when a patient and family can openly discuss their situation together, their relationship can be deepened and this can give great comfort to the bereaved person afterwards. It also creates a basis of honesty and trust which facilitates the relationship between patient, family and carers. Ann Oakley (1985) described when her father, Richard Titmuss, was dying: "You said things you never would have said had you not known you were dying – and that is how I knew you were."

That families fail to share their feelings openly with one another when faced with terminal illness may be due to the defence of denial and also a function of experience. Although we, the health workers, have been enlightened about combating this so-called conspiracy of silence which surrounds the topic of death, it is also possible that some families have been over-exposed to that viewpoint. As Bowen, (1978) points out, in spite of whatever attitudinal change that may have taken place the "basic problem is an emotional one and a change in the rules does not automatically change the emotional reactivity."

Support

So, should staff be so involved as to sit and weep with the relatives? Is this what sharing and support is about? Kubler Ross, (1974), suggests that we ask ourselves whether we would judge someone who cared enough to cry for us. "A display of emotions on the part of the therapist is like drugs, the right amount of medicine at the right time can work wonders. Too much is unhealthy – and too little is tragic."

It has been suggested that nurses are in a prime position to meet the family needs through active listening and supporting. They found that relatives wanted support but they tended to feel they should not burden the 'too busy' nurses with their problems. It is important, therefore, that a sense of availability is conveyed to families so that they will not feel guilty when sharing fears and worries with the nurse. Families usually appreciate information and explanation about nursing procedures, tests, treatments, medications. This helps them to feel they are part of the life of the patient and increases feelings of control, which can enable them to cope more realistically and effectively with the immediate future.

Relatives who feel that they have not been 'told enough' are suffering from a lack of sustained professional interest. Effective nursing care is *planned* care and relatives can and should be involved in this. Short-term objectives for the patient such as an improved night's sleep, can be explained to relatives and are positive indicators that there are always things which can be done to improve the quality of life for the patient.

There is often an accompanying aspiration or, for many people, a desperate need to find that the experience of grieving does have some meaning. This may lead to a turning or returning towards religion, or other philosophies of living. The nurse can often meet this need with tact and sensitivity by introducing the hospital chaplain or family priest at an appropriate moment. Their availability to families as well as patients gives comfort, and helps them to explore their own beliefs and what they mean.

Physical fitness is related to the ability to cope with stress and measures to maintain health may be more acceptable to the family if they are seen in terms of enabling him to support and be with the dying patient. They also serve to reinforce the message that the grieving relative *is* an important individual whose needs are also the nurse's concern. Simple relaxation techniques to promote sleep and encouragement to eat regularly are all part of this care.

Interpersonal skills

It is important, therefore, for nurses to develop interpersonal skills to enable them to meet the needs of the patient's family. The creation of a trusting relationship, the ability to give information in a clear and sympathetic manner, the ability to listen actively to their concerns and to help them to clarify problems and options all involve skills which can be learned and practised.

As Frederick and Frederick (1986) point out, although there is a great deal of controversy surrounding anticipatory grief, it appears that it may be a way of doing some of the work of mourning before the death occurs. In this way, it may soften the impact of the actual death on the bereaved. The nurse is in a unique position, being in constant contact with the family. Her attention to their needs may have long-term beneficial effects on their adjustment to bereavement and is likely to enhance the quality of their remaining time with the dying patient.

References
Bowen, M. (1978) Family reactions to death, In: Family Therapy and Clinical Practice. Aronson, New York.
Caplan, G. (1964) Principles of Preventive Psychiatry. Basic Books, New York.
Frederick, J.F. and Frederick, N.J. (1985) The hospice experience: possible effects in altering the biochemistry of bereavement, *Hospital Journal*, **1**, 3, 81–89.
Hampe, S. (1975) Needs of the grieving spouse in a hospital setting. *Nursing Research*, **24**, 20.
Kubler-Ross, E. (1970) On Death and Dying. Tavistock, London.
Kubler-Ross, E. (1974) Questions and Answers on Death and Dying. Macmillan, London.
Lindemann, E. (1944) Symptomatology and management of actue grief. *American Journal of Psychiatry*, **101**, 141–149.
Molter, N.C. (1979) Needs of critically ill patients: a descriptive study. *Nursing Research*, **8**, 2.
Oakley, A. (1985) Taking it Like a Woman. Penguin, London.
Solzhenitsyn, A. (1971) Cancer Ward. Penguin, London.
Ward, A.W.M. (1976) Mortality of bereavement. *British Medical Journal*, **11**, 700–702.

Bibliography
Penson, J. (1990). *Bereavement: A Guide for Nurses*. Harper & Collins, London.

41
Screening elderly people

Maggie Rogers, SRN, SCM, HV, Cert Ed
Avon Family Health Services Authority, Bristol

This chapter does not intend to discuss in detail the feasibility or effectiveness of screening elderly people, but will consider the implications of this type of work on the training needs of practice nurses, and how their growing role in this field interacts with the other members of the Primary Health Care Team. Many practice nurses have been employed specifically to undertake this task since April 1990.

It is known that the population range of the UK is getting older, with the projected numbers of people aged 75 years and over expected to rise by 30% over the next few decades. There are obvious implications for the planning and provision of services in trying to cope with the growing demand on resources, as a result of increased morbidity associated with ageing.

Systematic screening

Members of the Primary Health Care Team are often the first point of contact with the health service for people when problems occur, and are well placed to identify changes in a person's health or functional ability, as well as being able to assess future needs.

Attendance audits have shown that approximately 90% of people aged 75 years and over consult their GP at least once a year, and so general practice would appear to be an ideal starting point for screening and assessing the needs of the elderly population. The current situation regarding this is very variable with some Primary Health Care Teams already having a well established screening programme, while others do not have a coordinated system and contact with older people is often on a reactive or ad hoc basis.

In many practices the district nurses and health visitors may have contact with a large number of elderly patients on their case load, but not necessarily as part of a routine or regularly ongoing programme. In the case of health visitors, pressure of work involving the under 5s group often means that, however well motivated, the screening of elderly people often has to take second place. Some health authorities employ health visitor assistants who take on follow-up and routine visits for the elderly population while others employ health visitors with particular responsibility for older people.

The new contract The new contract for GPs, which was implemented in April 1990, gave recognition to the growing workload associated with 75 year olds, by increasing the capitation fee for this patient group. The 'Terms of Service for Doctors in General Practice' (DOM, 1989) requires that for all people aged 75 years and over, registered with a doctor, in each period of twelve months beginning on April 1st, the GP should:

- invite each patient on his list who has attained the age of 75 years to participate in a consultation,
- offer to make a domiciliary visit to each such patient for the purpose of assessing whether he needs to render personal medical services to that patient.

The GP is able to delegate this task to another professional, provided they are competent to carry it out. No matter which member of the Primary Health Care Team carries out the consultation the GP remains responsible and should make an assessment of the patient's needs and act accordingly.

Workload and role of the team   Initially the extra workload which was implied by this appeared to be a daunting task for general practice, and many practice nurses were employed specifically for this purpose. This caused some anxieties amongst community nurses already involved with the care of elderly people as to whether their role would be eroded, or whether there would be unnecessary duplication of work. Many of the anxieties about workload and role could be allayed by good communication and teamwork.

Setting up a screening programme

All members of the Primary Health Care Team should be involved in the planning process to establish a systematic screening programme. Many decisions need to be made before the programme starts such as who should carry out the screening and where this will be done, and who should be responsible for sending letters of invitation and recording the responses. The age sex register also needs to be accurate and up-to-date.

There should be agreement as to the recording of findings, and to assist practices in Avon the FHSA designed a simple record card which was available for their use.

A large proportion of the practice population aged over 75 years are already visited in their own homes by members of the Primary Health Care Team, particularly health visitors and district nurses. Their expertise and knowledge make it appropriate that they should continue to carry out full assessment for health needs as is their normal practice.

Within Avon the District Health Authority community managers have recognised that if community nurses are already visiting over 75 year olds that it would seem sensible for them to complete the screening requirements in accordance with the doctors' 'Terms of Service', during their routine visit, providing this was with the patient's informed consent. They would then report back their findings in order for the GP to assess whether the patient required his or her personal medical services.

If the screening is delegated by the GP to the practice nurse then it is not anticipated that she should duplicate or take over the role of either the health visitor or district nurse. If the practice nurse's screening consultation identifies the need for further assessment, the GP should refer to the health visitor, district nurse or other professional as appropriate for them to carry out this assessment.

Good liaison between professionals should ensure a coordinated approach to screening, and thus avoid duplication of visiting and consequent wasting of resources, as well as confusion to the patients.

Contacting all elderly patients   Before any screening is undertaken it is essential to identify which patients have not been seen by any member of the Primary Health Care Team in the previous twelve months. After checking whether these people are still registered with the practice, they would be the first group to be sent a written invitation, offering either a domiciliary visit or a consultation at the surgery.

Patients who accept the offer of a domiciliary visit in this group are the ones who could most appropriately be delegated to the practice nurse to carry out the initial screening visit.

Patients attending the surgery for other reasons can be offered a home visit at that time and their response recorded in their notes. GPs can collect most of the information required by their 'Terms of Service' opportunistically during routine consultations. The requirement to offer a domiciliary visit still holds, but many people will decline this offer, particularly if they are fit and active.

It would again be appropriate for this group of patients who accept the offer of a home visit to be delegated to the practice nurse. If the system of invitation and response is properly monitored approximately ten per cent of people aged over 75 years would need to be visited by the practice nurse, as the others would be seen either opportunistically by the GP in surgery or during visits, or by other members of the Primary Health Care Team. Good record keeping is essential to ensure people are not missed and it is a good idea to make one member of the team responsible for coordinating the system.

Issues of competency
As has been previously stated the doctors' 'Terms of Service' allow them to delegate this task to a person authorised by the doctor and who is considered competent to carry it out. This issue of competency initially caused some problems, as there were misconceptions that screening people aged over 75 years was an easy task, that required minimal skills beyond a basic nursing qualification.

The UKCC produced some guidelines which helped to clarify the the position to some extent; these stated that: "An assessment of the type required is complex and requires a high level of skill. Courses in District Nursing and Health Visiting are prime examples of the professional education and training which prepare nurses for such responsibilities." (UKCC, 1990).

However very few of the practice nurses employed to undertake the screening had either a district nurse or health visitor qualification, which highlighted the need for extra training for these nurses. The variation in experience amongst practice nurses was very broad. Some nurses had a wealth of experience in particular aspects of clinical nursing, but had little or no experience of community working. Other nurses were inexperienced generally, or had returned to work after a long break in their career. It was apparent therefore that many nurses employed to carry out domiciliary screening of elderly people needed extra training before they could really be considered competent to undertake this work.

In view of the extent of activities already carried out by the community nurses with regard to the over 75 age group, any training for practice nurses needed to take this into consideration. This was to ensure that the practice nurse's work was complementary to, and coordinated with the community nurse's. It was considered essential that any training programme for practice nurses should be planned in close liaison with the DHA training department and nurse adviser.

Screening process

It is important to clarify the difference between screening and assessment, and that here the practice nurses' training should be concerned with the screening of people over 75 years. Screening is an activity which identifies patients who require further follow-up, and is not in itself an activity to provide detailed assessment and intervention.

It was also recognised that in the majority of cases the practice nurse would only be visiting patients once annually, and would not be building up a case load in the way in which a district nurse or health visitor would.

Training needs The first step in organising training for practice nurses in this area was to be clear about the aims and objectives that it was hoped to achieve. The overall aim of the training was: to increase the nurses competence in screening elderly people both in the domiciliary setting and in the surgery. Also to be aware of the roles of the other members of the Primary Health Care Team in this area, and how they interlink.

The objectives to meet these aims were:
- To be aware of the UKCC guidelines relating to home visiting of the over 75 age group, and the nurse's own accountability.

- To be able to carry out a domiliary screening visit in a competent and professional manner.
- To be able to carry out an effective screening interview.
- To understand the delineation of the practice nurse's role, and the role of other health professionals in this situation.
- To be able to identify those patients over 75 years old who require screening.
- To understand the screening requirements of the GP's 'Terms of Service'.
- To be able to recognise problems and potential problems and report findings back to the GP.
- To keep accurate records.
- To have an understanding of the basic principles of health promotion with regard to the elderly population.
- To be aware of the routes of referral to other health professionals.

Setting up the study day course   A course of three, linked, study days was planned with one of the DHA's community training officers and the nurse adviser. Although many nurses would benefit from the training it was decided to limit places on the course to twenty, as it was felt that this would give the opportunity for more interactive learning and group work.

It was anticipated that the course would need to be repeated to meet the demand, but that organising this would be left until after the initial course had been evaluated. The plan for the course was that each day would be structured in such a way as to include a mixture of information giving, provided by appropriate professionals in the field, and experiential learning for the nurses.

A range of speakers are to be invited to contribute over the three days, including a geriatrician, psychogeriatrician, community pharmacist, incontinence adviser, home care organiser, health visitor for the elderly and a health promotion officer.

Although the course would not be able to award a certificate of competence as such, it was felt that it was necessary to build into the course some form of assessment. This was to take the form of asking the nurses to complete specific tasks between the study days, which would then be reported back on and discussed in small groups as a form of self-assessment.

Another part of the assessment process was asking the nurses to analyse and discuss case studies. This was to discuss how they would approach the visit if they were making it, and what aspects they would consider relevant to record and report back to the GP.

Between the first and second study day, the nurses would be asked to find out about the roles of the health visitors and district nurses in their own Primary Health Care Teams, with regard to their involvement with the over 75 year olds. Hopefully then in discussion with the community nurses they can consider how their roles differ and interlink with the practice nurse's own role. This discussion may also help to foster better communication and teamworking.

Between the second and third study days each nurse would be asked to make a critical assessment of one home visit that they felt went particularly well or particularly badly. This visit could either be made by the nurse alone, if she was already making home visits, or if not, this assessment could be made on an observation visit. These assessment visits would once again be discussed in detail in small groups and the wider issues discussed with the whole group.

By the end of the three days all the aspects of screening stated in the 'Terms of Service' would have been covered. These aspects are: sensory function, mobility, mental condition, physical condition including continence, social environment and use of medicines.

Other areas which need to be addressed on the study days are general aspects concerned with domiciliary working, such as carrying and using identification cards, and the etiquette of visiting someone in their own home rather than them being a patient in the surgery where they have initiated the consultation. Nurses should also be conscious of their own personal safety whilst visiting alone, and try not to allow themselves to be placed in positions of risk.

Providing a valuable service

Screening of people aged over 75 years can be a worthwhile task particularly if all the members of the Primary Health Care Team share in the responsibility. At worst the requirements of the doctor's 'Terms of Service' can be fullfilled by an ineffectual 'tick the box' approach, but in a well coordinated team, with a systematic screening system, it can provide a valuable service to patients and will identify unmet needs. This in itself could cause a problem by raising expectations that these unmet needs can be met, but on the other hand gathering this sort of information about needs will be essential to future planning.

References

Department of Health (1989) *Terms of Service For Doctors in General Practice*, HMSO, London.

Freer, C. (1990) Screening the elderly. *British Medical Journal*, **300**, 1447–8.

Mead, M. (1989) Screening the elderly. *Practice Nurse.*

RCGP. Care of Old People: A Framework for Progress. Occasional paper 45.

Stone, D. (1991) Looking for ill health in the elderly. *Medical Monitor.*

UKCC (1990) *Statement on Practice Nurses and Aspects of The New GP Contract*, UKCC, London.

42

The age gap: teaching students about health education for the elderly

Beverley Holloway, MA, RGN, RNT
Nurse Tutor, The Portsmouth District School of Nursing, Portsmouth

Evidence shows that the average age of the UK's population is increasing (Phillipson, 1985). With continuing general improvements in healthcare helping people to live longer, the elderly are an increasingly large group of the hospital population. Student nurses will therefore be exposed to large numbers of elderly people throughout their training and future careers, so it is important that aspects of caring for the elderly well, rather than simply the elderly sick are considered.

When teaching student nurses about the health education needs of the elderly, the teacher is confronted with the same problems that have made the appropriate and effective provision of health education for elderly people so difficult. This in itself can provide a powerful experiential tool with which to examine the issues surrounding this area of health promotion. These problems include ageism, stereotyping and a difference between normative and expressed needs.

The students reach their care of the elderly module at the end of the first year. At this stage, each has experienced three clinical placements: a basic care ward – which may be medical, surgical, or elderly nursing, – followed by medical and surgical placements. Consequently, some will have already come into contact with elderly people.

Students' attitudes

A useful starting point when teaching student nurses about health promotion in elderly people is to encourage exploration of their own attitudes to them. Despite the fact that many are familiar with elderly people on a personal level, or have worked in nursing and rest homes, and claim an affection for them, accurate analysis of perceptions often reveals issues which need to be discussed and clarified. Skeet (1985), claims that: "Looming over all these major issues is ageism – the deeply rooted discrimination against the elderly . . . one source of this prejudice is the fear among young and middle-aged people of joining the ranks of the ignored and the dispensable. . ." To allow student nurses to function with elderly people they must be given the opportunity, through discussion, to free themselves from the constraints of an ageist approach. This does not detract from the effect of the attitudes of the elderly themselves, and students need to be made aware of the often fatalistic view adopted by the elderly: Muir-Gray (1983) found that some elderly patients felt they should avoid exercise as 'the body will wear out'.

Students are asked to write down their feelings about being old, and how they imagine they will be when they reach old age. Responses vary; some students openly admit they are frightened by the prospect of being old and alone; others feel they would be frustrated by not being able to do things they wanted. Overwhelmingly however, students find it almost impossible to imagine what it is like to be elderly, and it is generally found enlightening to discuss what effects this inability to imagine has on the care given to the elderly.

A further productive exercise is to ask students to describe elderly stereotypes; these frequently resemble those cited by Brearley (1975) "the rigid, inflexible, dogmatic elder or the charitable, loyal, upright figure." A recent addition to this list was described by one student nurse as "a cantankerous old so-and-so". The effects of stereotyping can then be discussed, for as Brearley points out "it is a small step from the acceptance of the stereotype to the adoption of it personally."

Thus, attitudes and images, particularly in the negative sense with ageism and stereotyping, can be raised as important influences in health promotion for the elderly. Comparing different perceptions of needs of the elderly appears to generate interest and concern for them in the students. They are asked to determine what they see as the health education needs of the elderly. They are then asked to examine either normative needs or felt and expressed needs. Various methods of data collection are used, as the students feel appropriate, and this will usually include interviews with professionals and elderly people, literature reviews, and amassing available health education or promotion material.

Role play

An alternative method, depending on time availability, involves dividing the students into small groups, and asking them to imagine that they are either a group of elderly people or nurses working in a care of the elderly unit. They are then asked what they feel the health education needs of the elderly might be. Each group can be carefully selected depending on their responses to how they feel about becoming old themselves. The exercise appears to work well in that each group tends to identify different aspects of health education.

Students are usually surprised to discover a gulf between normative needs and expressed needs of the elderly. Their own beliefs are frequently similar to those of health professionals, such as emphasis on hypothermia or the need for mobility. The greatest impact, however, occurs when the students analyse the responses of the well elderly people they have interviewed (where possible), and discover the elderly themselves are less concerned with physical or even specific aspects of health, but see social and psychological health as most important. Overwhelmingly the elderly articulate their problems in financial terms, expressing particular needs such as assistance with telephone installation and bills. The lack of awareness regarding the services and schemes that are available to assist them financially enforces the sometimes inadequate or inappropriate provision of health education or promotion. To simply criticise existing provision would not only be a negative exercise, but would also deny the valuable contribution made by many groups, organisations and individuals concerned with caring and providing for the health of the elderly.

The next activity requires the students to find out what exists in terms of health education, and who is making the provision. They are asked to find examples from each tier of the national framework which exists to meet the needs of the elderly. At central government level they can explore provision made by the Department of Health, and that of Social Security, at a local level how the NHS and local authorities provide for their elderly, and – importantly – the work of the voluntary organisations. This latter group is particularly welcoming, encouraging students to look at their work. Age Concern West Sussex has developed an especially close liaison with the local nurse students; the group, and in particular their health education adviser (jointly appointed with three health authorities), are keen for the students to become involved in the awareness of health education problems affecting the elderly.

Purpose-made materials

Apart from a global view of how organisations work, students are encouraged to examine specifically produced materials for the elderly, such as 'Helping Yourself to Health', a resource pack produced as part of the Pensioners' Link Health Education Project (1987). Our district health authority's education department is extremely helpful in allowing students to explore the resources they have on offer for groups and individuals within the district. With this information, the students can identify and piece together a picture of what material is available locally for health professionals to use when providing elderly people with health education. At this point it is useful to look at the disciplines involved, and it is important to air feelings about other professional groups, as this may uncover negative attitudes. An understanding and acceptance of contributions made by all the different groups and individuals encountering the elderly is desirable to maximise and coordinate efforts. Nurses, working in a variety of settings, form one of the many groups, and the student nurses are asked to think about their possible contribution, before going on to list other groups whom they believe contribute to the health education of the elderly.

Planning to meet needs

As a final exercise the students are divided into groups of three or four and asked to draw up a plan to meet the health education needs of the elderly. They are asked to look at what provision is required nationally, locally and individually and to say how they feel this could be best achieved. The students are also asked to think about how they could provide health education for those already in hospital. It is encouraging that by this stage they usually state the importance of listening to what the patient says. Having shared their ideas, the session closes with a look at the work of Brocklehurst (1976) and Phillipson (1985) whose contributions to this field have been significant.

While these exercises have been designed to be carried out in the classroom-based setting, they are readily adaptable for use in clinical placements, be it in hospital or the community. Caring for the elderly has historically been seen as lacking both appeal and glamour. However, more recently there has been a thrust towards promoting interest and a positive image in this field. It is hoped that by teaching today's students about this vital area and by facilitating their confrontation of the issues surrounding the elderly, they will be able to competently make useful contributions to an already committed team.

Bibliography
The following sources of information are recommended to those wishing to further explore this subject.
Garrett, G. (1987) Health Needs of the Elderly, Macmillan, London.
   An extremely readable book, this would be an excellent place to start for anyone wanting to gain an overview of the health needs of the elderly.
McClymont, M., Thomas, S., Denham, M. (1986) Health Visiting and the Elderly. Churchill Livingstone, Edinburgh.
   A useful book, not only for health visitors, but for any health professional wanting to understand more about the application of health education theory to practice with the elderly.
Muir-Gray, J. and McKenzie, H. (1986) Caring For Older People. Penguin, Harmondsworth.
   A comprehensive, practical book, focusing clearly on the health needs of the elderly. The information is useful to professionals, families with elderly members, and the elderly themselves.
Tinker, A. (1986) The Elderly in Modern Society, Longman, Harlow.
   A background of how the elderly have come to be in their present position in society. The book not only presents information clearly, but looks at existing literature and relevant research.
   For further resources, or specific information the reader is advised to contact their local Health Education Department, local voluntary organisations such as Age Concern or the Health Education Authority.

References
Brearley, C.P. (1975) Social Work, Ageing and Society. Routledge and Kegan Paul Ltd., London.
Brocklehurst, J.C. (1976) Health education in the elderly. *Journal of the Institute of Health Education*, **14**, 4, 115–20.
Muir-Gray, J. (1983) Beliefs and attitudes – the ageing process (2), August 17, *Nursing Mirror*, 36–37.

Pensioners' Link Health Education Project (1987) 'Helping Yourself To Health'. Pensioners Link.

Phillipson, C. (1985) Developing a health education strategy with older people. *Journal of the Institute of Education*, **23**, 3, 184–87.

Skeet, M. (1985) 'Some international concepts of old age'. *Nursing*, **41**.

43

Happy to be home? A discharge planning package for elderly people

Jo Booth, Bsc (Hons), RGN
Lecturer, Department of Nursing, University of Manchester; and Clinical Developments Nurse, Nursing Development Unit, Manchester Royal Infirmary.

Cath Davies, MSc, Bsc (Hons), RGN, RNT
Former Nursing Development Unit Leader, Manchester Royal Infirmary

Adequate provision for discharge of patients from hospital is now regarded as a priority by all healthcare professionals concerned with the quality of care offered to elderly people. This has arisen as a result of extensive research conducted over the past 25 years which has highlighted the numerous and varied areas where deficiency occurs.

The impetus for such research comes not only from the desire to improve care and outcomes of care, but also from the need to minimise readmission due to inadequate aftercare which tends to be both expensive and, in many cases, unnecessary. Improvements in practice have also been instigated at government level with the publication of documents such as the Department of Health circular HC/89/5 which bemoaned the lack of recent guidance on discharge arrangements from health authorities. There has, therefore, been a double stimulus to review the discharge procedures - a bottom up and a top down approach.

Planning discharge goals
Members of the multidisciplinary team must agree on the clear definition of terms before improvements in preparing for discharge can be put into practice. The term 'discharge', for example, may best be viewed as a process rather than a single event. "Discharge is regarded as a stage in patient care which has both a period of preparation and from which there are consequences. It cannot be examined in isolation from what has gone before or separated from what follows after the event when the patient leaves hospital" (Armitage, 1981).

This definition emphasises the complexity of the process, and raises two important issues for healthcare professionals responsible for planning discharges: successful discharge should reflect the care given throughout the hospital stay, and our role as coordinators of discharge extends beyond the hospital into the patient's home life. The ability to assess and meet needs accurately will mean the difference between success and failure for many patients. Embarrassing though a break-down in arrangements may be for the multidisciplinary team, it can be devastating for elderly clients who depend on these arrangements for their health, safety and ability to remain independent in the community.

'Discharge planning' according to Armitage (1981) refers to the 'period of preparation' necessary for arrangements to be made. Four key elements comprise discharge planning (Victor and Vetter, 1988):

- adequate notice of discharge;
- discussion of arrangements for aftercare;
- arrangements for aftercare;
- liaison with primary care services.

A fifth element could usefully be added to this, concerning the education of patients and carers on needs and arrangements.

Preparing a discharge package

The term 'aftercare' was first used by Roberts in 1975 as an outcome measure. She stated that aftercare is successful if it: "counteracts the disabling effects of any current stage of illness or disability, that is, it should make good any deficiency in an individual's ability to care for himself". Recent research, however, has indicated that an increased level of aftercare services is essential for many elderly people following discharge, as their level of independence in activities of living tends to be lower than it was before admission (Bowling and Betts, 1984; Waters, 1987; Victor and Vetter, 1988).

The nursing development unit at Manchester Royal Infirmary has developed a discharge package, based on research findings (Table 1). This will be discussed using Victor and Vetter's key elements as a framework.

Adequate notice of discharge

Skeet (1970) conducted a survey of 1,550 structured interviews with elderly people following discharge, and found that 12 per cent had less than 24 hours warning that they were to be discharged. A survey in 1979 (NCCOP, 1979) found that most elderly patients had two days or less notice of discharge, which is inadequate considering the range of needs which may have to be met. A small study carried out by Bowling and Betts (1984) suggests the situation may have worsened since the '70s, especially in the light of the move towards early discharge. The results showed that 42 per cent of patients were given two or more days notice of discharge, 34 per cent were told the day before and 24 per cent had no prior notice at all. Short notice may, therefore, be a major reason for the lack of accurate assessment of potential post-discharge needs, and subsequent poor planning and coordination of the discharge process, with the almost inevitable consequences of inadequate aftercare.

Discussion of aftercare arrangements

This involves accurate and thorough assessment of each individual's present home circumstances and healthcare needs to maintain or improve on their current health status and reduce levels of dependence. It is pointless investing effort and resources into patient care if discharge proves unsuccessful because nobody bothered to accurately assess and address the patient's homecare needs. Skeet (1970) showed that nurses are often not aware of the home situation of many of their patients and therefore unable to accurately determine special needs and requirements. Reports also suggest that elderly people are likely to require a greater level of aftercare support after discharge than they did before admission (Walters, 1987; Victor and Vetter, 1984; Bowling and Betts, 1984). This is true for both personal needs such as washing and dressing and household needs such as shopping, cleaning and cooking. Many health professionals are unaware of this, believing rehabilitation leads to a lowered dependency at home with less reliance on formal and informal community facilities. Skeet (1970), however, found almost half of the people interviewed had to cope with unmet needs after discharge; these included the need for equipment, advice, help with personal care, domestic support and treatment.

1. Core care plan
2. Health educational needs assessment checklist
3. Patient discharge booklet
4. Multidisciplinary team checklist
5. Information file

Table 1. Components of the discharge package.

Hockey (1968) suggested that greater anticipation by ward staff of needs for domestic assistance could allay many elderly patients' anxieties about going home. This is of vital importance given anxiety's negative effects on consequent recovery (Hayward, 1975; Seyle, 1974).

To achieve both adequate notice of discharge and discussion of aftercare arrangements, parts one and two of the discharge package are used (Table 1). A discharge planning core care plan is incorporated into each patient's complete care plan on admission, and any individual needs are documented as they arise. This usually follows discussion between primary nurse, patients and carers about healthcare needs following discharge, using the health educational needs assessment checklist to ensure that potential problem areas are not missed (Table 2).

Arrangements for aftercare

There has been little interest, until recently, in the plight of elderly people in the community following discharge, even though it was recognised as a problem as early as 1966 (Brocklehurst and Shergold, 1968). This situation has remained fairly static - evidence was available to justify major improvements in the types and quality of arrangements made, but

Activities of living
Mobility around the house
Getting up in the morning
Dressing/undressing; going to bed
Washing and bathing
Footcare
Eating, drinking; preparation of meals
Shopping
Maintenance of continence
Sexuality
Stress management/relaxation
Communication eg, care of hearing aids
Comfort needs and keeping warm
Social needs
Support of carers eg, lifting techniques and how to prevent pressure sores
Relief for carers (respite care)
Companionship
Advice on financial needs
Advice on how to obtain information
Self-help groups
Security needs
Worship needs
Nursing/medical needs
Understanding of diagnosis
Understanding of medication
Nursing procedures eg dressings
Arrangements for emergencies
Medical and nursing follow-up

Table 2. Health educational needs assessment checklist.

change tended to be limited to isolated examples. In 1989, however, two powerful documents were published which may have permanent and positive effects on discharge preparation. The first was the British Geriatric Society/Director of Social Services joint statement, Discharge from Hospital/Readmission to the Community, and the second the Department of Health circular HC(89)5, issued in response to the findings of the Select Committee on the Parliamentary Commissioner for Administration.

One guideline common to both documents is that planning for discharge should begin as early as possible - in cases of booked admissions, before the patient is even admitted to hospital. Another important guideline is that patients and carers should be at the centre of the planning, and written information be provided on medication, diet, treatment, lifestyle and symptoms to look for and where to obtain help if needed. These guidelines have been welcomed by professionals as they formalise the basic principles underpinning individualised, patient-centred preparation for home. In the nursing development unit, once the healthcare needs have been elicited, the primary nurse and patient complete the patient's discharge booklet. This is the patient's property and is retained by her or him from admission to hospital on into the community. It contains all the relevant information on discharge and aftercare, including the names of all professionals involved with the patient's case, what the patient should or should not do after discharge, symptoms and treatment to expect and information regarding medication. The booklet serves as a reference source for patients and their families and carers. It includes, when relevant, all the aspects highlighted for inclusion by the DoH and BGS/DSS documents.

Liaison with primary healthcare services

Nurses should coordinate discharge arrangements with the patient. It must be stressed, however, that research has found a number of potential problem areas for people holding this role. Waters (1987) and Roberts (1975) indicate that discharge planning for elderly people is not a high priority, which is reflected in the nature of the communication between hospital and the community.

Skeet (1970) suggests there is a distinct lack of communication between multidisciplinary team members and patients regarding discharge arrangements. The coordinator of the discharge procedure, therefore, faces the often onerous task of ensuring a breakdown in communication does not occur. Bowling and Betts (1984) suggest the answer lies with structured planning and documentation of each arrangement in such a way that is obvious and available to everyone involved in the care and discharge of clients. This recommendation is in keeping with the DoH circular and the BGS/DSS document, which propose that written discharge procedures be agreed and made available to all concerned with the discharge process in hospital and the community.

A multidisciplinary team checklist was therefore devised for use in the unit (Table 2), containing information on specific arrangements relating to discharge which may be of use to the team but not necessarily to the patient (for example, who booked the ambulance and when). This document is kept in a central point, rather than with the patient, so that it is easily accessible to all team members. Completion is the responsibility of the primary nurse, although all team members may make entries where appropriate. This focus of responsibility is in line with the DoH document which recommends that responsibility for coordinating discharge planning should be given to one member of staff caring for that patient.

The discharge package devised by the staff of the nursing development unit in Manchester Royal Infirmary attempts to rectify the problems that can lead to inadequate discharge planning. It has been designed to facilitate a comprehensive and systematic approach towards the process of adequately preparing patients for discharge.

References

Armitage, S. (1981) Negotiating the discharge of medical patients. *Journal of Advanced Nursing*, **6**, 385–89.

Bowling, A. and Betts, G. (1984) Communication on discharge. *Nursing Times*, **80**, 32, 31–33.

British Geriatric Society/Association of Directors of Social Services (1989) Discharge to the community of elderly patients in hospital. BGS/ADSS, London.

Brocklehurst, J. and Shergold, M. (1986) What happens when geriatric patients leave hospital? *The Lancet*, **2**, 1135–35.

Department of Health (1989) Discharge of Patients from Hospital. DoH Circular HC/89/5, London.

Hayward, J. (1975) Information: A Prescription Against Pain. RCN, London.

Hockey, L. (1968) Care in the Balance. Queen's Institute of District Nursing, London.

National Corporation for the Care of Old People (1979) Organising Aftercare: Continuing Care Project. NCCOP, London.

Roberts, I. (1975) Discharge From Hospital. RCN, London.

Royal Commission on the NHS (1978) Patients Attitudes to the Hospital Services, Research Paper 5. HMSO, London.

Selye, H. (1974) Stress without Distress. New American Library, New York.

Skeet, M. (1970) Home from Hospital. Dan Mason, Nursing Research Committee, Macmillan, London.

Victor, C. and Vetter, N. (1988) Preparing the elderly for discharge from hospital: a neglected aspect of care? *Age and Ageing*, **17**, 155–63.

Waters, K. (1987) Discharge planning: an exploratory study of the process of discharge planning on geriatric wards. *Journal of Advanced Nursing*, **12**, 71–83.

Waters, K. (1987) Outcomes of discharge from hospital for elderly people. *Journal of Advanced Nursing*, **12**, 347–55.

44

Encouraging compliance

Ruth E. Smith, BSc, RGN, RMN, DNCert
Deputy Officer in Charge, Thornybank Hostel, Edinburgh

Jill Birrell, MA(Hons), MSc, AFBPsS, C.Pychol
Principal Clinical Psychologist, Royal Edinburgh Hospital

Compliance is generally used to refer to adherence or co-operation — doing as the health professional says concerning health matters. Taking medicine when one is supposed to, going on a prescribed diet or stopping smoking when advised are all examples of compliance. Non-compliance, may cause a breakdown in a treatment programme. It may put an individual at risk of a more serious illness or prolong the current difficulty.

'Non-compliance is not restricted to medicine. Not every bit of advice given by solicitors, architects, business consultants and other professionals is followed by those who have sought their services. Clients exercise their judgement, as is their right, when presented with professional advice even though they may not have the experience claimed by their advisers . . . clients' failure to follow advice may have serious consequences, yet these professions tend to see this independence as part of a client's rights and if they study non-compliance at all, do not do so in terms of client deficiency but in terms of necessary improvement in the services they offer.' (Thompson, 1984).

The nature of compliance
An early study by Stockwell (1972) describes the views of nurses in the inpatient setting where patients are described as 'popular' or 'unpopular'. 'Popular' patients are passive in interactions with staff, unquestioning and undemanding. Patients who question their treatment and express views about the nursing care they receive are regarded as 'unpopular'. Perhaps unpopularity and non-compliance have similarities?

Compared with inpatient settings, hospital outpatient clinics and general practice consultations have far greater difficulties regarding compliance – they have a less captive audience. Non-compliance can take many forms, among them failure to turn up for an appointment, failure to file prescriptions, discontinuing medication early, failure to make recommended changes in daily routine and missing follow-up appointments. Studies of a wide variety of illnesses, including coronary heart disease, hypertension, glaucoma and diabetes, have indicated that only 40 to 70 per cent of patients comply fully with physicians' prescriptions and advice. It is also worth noting that problems of non-compliance are often aggravated in elderly people who have no family support to ensure they follow instructions correctly. Macdonald et al (1977) found that twelve weeks after discharge from hospital, half of the elderly people studied were taking less than 50 per cent of their tablets while a further 25 per cent were seriously overdosing themselves. Less than 25 per cent were still taking medicine as prescribed. Clearly consultations often fail to convince patients of the wisdom of the proposed treatment. It is also important to remember the economic consequences of non-compliance, including cost of drugs, salaries and valuable time lost by staff members as well as the consequences to the patient's health.

Peck (1978) noted that a large number of studies have endeavoured to find an association between compliance and demographic variables such as sex, educational level, age, race, income and religion. If an association is present at all, it is very low. Studies have also been conducted on disease variables and it has been found that the diagnosis, severity of illness, duration of illness, previous hospitalisation and degree of illness or disability also have little or no association with compliance. The only reasonably consistent finding seems to be that psychiatric patients tend to be less compliant than patients with a physical illness.

Most important factors in determining the degree of compliance are more subjective than objective. Patients' satisfaction with contacts with health professionals and beliefs about illness are important. Rosenstock

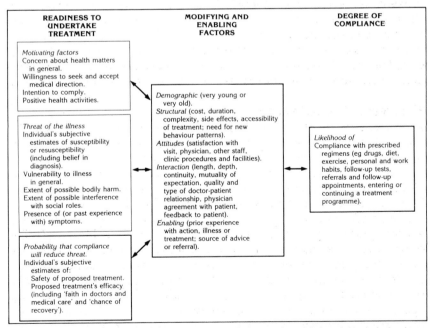

Table 1. Summary of Health Belief Model for predicting and explaining sick role behaviour, adapted from Becker, M.H.: The health belief model and sick-role behaviour reproduced with kind permission of the Society for Public Health Education, Inc.

(1966) and Becker (1974) present the Health Belief Model (Table 1).

Clearly patients' readiness to act is paramount. Action comes from their perception of the severity of the disease or possible progression and their perceived susceptibility to illness. If a patient does not believe that an illness is serious or does not believe he or she is likely to become ill, the readiness to act is low, whereas if the patient believes the illness is severe and there is a high chance of him or her contracting it, readiness to act is high. Important too are patients' considerations of the costs and benefits of compliance. They must believe that treatment will be effective.

Increasing compliance

Patients must understand and remember advice if they are to pay attention to it. Compliance is likely to be higher if the doctor or other health professional has a warm and friendly manner, heeds the patient's need for information, talks about non-medical topics and tests out and corrects any misunderstandings the patient may have. Written information seems effective in improving compliance in the short term. Categorisation of material into blocks has also proved useful. For example, saying "I am going to tell you what you must do to help yourself, what treatment you will receive, what tests need to be done" and suchlike, leads to greater recall of information. Also, the more specific the information given, the more compliance will be achieved. Telling a patient to lose half a stone is more effective than simply saying that he or she must lose weight. Supervision by a health worker can effectively increase compliance, as the act of reporting regularly to someone is reinforcing to the patient. When that constant supervision is removed, however, compliance returns to its lower initial rates. Finally, attempts to improve the communication skills of health care workers by further teaching and discussion have also shown promise. Research must continue to look for ways of removing barriers that prevent patients working well with health professionals and as Thompson (1974) states "a fuller understanding of attitude change required if the generally poor record of medical advisers is to be improved".

Bibliography

Fitzpatrick, R. et al. (1984) The Experience of Illness, Tavistock Publications, London and New York.
  The most comprehensive discussion of the literature to date. The book covers most areas of patients' experiences of illness.
Gatchel, R.J. and Baum, A. (1983) An Introduction to Health Psychology. Addison Wesley Publishing Company, London.
  Easier reading than Fitzpatrick et al – covers patients' experiences of illness but with less research data. Chapter seven is a precise summary of the main points.
Rachman, S.J. and Phillips, C. (1978) Psychology and Medicine. Penguin Publications, London.
  Chapter three is a short introductory text.

References

Becker, M.H. (1974) The health belief model and sick role behaviour. *Health Education*

Monograph, **2**, 409–419.

MacDonald, E.T., MacDonald, J.B. and Phoenix, M. (1977) Improving drug compliance after hospital discharge. *British Medical Journal*, **2**, 618–621.

Peck, D. (1978) Communication and compliance. *Bulletin of the British Psychological Society*, **32**, 348–352.

Rosenstock, I.M. (1966) Why people use health services. *Millbank Memorial Fund Quarterly*, 94–127.

Stockwell, F. (1972) The unpopular patient. Royal College of Psychiatrists, Series 1, No. 2.

Thompson, J. (1984) Compliance. In Fitzpatrick, R., Hinton, J., Newman, S., Scrambler, G. and Thompson, J. (Eds) (1984) The Experience of Illness. Tavistock Publications, London and New York.

45
Patient advocacy

Mary Watkins, RMN, RGN, DN, Dip NEd, MN
Principal, South West College of Health Studies, Devon

To what extent should nurses act as advocates for elderly clients? In order to address this question, it is necessary to examine the relationship between advocacy and accountability.

Accountability

Accountability is defined in Longman's dictionary (1984), as an area for which one is responsible, to explain one's conduct, to account for behaviour. Clearly this definition is orientated towards the individual being held to account for their own rather than someone else's behaviour.

In nursing, however, there are more complex issues involved than just being responsible for oneself. In particular, qualified nurses can be held to 'account' for the behaviour of those they supervise. As patients are by the very nature of their 'sick role' frequently dependent, nurses are held accountable for not only their own behaviour but that which they conduct on behalf of the patient. These 'acts' may be as diverse as bed-bathing to assisting in applying for financial allowances to which the patient is entitled.

Advocacy

Here the 'advocacy' role begins to become evident. The word 'advocate' is defined as "one who pleads the cause of another" (Longman's, 1984). This has traditionally been seen as a lawyer's role in that he or she actively supports and pleads for clients in adversity. Is it the role of the nurse? Should it be the role of the nurse?

Opinions differ, Brown (1985) suggests that it is an essential element of the nurse's role and other writers support this view, (Salvage, 1987). The alternative opinion given by Porter (1988) is that nurses are too involved in the health structure to really act as patients' advocates and ideally this role should be adopted by someone outside the system. To some extent this is the role of bodies like Age Concern and the Patients' Association.

Professional accountability

The problem of nurses' involvement in the health care structure is also recognised within the Code of Conduct (UKCC, 1984), which indicates that nurses have a responsibility in terms of accountability to both their profession and employer. This dual accountability can lead to conflict, but there is a widely held belief that accountability to the professional body must come first. In other words, the patient must be the nurse's first responsibility not her employer. The question arises: does this accountability include the role of advocacy? Again the Code of Conduct guides practitioners by stating: "Each registered nurse is accountable for his/her practice and shall have regard to the environment of care and its physical, psychological and social effects on patients/clients, and also to the adequacy of resources, and make known to the appropriate persons or authorities any circumstances which could place patients/clients in jeopardy or which militate against safe practice."

This paragraph indicates that the nurse is expected to act as a patient's advocate, in terms of pleading for his safety when necessary. In 1987, Pyne, then Director of Professional Conduct at the UKCC, warned: "Nurses who tolerate bad practice in silence are surely guilty of professional misconduct."

Silence
It is our job to "act always in such a way as to promote and safeguard the well-being and interests of patients and clients." (UKCC, 1984). Yet the conspiracy of silence between health care professionals is well illustrated by the Cavendish-Boyd case. She was told by a doctor that she had had a mastectomy for a 'fat necrosis' (McSweeney, 1990). Only when reading up the definition did her husband establish that this was unnecessary but not one health care worker involved in her care pointed out the mistake. Clearly health care professionals sometimes put loyalty to colleagues above patients' interests.

Collaboration not conflict
The important thing about advocacy is that it is concerned with safeguarding patients *not* with conflict for its own sake.

It is essential that nurses work in a collaborative manner with others but that this is not at the expense of patient advocacy. The dramatic cases such as Cavendish-Boyd are well documented. What is rarely reported is the nurse who has said to the doctor "Is that really the drug dose you want?" Or the nurse who has said to a colleague "Have you read the research which suggests that egg white and oxygen on pressure sores may do more harm than good?" In both cases the nurses are acting as advocates but *not* creating conflict. Good working relationships do exist and are in many people's perceptions the catalyst of advocacy, where the role is seen as positive rather than as whistle-blowing.

Whistle-blowing
Where collaboration exists, whistle-blowing should be unnecessary. However, in certain circumstances, the nurse must speak out to protect

patients' interests. This is frequently necessary in care of the elderly areas, where financial cutbacks have resulted in unacceptable standards of care. The manager who uses phrases like: "You can manage nurse, can't you?" or "I am leaving you with only one nursing assistant because you are so competent" is trying to manipulate the nurse into managing with insufficient resources. Once the nurse has accepted the responsibility for caring with insufficient staff, it ceases to be the concern of the manager. In this instance, the qualified nurse must speak up if patients are to receive quality care. Although nurses may request additional assistance and resources, inevitably there will be times when they have to make judgements concerning the allocation of resources to individual patients.

Professional judgments

On a day-to-day basis, all nurses are faced with the problem of which patient to allocate time to before another. For example, the district nurse has to decide whether to visit elderly people who live alone and are at-risk early in the morning, or to initially visit the most acutely sick individuals on her books. Similarly, the hospital nurse may be faced with one patient needing assistance with feeding while another calls urgently for a commode. It is up to the individual nurse to make a judgement about these matters while attempting to ensure that no patient is unduly disadvantaged. This complex issue is closely related to that of advocacy in that the nurse must try to protect the interests of all her clients, not just an elite few. When professional judgements become impossible, due to completely inadequate resources, the nurse must inform management of this problem in order to plead her client's entitlement to quality care.

Having identified some of the problems which may face nurses, in the clinical area, ways in which nurses can act as advocates for clients and enhance care through this role, will now be discussed.

Standards of care

One way of ensuring advocacy is achieved, is for management and clinical staff to identify clear standards of care. The question arises, "Should standards be set at an optimal or a minimal level?" For purely pragmatic reasons, it is suggested that nurses try to agree with their employers' minimal basic standards which can actually be achieved within the resources available. This does not negate the need to fight for additional finances to enhance care, but should prevent care falling below the accepted baseline.

There are three types of standard: structure, process and outcome (Kitson, 1990). Structural standards refer to the equipment and staffing available in a given area. For example, a standard may be agreed for a ward, which *states* that there must always be a minimum of one Grade D nurse and two health care assistants on duty. Similarly, it may be necessary to list the minimum number of commodes, wheelchairs etc that are required to deliver quality care.

Process standards in nursing terms refer to the 'actions' of nursing staff. A process standard could be phrased as follows: "All patients will have a member of nursing staff assist them with eating at every meal should this be judged necessary by the qualified nurse who assesses their nursing needs."

Outcome standards involve patient behaviour and should, when possible, like structure and process standards, reflect research findings. Millar (1985) has demonstrated that nurses sometimes create dependence in elderly patients by acting for them rather than encouraging independence. A process standard may be defined to involve 'encouraging patient independence' together with a related outcome standard. The latter could be stated thus: "only five per cent of patients will become more dependent in terms of activities of living between their admission and one week following admission."

The five per cent figure is realistic, in that due to changes in patients' illness patterns, a proportion will become more dependent. The important aspect of 'outcome standards' with regard to advocacy is that when these standards are not achieved, the nurse investigates why, and changes care if necessary to enhance patient outcome. The changes in care may involve altering nursing actions and/or the environment in which care is conducted.

Environment of care/patient choice

When acting as advocates, nurses have a responsibility to monitor patients' environment and this can be achieved by answering the following types of questions on a regular basis: "Is there enough space for walking frames and wheelchairs so that elderly people can get around in the environment in which they are living? Is the lighting sufficiently strong for patients to read? Is the ward or nursing home warm enough for patients to sit still comfortably?"

The psychological environment is perhaps even more important than the physical. There is a clear relationship between patients having choice in their lives with regard to activities of living and not being exposed to monotonous daily routines. There is a danger that nurses may confuse 'advocacy' with 'paternalism' and take over the patients' responsibility for making decisions about their own lives. The nurse's role as advocate has been interpreted as "performing a function for the patient which for a number of reasons he cannot perform himself" (Sawyer, 1988); while Clark (1982) believes it involves giving sufficient information to individuals so that they can make informed choices and subsequently supporting the patient's decision. It is suggested that these definitions are particularly pertinent to the nurse/patient relationship where partnership in care should be the predominant feature. In some instances, relatives of dependent patients are in a better position to act as 'advocates' than nurses, because their previous knowledge of the individual's beliefs and desires will outweigh that of nurses. Nurses need to consider relatives' opinions in such instances so that patients are represented effectively.

National role

In addition to the advocate role nurses experience within their day-to-day practice, Clarke (1989) believes that nurses have a collective responsibility to act as advocates at a national level. She cites the fact that 80% of fractured necks of femur occur in elderly women with the predominant cause being osteoporosis. As osteoporosis is preventable, she argues that the nursing profession should lobby for hormone replacement therapy to be more easily available, thus preventing ill health in the future.

Accepting professional responsibility

It has been argued that nurses do have a responsibility to act as patients' advocates but that this role is not exclusively theirs; patients, their relatives and national bodies, such as Age Concern, should also be involved. The relationship between standards of nursing care, the instigation of research findings in practice and the advocacy role has been explored. In particular, it has been suggested that nursing research is increasingly indicating ways by which nurses can enhance care and that it is their responsibility to do so.

The competent practitioner who acts for the elderly person when they are incapacitated and gives them sufficient information to help them choose when they are able, fits with the nursing process philosophy of partnership in care.

Advocacy does not involve fostering dependence, but being the protector of the client's self-determination (Nelson, 1988). This can be achieved in the following ways:

- practising high standards of care.
- working in partnership with patients; giving them sufficient information to make choices for themselves.
- incorporating research into practice.
- acting always in such a way as to safeguard the patient.
- fostering good interdisciplinary relationships.
- speaking out when necessary to ensure that clients are properly protected.

While advocacy is not perceived as the exclusive role of the nurse, it does appear that nurses cannot practice effectively without adopting this role at some time. There is therefore no room for only obeying orders. Nurses must accept their professional responsibility and make the necessary professional judgments if they are to truly act as clients' advocates.

References

Brown, M. (1985) Matter of commitment. *Nursing Times, 81* (18), 26–7.

Clark, J. (1982) Nursing matters patient advocacy. *The Times Health Supplement, 19*, 2.

Clarke, M. (1989) Patient/client advocates. *Journal of Advanced Nursing, 14*, 7, 513–4.

Kitson, A. *et al* (1990) *Quality Patient Care: The Dynamic Standard Setting System*, Scutari, London.

Longman (1984) *Longman Dictionary of the English Language*. Longman, London.

Millar, A. (1985) Nurse/patient dependency: is it introgenic? *Journal of Advanced Nursing, 10* (1), 63–9.

McSweeney, P. (1990) Accountability in nursing practice. *Nursing Standard, 4* (18), 30–1.

Nelson, M.L. (1988) Advocacy in nursing: how has it evolved and what are its implications for practice? *Nursing Outlook* **36** (3), 136–41.

Porter, S. (1988) Siding with the system. *Nursing Times*, October 12, **84** (41), 30–1.

Pyne, R. (1987) The UKCC Code of Conduct: accountability and implications. *Nursing, 3* (14), 510–1.

Salvage, J. (1987) Whose side are you on? *Senior Nurse*, **6** (2), 20–1.

Sawyer, J. (1988) On behalf of the patient. *Nursing Times* Oct 12th, **84** (41), 27–30.

UKCC ((1984) *Code of Professional Conduct for the Nurse, Midwife and Health Visitor*. UKCC, London.

Index

INDEX

Abuse 55–61
  in residential care 8
Accountability 256–7
Activities of daily living
    14–67
Advocacy 256–61
Aftercare 247–51
Ageing 1–5
  dyamics 210–14
  physiological effects 21–2
Ageism 3, 7
  and sexuality 34
  student nurses 241–2
AIDS, residential care 8
Alcohol
  falls 78
  hypothermia 72
  sexual dysfunction 38
Alzheimer's disease 179–80
  residential care 8
  see also Dementia
Ankle flare 97–8
Antiseptics, pressure sores
    164
Appliances, urinary
    incontinence 127–8, 135,
    137–40, 146–7
Arterial ulcers 104
Art therapy 185–6

Bandaging, compression,
    venous ulcers 106–11
Bereavement 62–7, 230–34
  see also Death; Loss
Bladder function, normal
    131–2
  see also Incontinence
Blindness see Visual changes
Boredom 40–45

Carers 6–11
  abusing 55–61
  elderly 48–9
  family as 46–51
  informal 8
  nurses see Nurses
  stroke victims 89–93
  support for 52–4
Catheters, urinary
  care of at home 141–3
  incontinence 128
  and sexuality 148

Cerebro-vascular accident
  see Stroke
Co-counselling 222
Communication problems
    215–19
  hearing loss 27–9
  pain assessment 82–3
  touch 31
  visual changes 29
Compliance 252–5
  drugs 188–93, 194–6
Compression bandaging,
    venous ulcers 106–11
Confusional states 176–7
Consent, informed 197–8

Daily living 14–67
Deafness see Hearing loss
Death 62–7
  bereavement 62–7, 230–34
  dying: home or hospital
    231–2
  falls as precursor 76
  grieving 63, 226, 232–3
  recognition of mortality
    213–14
  see also Loss
Debridement of wounds 163
Deep venous thrombosis
    and leg ulcers 96–8,
    113–14
Dementia 179–80
  boredom 45
  drug therapy 186–7
  hypothermia 72
  residential care 8
Depression 177–8
  drug therapy 186–7
  versus dementia 178
Diabetes, leg ulcers 94
Diet see Nutrition
Disability and relationships
    38–9
Discharge home from
    hospital 201–2
  planning 246–51
Disorientation 218
Domiciliary services 18
Dressing and visual loss 30
Dressings
  leg ulcers 102–3
  pressure sores 161–6
Drug rounds as part of
    learning process 195

Drugs
  compliance 188–93, 194–6
  contributing to
    incontinence 126, 129
  dementia 186–7
  depression 186–7
  failure to comply 188–93
  falls 78
  hypothermia 71
  instructions 191–2
  labelling 191
  mental health problems
    186–7
  packaging 190–91
  pain control 85–7
  and sexual function 38
Dying
  home or hospital 231–2
  self-esteem 64
  support for relatives 232–3
  see also Death
Dynamics of ageing 210–14

Eating difficulties 22, 30–32
Eczema, with leg ulcers 101
Education see Health
    education; Nurse
    education
Elderly carers 48–9
Elimination
  falls 77–8
  fully dependent people
    127–9
  post-operative 201
  see also Incontinence
Emergency surgery 199
Emotions 220–24
Environment of care 259–60
Ethnic minorities
  recreation 44
  residential care 8
Exercise, leg ulcers 116
Exudate, pressure sores
    164–5

Faecal incontinence 128
Falls 76–81
Family
  as carers 46–51
  as part of caring team 205
  of terminally ill patients
    230–34
Foot pulses 95–8

GPs new contract 236–40
Grieving 63, 226, 232–3
Group psychotherapy 183, 212–13
Groupthink 207–8
Growth groups 222

Health Care Assistants 10
Health education 241–5
and discharge planning 248–9
about drugs 192–3, 194–6
after a fall 80
Health screening 9, 235–40
study day course 239–40
Hearing loss 27–9
falls 77
Helping skills 225–9
Holidays 45
Home
choice of living environment 16–20
improvements 18
residential care 7–8
see also Housing
Homosexuality 34–9
Hospitalization
falls 78
surgery 198–201
Housing 16–20
hypothermia 72, 74
Hypothermia 71–5
post-operative 200

Incontinence 118–23
appliances 127–8, 135, 137–40, 146–7
assessment 124–5, 132–3
care of the patient 121–2, 131–6
catheters 128
causes 132
the elderly 124–30
faecal 128
male 137–40
and pressure sores 152
and sexuality 144–9
treatment 121–2, 131–6
Infection
leg ulcers 103–4
wounds 163–4
Informal carers 8
Information
to dying patients 232
silence 257
Interpersonal skills 233–4
Intervention 223–4
Ischaemia, leg ulcers 94–8

Leg ulcers
arterial 104
diagnosis 94–9
treatment 100–105
venous 94–8, 100
compression bandaging 106–11
prevention 113–17
Leisure activities 40–41
and hearing loss 28–9
and visual changes 30
Life history review 43–4, 65
Loss 212–13, 225–9
see also Bereavement; Death

Malnutrition see Nutrition
Maslow's hierarchy of needs 50–51, 64
Medication see Drugs
Memory loss and drugs 192
Menopause 36
Mental health problems 175–80
assessment 181
drugs 186–7
falls 78
and incontinence 128–9
management 181–7
Mentally handicapped, residential care 8
Mobility
and continence 126
falls 76–81
stroke victims 89–93
and visual changes 29–30
Mortality rates 2
falls 76
Mortality, recognition of 213–14
Motivation, stroke victims 89
Mourning, tasks of 225–6
Moving to a new home 17
Music and art therapy 185–6

Neural blockade 86
Newspapers 44
Non-compliance see Compliance
Norton Scale for pressure sore risk assessment 153–4
Nurse education 9–10
health education for the elderly 241–5
Nurses
care of the dying and bereaved 67
involvement in recreation 42–3, 44–5
as lobbyists 260
practice nurses 238
standards of care 258–9
team approach 205–9
Nursing home care 7–8
Nutrition 21–6
eating difficulties 22, 30–32
healing of leg ulcers 101
post-operative 200–201
pressure sores 152–3

Odour, pressure sores 164
Oedema and leg ulcers 94–8, 100–101

Pain management 82–8
post-operative 200
Parkinson's disease 77
Patient advocacy 256–61
Patients
choice 259–60
as directors of caring team 206
popular and unpopular 252
terminally ill 230–34
Personal alarms 18
Personal cleansing and visual loss 30
Pets 42
Practice nurses 238
Pressure sores
assessment of the wound 156–60
early assessment of risk 150–55
local treatment 161–6
measuring 159
ongoing assessment 168–9
prevention 167–74
relief of pressure 169–71
support systems 171–2
Primary Health Care Team
liaison over discharge arrangements 250
screening 235–40
Private sector care 7
Professional judgements 258
Professional responsibility 260
Psychotherapy, group 183, 212–13

Quality added life years 7
Quality of care 10

Reality Orientation 181–3
Recreation 40–41
  nurse involvement 42–3,
  44–5
Rehabilitation, stroke
  victims 89–93
Relationships 34–9
Reminiscence 43–4, 65, 185,
  211
Residential care 7–8
Resolution therapy 184
Rest, leg ulcers 116
Retirement 37
Role play 242–3

Safety
  environment 15–20
  falls 76
  hearing loss 28
  loss of sensation 31
  loss of taste and smell 32
  visual changes 29–30
Screening 9, 235–40
  study day course 239–40
Self-esteem in the dying 64
Self-help, leg ulcers 115
Senses 27–33
  and recreation 44
  and relationships 36

Sexuality 34–9
  and incontinence 144–9
Sheaths, incontinence
  137–40
Sheltered housing 18–19
Sight see Visual changes
Slough, leg ulcers 103
Social change
  the family 47–8
  and relationships 37
Standards of care 258–9
Stroke
  falls 77
  rehabilitation 89–93
Support for relatives of
  dying patient 232–3
Support groups 221–2
Surgery 197–202

Taste and smell 31–2
Teamwork 205–9
Technology and leisure 44
Therapeutic touch 223
Thrombogenic events 96
Toilets 127, 129
Touch 31
  therapeutic 223
Transcutaneous nerve
  stimulation (TCNS) 87

Ulcers see Leg ulcers
Urinary incontinence see
  Incontinence

Validation therapy 184
Venous ulcers see Leg ulcers:
  venous
Voilence towards the elderly
  55–61
  in residential care 8
Visual changes 29–31
  falls 77

Whistle-blowing 257–8
Women as carers 47–8
Work
  and hearing loss 28
  and visual changes 30
Wounds
  assessment chart 156–9
  debridement 163
  dressings see Dressings
  healing, surgical 200–201
  infection 163–4
  see also Leg ulcers;
    Pressure sores